THE VIRTUOUS
READER

STUDIES *in* THEOLOGICAL INTERPRETATION

THE VIRTUOUS READER

Old Testament Narrative and Interpretive Virtue

RICHARD S. BRIGGS

Baker Academic
a division of Baker Publishing Group
Grand Rapids, Michigan

© 2010 by Richard S. Briggs

Published by Baker Academic
a division of Baker Publishing Group
P.O. Box 6287, Grand Rapids, MI 49516-6287
www.bakeracademic.com

Printed in the United States of America

Library of Congress Cataloging-in-Publication Data
Briggs, Richard, 1966–
   The virtuous reader : Old Testament narrative and interpretive virtue / Richard S. Briggs.
       p.   cm. — (Studies in theological interpretation)
   Includes bibliographical references (p.   ) and indexes.
   ISBN 978-0-8010-3843-3 (pbk.)
   1. Bible. O.T.—Hermeneutics. 2. Virtues. I. Title.
BS476.B617 2010
221.601—dc22   2009029848

10   11   12   13   14   15   16   7   6   5   4   3   2   1

To
Robert Briggs
and
Maureen Briggs
with love

CONTENTS

SERIES PREFACE

As a discipline, formal biblical studies is in a period of reassessment and upheaval. Concern with historical origins and the development of the biblical materials has in many places been replaced by an emphasis on the reader and the meanings supplied by present contexts and communities. The Studies in Theological Interpretation series seeks to appreciate the constructive theological contribution made by Scripture when it is read in its canonical richness. Of necessity, this includes historical evaluation while remaining open to renewed inquiry into what is meant by history and historical study in relation to Christian Scripture. This also means that the history of the reception of biblical texts—a discipline frequently neglected or rejected altogether—will receive fresh attention and respect. In sum, the series is dedicated to the pursuit of constructive theological interpretation of the church's inheritance of prophets and apostles in a manner that is open to reconnection with the long history of theological reading in the church. The primary emphasis is on the constructive theological contribution of the biblical texts themselves.

New commentary series have sprung up to address these and similar concerns. It is important to complement this development with brief, focused, and closely argued studies that evaluate the hermeneutical, historical, and theological dimensions of scriptural reading

and interpretation for our times. In the light of shifting and often
divergent methodologies, the series encourages studies in theological
interpretation that model clear and consistent methods in the pursuit
of theologically engaging readings.

An earlier day saw the publication of a series of short monographs
and compact treatments in the area of biblical theology that went
by the name Studies in Biblical Theology. The length and focus of
the contributions were salutary features and worthy of emulation.
Today, however, we find no consensus regarding the nature of biblical
theology, and this is a good reason to explore anew what competent
theological reflection on Christian Scripture might look like in our
day. To this end, the present series, Studies in Theological Interpretation, is dedicated.

AUTHOR PREFACE

W hat sort of reader should one be in order to read the
Bible? I have come to think that this question is at least
as important as the perennial question of how we should read the
Bible, but equally I have not wanted to give up on the notion that
scriptural texts will have their own particular contribution to make
toward one's reflection on the question of what sort of reader one
should be. There has to be some kind of hermeneutical give-and-
take between text and reader, allowing the reader to work on the
text at the same time as the text works on the reader. In this book,
I attempt to explore the feedback loop that this dynamic represents
by exploring the virtues implied in certain Old Testament narratives.
These virtues, in turn, might be commended to those who wish to
read the Old Testament. The opening chapter explains in detail the
project of the book and some of its goals, working assumptions, and
limitations. The closing chapter also recognizes some of the obvious
ways in which the present study will need to be developed and taken
further before anything like a full answer can be given to the question
of what sort of reader one should be.

My experience of teaching, first the New Testament for four dizzy-
ing years, and now, in Durham, the Old Testament, has left its mark
on this book. My background lies in philosophy and in hermeneutics,
but the weekly labor of leading classes through rich, puzzling, and

yet rewarding biblical texts has gradually led me to want to harness whatever hermeneutical theory is in play to the ultimately practical and formational task of actually reading the text in front of us. This is not easy. But then it is a transformative task in part because it is not easy. I rather like the way Hugh Pyper puts it: "Part of the excitement of reading these texts, and the reason why three millennia after their composition they are still provoking the arguments of commentators, is that we can never be assured of having fully appreciated them. . . . Any text that one could fully appreciate would be unlikely to be worth the effort" (Pyper 1993: 30). So in the end, I have endeavored to write a book that is engaged with the actual practice of interpreting Scripture. While I do think that this is a profoundly hermeneutical task, I appeal to hermeneutics only as and when necessary rather than as prolegomena. At just the right moment, I was helped to take this overall direction by chancing upon this pointed reflection on Thomas Aquinas, who himself gets relatively short shrift here (at least compared to the hours spent exploring what was to me the previously undiscovered treasure of the *Summa*): "Thomas has little to say of a strictly hermeneutical nature. This may be because Thomas is more interested in actually interpreting Scripture than in thinking about interpreting Scripture" (J. Boyle 1995: 95; cited in Hahn 2003: 62). In writing this book, I have discovered, or perhaps rediscovered, just how much there is to say on almost any verse or passage of Scripture. Aquinas, therefore, must be left to fend for himself; the mass of scholarship on his view of the virtues attests that he can do more than ably. I use the opening chapter to say as much as I think I need to about virtue, about Aquinas, and even a little about Aristotle, but the task is conceived in such a way as presses me on to look at the biblical text.

Likewise, I reluctantly decided not to include a discussion of Aristotle's own account of the virtues in his *Nicomachean Ethics*. To summarize what I will not discuss here: I am aware that *aretē* may best be translated as "goodness" or "excellence" rather than "virtue," and I searched at length in the various accounts of specific virtues in the *Ethics* in the vain hope that I would uncover a principle of classification that I could adapt to my own hermeneutical ends. Chapter 1 recounts (in part) why this turned out not to work and why, in the end, it did not matter too much.

One or two brief points of practical explanation are required. Among conventions adopted in this book, I use "interpretive" throughout rather than "interpretative," simply because most of the authors discussed follow this standard American usage. I have tried to adopt a relatively unobtrusive way of referring to secondary literature and have tried (though not always successfully) to keep lengthy footnotes to a minimum. I have also tried in general to avoid technical discussions of Hebrew or Greek texts and have employed transliterations accordingly in the hope that readers without facility in these languages may not be disadvantaged. This does come at a price, but other ways of handling the matter would simply have paid a different price.

Though none of the material here has been published before as it stands, I have in some places drawn briefly on my previous writings. I am indebted to the editor of *Theology* for permission to use some aspects of an article on trust and suspicion (2009a) in chapter 4 from a paper originally given to local church leaders in Durham in summer 2008, where stimulating discussion helped me to see which lines of argument it was most important to develop. Chapter 4 also contains a paragraph summarizing some of (and drawn in part from) the argument of my article on Numbers 5 (2009b), and I am grateful to the editors of *Biblical Interpretation* for permission to make use of it here. A considerably less lucid version of chapter 2 was read at the Durham University Old Testament research seminar as I was beginning this project, and I benefited from the seminar's friendly but probing critique in many ways that helped to shape the overall project. This in turn meant that by the time I got around to presenting chapters 3 and 5 to them, I had a clearer idea of what I was doing. An abbreviated version of chapter 1 likewise benefited from a lively discussion at the Durham-Duke symposium on identity in Durham in May 2008, where feedback ranged from hugely encouraging on through to profoundly unconvinced and where I was at least able to shift the section on "anticipated objections" to one on "actual objections." Many of the formulations of the final chapter now owe their substantive concerns to points first raised at that session by one or another attentive critic.

The writing of this book has been a real joy, and for that I am indebted to many friends and colleagues who have discussed it, probed it, and offered various kinds of feedback on the work in progress. In particular, I owe much to Walter Moberly, who has regularly and generously offered both wide-ranging encouragement and friendly critique marked by meticulous attention to detail. He has consistently helped me to shape constructive agendas for taking Scripture seriously. I would like to thank also Debbie and John Chapman for wisdom, counsel, and enthusiastic interaction at many points along the way; my colleagues at Cranmer Hall for a stimulating environment in which to work and write, and in particular David Clough, Anne Dyer, and David Wilkinson for specific encouragements; and the council of St. John's College, Durham University, for a term's research leave in 2008, when the bulk of this book was drafted. I continue to learn more from my students than they do from me (though it is unnerving when they agree with this estimation). And warm thanks to Jim Kinney, Wells Turner, and the wonderful staff at Baker Academic for encouraging this book all the way through the writing and publication process, and to Craig Bartholomew, Joel Green, and Christopher Seitz for accepting it into their Studies in Theological Interpretation series. I am especially grateful to Craig for careful editorial perusal of a final draft. None of these good people should be held responsible for errors and omissions in what follows, all of which are my own achievement. I have taken comfort from the delightful word of Alan Jacobs in his exceptional book *A Theology of Reading*: "Avoiding error is a good thing, but it is probably not central to hermeneutics" (2001: 14), but not, I hope, too much comfort.

Finally, on a personal level, the most significant thanks. To Mum and Dad: it is a pleasure to dedicate this book to you in grateful acknowledgment of the lifelong gift of growing up in a house full of books and with a love of reading, and with your patient endurance of wondering how long it would be before I "got a proper job." To Joshua, Kristin, and Matthew—three wonderful children—for so much joy and for the persistent reminder that no writing project is so significant that it shall not stop for family viewing of *Dr. Who*. And above all, and always, to Melody, my life partner and my best friend. She has never ceased to encourage me in all my thinking and writing and has selflessly taken time out of her own teaching and research to help make this book possible. She is also an excellent reader of texts, including this one—a virtuous reader indeed.

ABBREVIATIONS

Bibliographic and General

AT	author's translation
b.	Babylonian Talmud
BDB	Francis Brown, S. R. Driver, and Charles A. Briggs, *A Hebrew and English Lexicon of the Old Testament* (Oxford: Clarendon, 1907)
DQVirtGen	Thomas Aquinas, "On the Virtues in General: Thirteen Articles," in *Disputed Questions on the Virtues* (ed. E. M. Atkins and T. Williams; trans. E. M. Atkins; Cambridge Texts in the History of Philosophy; Cambridge: Cambridge University Press, 2005)
J-M	Paul Joüon, SJ, *A Grammar of Biblical Hebrew* (trans. and rev. T. Muraoka; Subsidia biblica 14; Rome: Pontifical Biblical Institute, 1991)
JPS	Jewish Publication Society
LXX	Septuagint
Mak.	tractate *Makkot*
Midr.	midrash
Ned.	tractate *Nedarim*

NETS	*A New English Translation of the Septuagint* (ed. Albert Pietersma and Benjamin C. Wright; New York: Oxford University Press, 2007)
NIV	New International Version
NRSV	New Revised Standard Version
Qoh.	Qohelet (Ecclesiastes)
Rab.	Rabbah
Roš Haš.	tractate *Roš Haššanah*
SBL	Society of Biblical Literature
Sanh.	tractate *Sanhedrin*
ST	Thomas Aquinas, *Summa theologiae* (59 vols.; London: Blackfriars, 1964–76)
Tanakh	*Tanakh: A New Translation of the Holy Scriptures according to the Traditional Hebrew Text* (Philadelphia: Jewish Publication Society, 1985)
Tg.	targum

Old Testament

Gen.	Genesis	Prov.	Proverbs
Exod.	Exodus	Eccles.	Ecclesiastes
Lev.	Leviticus	Song	Song of Songs
Num.	Numbers	Isa.	Isaiah
Deut.	Deuteronomy	Jer.	Jeremiah
Josh.	Joshua	Lam.	Lamentations
Judg.	Judges	Ezek.	Ezekiel
Ruth	Ruth	Dan.	Daniel
1–2 Sam.	1–2 Samuel	Hosea	Hosea
1–2 Kings	1–2 Kings	Joel	Joel
1–2 Chron.	1–2 Chronicles	Amos	Amos
Ezra	Ezra	Obad.	Obadiah
Neh.	Nehemiah	Jon.	Jonah
Esther	Esther	Mic.	Micah
Job	Job	Nah.	Nahum
Ps(s).	Psalms	Hab.	Habakkuk

| Zeph. | Zephaniah | Zech. | Zechariah |
| Hag. | Haggai | Mal. | Malachi |

New Testament

Matt.	Matthew	1–2 Thess.	1–2 Thessalonians
Mark	Mark	1–2 Tim.	1–2 Timothy
Luke	Luke	Titus	Titus
John	John	Philem.	Philemon
Acts	Acts	Heb.	Hebrews
Rom.	Romans	James	James
1–2 Cor.	1–2 Corinthians	1–2 Pet.	1–2 Peter
Gal.	Galatians	1–3 John	1–3 John
Eph.	Ephesians	Jude	Jude
Phil.	Philippians	Rev.	Revelation
Col.	Colossians		

1

IN PURSUIT
OF THE VIRTUES
OF THE IMPLIED READER
OF THE OLD TESTAMENT

We need several interpretive virtues for wise and faithful
reading of Scripture. Prominent among them are receptivity, humility, truthfulness, courage, charity, and imagination. (L. Gregory Jones 2002: 32)

This study is an exploration of the moral character or virtues
most appropriate to the many and varied tasks of reading
the Old Testament. Its main thesis may be simply stated: implicit in
the Old Testament's handling of a wide range of moral and ethical
categories, we find a rich and thought-provoking portrait (or perhaps
series of portraits) of the kind of character most eagerly to be sought
after, and this in turn is the implied character of one who would read
these texts, especially one in search of their own purposes and values.

The main way of proceeding will be to build up a series of case studies of particular "interpretive virtues," as Gregory Jones calls them, as they are handled, either explicitly or implicitly, in various texts of the Old Testament. Not until the conclusion will we give a direct account of the question of what one does with an implied reader once such a character has been described. There we shall be concerned with the broader hermeneutical and ethical considerations that lie in the transition from ideal reading to actual reading. In this first chapter, four tasks need to be accomplished in order to map out the hermeneutical space within which we shall operate.

1. The idea of an "interpretive virtue" needs to be clarified, in dialogue with the concerns of virtue ethics and some issues in "theological interpretation" of biblical texts.
2. The notion of an implied reader needs brief clarification.
3. Some of the endless hermeneutical and theological questions surrounding the term "Old Testament" and its value as an independent topic of study need brief treatment, if only to avoid being waylaid by them in subsequent chapters.
4. Finally, a brief plan of the remainder of the study will be offered.

The Interpretive Virtues

The phrase "interpretive virtue" does not have a clear history or prominent tradition behind it. I can find no discussion of it in the fields of philosophical hermeneutics or literary theory.[1] It has not acquired prominence in either philosophical or theological inquiry into the virtues in general.[2] My starting point will be a significant discussion of it in the context of Christian concerns about interpreting biblical texts that occurs in Kevin Vanhoozer's discussion of hermeneutics, *Is*

---

1. Obviously such a statement may say more about me than about these fields, but at least in my search for it I have come across no indication that such a concept has left any particular mark. Lewis (1961) offers a comparable notion, though it is not developed in terms of virtues. See Vanhoozer 1998: 374–76; S. Wright 2000.
2. The exception of Zagzebski 1996 will be considered below. The significant essay of E. Rogers 1996 on "the virtues of an interpreter" will be considered in a later chapter.

There a Meaning in This Text? (1998). As part of its subtitle, this study indicates that it is occupying itself with questions of "the morality of literary knowledge." The book as a whole is a sustained plea for "hermeneutical realism," and in his final chapter, Vanhoozer explicitly addresses the question of the nature of the reader of the text, defending the moral virtue of "respect for what is there in the text." This leads him to develop an account of what he calls "the interpretive virtues": *An interpretive virtue is a disposition of the mind and heart that arises from the motivation for understanding, for cognitive contact with the meaning of the text*" (1998: 376, italics original). In addition to faith, hope, and love and their significance for hermeneutics, he suggests four further interpretive virtues in the first instance:

1. Honesty: "acknowledging one's prior commitments and pre-understandings."
2. Openness: being "willing to hear and consider the ideas of others . . . without prejudice."
3. Attention: the reader is "focused on the text," with respect, patience, thoroughness, and care.
4. Obedience: which means "not necessarily . . . doing what the text says, but . . . minimally, reading it in the way its author intended" (1998: 377).

As we shall see in a later chapter, the climax of his 500-page book is a call for a hermeneutic characterized by humility, though he does not explicitly list this as one of the interpretive virtues in view.

Taken together, we have here anything from four to eight specific virtues articulated as keys to right interpretation. One need not doubt that all of them are greatly to be sought after. Equally, to anticipate a point about the role of Scripture in our hermeneutical reflection, it seems that one need not have read the Bible in order to understand fully what Vanhoozer is talking about, although the status of "faith, hope, and love" as a foundational triad of virtues would perhaps be more evident to those who know 1 Corinthians 13:13 than to those who do not.[3]

---

3. In the Christian tradition, Aquinas adds these three virtues to the four "cardinal" virtues of Aristotelian thinking, to make seven. As far as I can tell, the symbolic signifi-

Vanhoozer does not do a great deal with his list of virtues, which may be partly because his overall agenda concerns how the Bible ought to be read, as a trinitarian communicative act with a definite (though possibly multilayered, or even multiple) content and illocutionary force. In this scheme, the virtuous reader is one who operates within this conception of what constitutes the task of reading the Bible, even to the point where the key quality of humility is characterized primarily as "a prime interpretive virtue" that "constantly reminds interpreters that we can get it *wrong*" (1998: 463–64). In other words, humility represents the stance of standing "under" the definite meaning and force of the text rather than "over" it: understanding rather than overstanding, as Vanhoozer puts it.

The overall merits of Vanhoozer's approach to hermeneutics are not our concern here. Instead, two points of specific evaluation may be ventured. First, it is not clear that this account of the virtues, which will serve as a springboard for our own inquiry, plays an especially significant role in the overall scheme of Vanhoozer's hermeneutics.[4] Vanhoozer's main concerns rest with meaning and force, tying together the classic speech-act triad of author, text, and reader in a productive and subtle proposal for considering questions of interpretation. His subsequent work broadens out these concerns in yet richer and more theologically nuanced ways but in fact does so without taking up the notion of interpretive virtue.[5] A similar point may be made about the brief discussion of "sapiential virtues" in his subsequent *The Drama of Doctrine*, where he notes the moral/intellectual and theological virtues that constitute the Aristotelian notion of *phronēsis* (2005a: 332–35). Elsewhere in this work he notes that "according to the canonical maps, . . . virtue requires a renewing not only of the

---

cance of seven is not a factor either of Vanhoozer's discussion or of the analysis offered by Aquinas (*ST* 1a2ae, 61–62).

4. We may note, for example, that Vanhoozer makes only light (though appreciative) use of the work of MacIntyre (described below)—for example, concerning his notion of making "rational judgments between traditions of hermeneutical inquiry" (1998: 334).

5. Especially worthy of note are Vanhoozer's two essays (2002: 159–203; 2005b) that work with notions of covenant and theological subject matter respectively. It is also worth noting that Vanhoozer remains in some disagreement with the approach of Stephen Fowl, which will be described below, thus inter alia suggesting that his own use of the virtues is not a fundamental part of his approach. Cf. the essays in Adam et al. 2006; also Fowl 2000.

mind but also of the whole being; it requires a work of transforming grace, a reorientation to truth" (2005a: 303). Again, one may recognize here a profoundly helpful characterization of the relevance of "virtue" thinking to the tasks of articulating theological understanding without going so far as to say that this insight is deeply woven into the fabric of the overall argument.

Second, especially given the way in which the notion of "interpretive virtue" does not particularly drive or even shape the argument, one may suggest that along the way to his own particular goal, Vanhoozer has coined a term that may usefully serve for purposes other than the (singular) one to which he puts it. In short, an "interpretive virtue" is a virtue relevant to the task(s) of interpretation, regardless of how one evaluates Vanhoozer's particular view of what that task is—"cognitive contact with the meaning of the text," in the definition quoted above (1998: 376). Thus one may extract the other part of his definition and work with it outside such a framework: an interpretive virtue is a disposition of the mind and heart that arises from the motivation for achieving good interpretation. In the quote from Gregory Jones with which we began, and which is without doubt operating with a different conception of the task of hermeneutics from Vanhoozer's 1998 work, one might render this definition in terms of interpretive virtues being those dispositions that lead to "wise and faithful reading of Scripture" (2002: 32).

There is of course some sense of circularity, or perhaps begging the question, about such formulations: virtues help you to achieve good/wise/faithful ends, but how does this get you past defining virtue in terms of what achieves the good, and the good in terms of what results from the practice of virtue? This apparent risk of circularity is a familiar one to those aware of the broader discipline of virtue ethics, of which we must offer here the briefest of accounts.

Virtue Ethics

The major articulation of virtue ethics in recent times is the seminal work of Alasdair MacIntyre, *After Virtue* (1984). In this and subsequent works, MacIntyre has put forward the claim that much modern thought (which he characterizes as an "Enlightenment project") has reduced moral language to "emotivism," the expressing of individual preference. This rootless moral language of disembodied values, he suggests, has taken hold in the wake of the collapse of a longer and more robust tradition of speaking in terms of virtues and practices that nourish and sustain human communities. The various definitions of the key terms that MacIntyre uses reveal that they interlock: "The virtues are to be understood as those dispositions which will not only sustain practices and enable us to achieve the goods internal to practices, but which will also sustain us in the relevant kind of quest for the good . . . and which will furnish us with increasing self-knowledge and increasing knowledge of the good" (1984: 219). The main definition of practices is harder work but essentially suggests that practices are cooperative human activities with their own internal "goods" and standards of excellence (1984: 187). In other words, practices have their own inbuilt values, which bring with them appropriate practice-specific recognitions of levels of achievement. The virtues facilitate excellence in practices, and all contribute to the quest for human good.

To what then does this quest for the good lead? The clearest passage on this in MacIntyre's book, to my mind, comes in the section where he is simply laying out Aristotle's own account of the virtues from the *Nicomachean Ethics*. It is worth quoting at length:

> What then does the good for man turn out to be? Aristotle has cogent arguments against identifying that good with money, with honor or with pleasure. He gives to it the name of *eudaimonia*—as so often there is a difficulty in translation: blessedness, happiness, prosperity. It is the state of being well and doing well in being well, of a man's being well-favored himself and in relation to the divine. But when Aristotle first gives this name to the good for man, he leaves the question of the content of *eudaimonia* largely open.
>
> The virtues are precisely those qualities the possession of which will enable an individual to achieve *eudaimonia* and the lack of which will frustrate his movement toward that *telos*. (1984: 148)

Much of MacIntyre's subsequent argument, in this and later works, is concerned with developing, correcting, and reappropriating this moral vision for today's world. In particular, this teleological category of *eudaimonia* works well as long as it is the only *telos* in view, but how is one to judge between competing views of what "the end of man" is? It is Aquinas who co-opts Aristotle's system into a Christian vision of how to live the moral life, and this raises an obvious question about *After Virtue*, which is how it can account (either in theory or in practice) for contested notions of *telos*. In particular, as MacIntyre notes in the second edition of the book, he has failed to discuss the competing claims of the Aristotelian and the biblical views of such a *telos* (1984: 278).

His subsequent work (in particular 1988; 1990) tackles the question of how to evaluate across competing systems of justice and rationality once more than one functioning set of virtues is in view (MacIntyre 1988), especially given that the kind of cross-tradition argument available to him is not that found in twentieth-century moral philosophy, where one may make judgments about whether a view is right or wrong on some metalevel independently of its place within its own tradition. (Such an approach, the encyclopedic view, is one of the "three rival versions of moral enquiry" that he finds wanting; MacIntyre 1990.)

Utilizing the Concerns of Virtue Ethics

For our purposes, it is not necessary to resolve all the questions raised by (and about) virtue ethics.[6] All we need to draw out of this discussion at this stage is the recognition of the tradition of virtue ethics that lies behind the notion of an "interpretive virtue," which we have developed from Vanhoozer's work. As for the plausibility of transplanting this kind of language into the concerns of hermeneutics,

---

6. Cf. van Hooft 2006; Porter 1990; 1995. Porter's 2001 essay is a concise historical survey of the ups and downs of the discipline. There is no shortage of critique, most notable of which is Stout 1988, who contests MacIntyre's gloomy perception of the current state of moral discussion by suggesting that we do manage to talk quite productively across tradition-constituted divides on all manner of ethical issues (Stout 1988: esp. 191–242, 266–72). Yet see Fowl 1991, who thinks that MacIntyre still has a substantive point, even if Stout is technically right. Critiques of the "logic" of virtue ethics (such as R. Smith 2003, who charges MacIntyre and Hauerwas with a philosophically confused relativism) seem to me to show that much analytic philosophy still often fails to grasp its own contextual commitments and embeddedness, indeed its own "traditions of inquiry." A most enjoyable account of what is at stake in virtue ethics is offered by Eagleton 2003: 110–39.

it is noteworthy that Vanhoozer himself develops the idea from the epistemological work of Linda Zagzebski, *Virtues of the Mind* (1996).[7] Zagzebski offers a penetrating account of how to reformulate many traditional epistemological questions (e.g., concerning knowledge, justification, and belief) in virtue terms. Along the way she makes several points helpful to a project of biblical interpretation, of which we may note three.

The basic point of her analysis is that knowledge is one form of the "good" (*eudaimonia*) noted in virtue-based approaches to human living, and that "if there are intimate connections between knowledge and happiness, it should not be surprising that the pursuit of one is not easily separable from the pursuit of the other" (1996: 338). This is not quite what philosophers mean when they talk of "virtue epistemology," largely for contingent reasons relating to the questions that happen to have fallen under that label (cf. the edited collection of Fairweather and Zagzebski 2001), but the shorthand will suffice for our purposes. In short, and allowing for all the caveats and recognitions that virtuous people do not act invariably on their best apprehensions, her thesis is that, all other things being equal, one who is morally virtuous is more likely to make wise judgments. An account of how one judges (epistemologically) finds congruence with an account of how one lives morally in other spheres.

Second, to make her case, she challenges the standard (philosophical) distinction between moral and intellectual virtues, drawing in part on the point that other disciplines (e.g., cognitive psychology) no longer find it plausible to separate out a notion of the intellect from the wider embodied nature of the brain. Zagzebski mounts a strong argument for maintaining that "an intellectual virtue does not differ from certain moral virtues any more than one moral virtue differs from another" (1996: 139; cf. 137–65). Indeed, in certain cases, such as honesty, the moral virtue is inextricable from intellectual ones (such as truth-telling; 1996: 158–59).

---

7. Cf. Vanhoozer 1998: 360n192, as well as his definition of interpretive virtue cited earlier. Zagzebski's work has now been substantially developed in the treatment of Roberts and Wood (2007: esp. 7–16), who in turn have also written fine psychological (Roberts 2007) and introductory (Wood 1998) texts on this topic. But for our purposes, Zagzebski's own treatment will suffice.

Third, she offers a concise analysis of the standard difficulty of finding a list of virtues sufficient to the task of characterizing what sort of concerns occupy virtue ethics. This difficulty goes back to the earliest attempts to make sense of Aristotle's own classification, or to compare it with that of Aquinas, or to search for some form of rationale for how many virtues there are or how they might be interrelated.[8] Zagzebski notes that there is a "pre-theoretic" notion of virtue, which serves as a constraint on any list put forward, and discusses how one may get past various culture and tradition-specific blocks that lie down the path of listing virtues (1996: 84–89).[9]

Zagzebski's work is an example of utilizing the concerns of virtue ethics in an allied but distinct field of inquiry and thus lends itself most helpfully to any concern to develop an account of how virtue ethics sheds light on interpretive questions. Indeed, it is this insight that underlies Vanhoozer's development of the notion of the "interpretive virtues." One may therefore take up the three points just noted as follows.

First, how one interprets is not an entirely separable activity from how one lives the human life. Mindful of caveats, and noting the variability of how wise readers do or do not follow their own best practices, one finds this precise point made by Stephen Fowl in a short dictionary article on the relevance of the virtues to theological interpretation: "Given that Christians are called to interpret Scripture as part of their ongoing journey into ever-deeper communion with God, it is not surprising that those who have grown and advanced in virtue will tend to be masterful interpreters of Scripture" (2005: 838). As Fowl observes, this is not a mechanical operation whereby wise people offer wise readings and others do not, but the caveats and variables should not obscure the general point.

Second, interpretive virtues may not be entirely divorced from the moral virtues more generally. A hermeneutic of trust, to anticipate a

8. See the survey of proposals in van Hooft 2006: 128–35; cf. MacIntyre 1984: 181–203.

9. It is interesting to note that in the subsequent work of Roberts and Wood (2007), the "intellectual virtues" that they select for consideration are love of knowledge, firmness, courage and caution, humility, autonomy, generosity, and practical wisdom. This list offers pointers for the present study. (The phrase "intellectual virtues" is the title of *ST* 1a2ae, 57.)

later discussion, is related in some sense at least to the general virtue of trust (cf. also Zagzebski 1996: 160–61). Third, and briefly at this stage, it will not be possible to offer a definitive listing of interpretive virtues, although clearly one may still assess the ad hoc claims of one or another hermeneutical category to be a virtue, such as, indeed, a hermeneutic of suspicion or of trust.

MacIntyre's work has been well received by Christian theologians and ethicists without it being assumed that one could simply transpose his Aristotelian argument into Christian tradition. Thus, in their robust theological analysis, Hauerwas and Pinches note that "if the language and logic of virtue tips in any direction, it is away from Christianity and toward the Greek context in which it originated. For Christians, it can be used with great reward, but it must be purified as used or else bear bad fruit" (1997: 57). Part of this purification, for them, is replacing the Greek notion of *polis* with a theology of participation in the body of Christ.[10] Indeed, as Gavin D'Costa has expressed it, MacIntyre has perhaps uncritically at times championed Aristotle and "has taken some time to ground his preference for virtue ethics in an actual community of practice (Roman Catholicism)" (2001: 161–62). With respect in particular to Roman Catholic reflection on the virtues, one should also note the rich tradition that operates in effect the other way around: beginning with a christocentric perspective that understands "the moral life of the Christian as a participation in the virtues of Christ, by means of the grace of one's incorporation into the Church" (Melina 2001: 7). In this tradition, "God has revealed the content of the virtues . . . in Jesus Christ and, in doing so, has communicated them to humanity in a manner accessible to our natures" (Cochran 2008: 82).[11]

One notably careful theological example of the appropriation of MacIntyre's approach is offered by Gregory Jones (1990), who sees

10. See Hauerwas and Pinches 1997: esp. 55–109. Others offering Christian appropriation of MacIntyre's ideas include Murphy et al. 1997; J. R. Wilson 1997; Rey 1999; and the work of Stephen Fowl and Gregory Jones 1991, discussed below.

11. An evaluation of this approach would take us into very different territory from what follows, though one may note that such works have perhaps tended to appeal to the biblical text within some predetermined scheme more than biblical scholars might find appropriate. For initial New Testament reflections here, see Harrington and Keenan 2002. Could a comparable Old Testament volume be imagined?

the fact that Christians live in the presence of the Triune God as essential to reorganizing MacIntyre's discussion around the practices of friendship and of discipleship in community. A year later, Stephen Fowl and Gregory Jones offered what remains to date one of the most significant analyses of how this approach to moral formation might be understood to relate to the specific practices of reading Scripture, in their *Reading in Communion* (1991). This programmatic work offers the following reflection on the particular tradition of biblical criticism: "In order that communities can embody wise readings of Scripture, they need to nurture and develop people who are capable of exercising the critical virtues of professional biblical scholarship" (1991: 43). These critical virtues, when they are introduced into the conversation a few pages earlier, are primarily associated with guarding against self-deception and allowing readers to make discerning use of the mass of critical scholarship that exists in biblical studies. Thus, "by characterizing the importance of critical biblical scholarship in terms of critical *virtues* we want to emphasize that this task involves the interdependence of people with well-formed character in particular communities, not the dependence on experts" (1991: 40). The book goes on to explore, in particular, readings of Jeremiah and exemplars of the embodied practice of biblical interpretation, such as Dietrich Bonhoeffer, in its analysis of how to conceive of the role of Scripture in Christian life. In subsequent writings, Fowl and Jones each have offered compelling accounts of the necessity of cultivating virtue if the Christian church wishes to make any progress in its practices of scriptural interpretation. We recall the list of interpretive virtues called for by Jones in the quote at the head of this chapter. In Fowl's case, he provides an illuminating case study of the need for charity in interpretation as an interpretive virtue (1998: 86–87), and elsewhere he writes of the key virtue that needs to be formed in biblical scholars as practical reasoning (or *phronēsis*; 1998: 188–90).[12]

12. See also Fowl 1995 for a summary version of the argument of Fowl and Jones 1991. One need not agree with all the arguments of Fowl 1998 in order to appreciate the significance of his approach to virtue, character, and formation. The judgment that such an approach is an *alternative* to concerns with meaning, for example, is perhaps too disjunctive (Fowl 1998: 56–61; and its origins as Fowl 1990, though there is some effective nuancing of this in Fowl 2000). See the perceptive discussion of Spinks 2007: 40–67.

It would be optimistic to say that these works have had a major impact on biblical studies, though one may discern signs of renewed attention to the character of the interpreter (e.g., J. Green 2007: 18–23, 138–40) and to the pressing need to pursue wisdom as one particular emphasis in biblical interpretation, as in the collection of essays gathered under the significant title *Reading Texts, Seeking Wisdom* (Ford and Stanton 2003). The SBL group "Character Ethics and Biblical Interpretation" produced three volumes of collected essays (W. Brown 2002; Carroll R. and Lapsley 2007; Brawley 2007), which represent major steps forward in the disciplined development of such an approach, though even here it is striking how few of the individual essays make explicit use of the concerns of virtue ethics.[13]

Some Objections to a Virtue Emphasis in Biblical Interpretation

But before one either celebrates such achievements too quickly, or laments the lack of work exploring this area, some prominent counterarguments to the whole approach need to be considered. First and foremost, a simple and perhaps rather obvious objection may be raised: on what grounds should one turn from many more well-trodden paths, both historical-critical and theological in nature, and embrace an approach to interpretation that has been so signally underrepresented in recent centuries, both in the academy and the church? One may put the point this way: from whence come these interpretive virtues? Surely an interpreter with a concern for the church of Jesus Christ might justifiably be wary of throwing over one set of traditions, no matter how problematic they may be at times, and embracing an Aristotelian line of inquiry. Arguably such concerns would be alleviated by recognizing the intradisciplinary debates of virtue ethicists regarding the perspectives of Aquinas as they relate to Aristotle, and certainly it seems prima facie far more plausible to propose a Thomist approach to the texts of Christianity than an Aristotelian one. Yet even on a simply hermeneutical level, one may well ask where the specific

13. The most notable exceptions are E. Davis 2002 (on which see below) and Carroll R.'s (2007) thoughtful piece on Micah. Most of the (relatively modest number of) works that make use of the concerns of virtue ethics in Old Testament (and some New Testament) interpretation are noted either later in this chapter (e.g., Wenham 2000; Whybray 2002) or in subsequent chapters (e.g., Mills 2001).

categories of interpretive virtues come from, what constitutes their content, and perhaps most pointedly, whether they are brought, fully formed, to the biblical text to do their work.

Doubtless such a case could be made, that the Aristotelian (and perhaps Thomist) categories are fundamental, with the concomitant perspective that "general" hermeneutics is rooted in the way God has made the world and therefore offers its resources to the specific "special" task of interpreting the Bible. Nevertheless it is worth noting the presenting oddity of a claim that one might bring moral categories to a text that is itself at least in part concerned with the shaping of moral categories, without also wanting to go on and ask whether scriptural texts might require us to rethink some of the content attached to those categorical labels as they are generally understood.

If a case is to be made against a "virtue-ethic approach" to biblical interpretation, then the two preceding paragraphs probably make it. What does Aristotle have to do with the wisdom of the Israelite sages, after all? Actually, there is more to be said in response to such a question than its rhetorical flourish might indicate. Ellen Davis, for example, proposes that "the Israelite wisdom literature, especially the book of Proverbs, [may be taken] as an exegetical base for renewing a biblically informed virtue tradition," a task that she describes as "useful" and even "urgent" for our day (2002: 186, 184).[14] One might conceivably argue that in such a case Davis is appropriating a vocabulary or a point of resonance with which to make a claim that she could make on purely exegetical and hermeneutical grounds without the language of virtue. Indeed, her commentary on the book of Proverbs suggests that there are many ways to articulate such insights, not all of which need to engage with the cardinal virtues or the insights of MacIntyre (2000: 9–155). But in any case, even if the discussion would be impoverished without such language, it is precisely the wisdom literature that does seem to foreground the subject

14. Indeed, William Brown (1996) has written an entire introduction to Old Testament wisdom literature from this perspective, though it is disappointing, given his approach, that he restricts himself to Proverbs, Job, and Ecclesiastes, given how much the Wisdom of Solomon would add to his study (which he notes; 1996: 21n94). Morgan (2002) offers much of interest for the tasks of today but, strikingly, does not make use of the categories or traditions of virtues.

matter that virtue ethics addresses, and the complaint against the "virtue-ethic approach" might be willing to concede the territory of Proverbs and suggest that elsewhere what is offered is a square tool for a round text.

Something like this critique of the emphasis on virtues may be found in a brief mention of it in the work of Christopher Seitz, who characterizes it as an emphasis on "the virtuous reader." Observing that this approach "is making a comeback in recent days," he writes, "One searches in vain in Stephen Fowl's recent work for any comprehensive, public, agreed-upon statement of what actually counts for virtue, such that we could see it and believe it was under God's providential care" (2001: 28–29). And this, it seems to me, is a valid concern, even if the stakes have been unnecessarily raised here by the use of adjectives such as "comprehensive" and "agreed-upon"—the issue is one of criteria, and it seems clear that few hermeneutical criteria of any sort have ever been comprehensively agreed upon. Nevertheless, the question of what counts as a virtue seems to be an entirely proper concern. It was of course a concern of Aquinas too (cf. *ST* 1a2ae, 57–62; as well as *DQVirtGen* 12), though Aquinas's social and theological location was sufficiently different, many centuries ago, to suggest perhaps that he would have been less troubled than many commentators today at the thought of having to negotiate between the categories of biblical tradition and Aristotelian philosophy. Seitz has thus put his finger on an issue deserving considerably more attention than it has so far received in the limited number of works that have explored this area. One may agree with Gregory Jones's concern to relate MacIntyre's thinking to trinitarian theological concerns (1990), or Fowl's desire to characterize relevant virtues as ecclesially located (1998: e.g., 202–6); but one may still ask what role Scripture might have in shaping our understanding of the virtues? It is not that one needs Scripture to shape our understanding of such virtues "in the first place," as if the alternatives were to start with either Aristotle or the Bible against a blank slate, but at least one will want to see the biblical emphases woven into any functioning account of the role of the virtues in biblical interpretation.

It is this precise area that we shall seek to address. In negotiating across the disciplinary backgrounds of biblical and Aristotelian thought, we shall not take the high road of grand systematization, after Aquinas, but we shall pursue a low-key, ad hoc approach through a series of exegetical and hermeneutical forays into particular texts.

But which texts? Where do biblical texts address themselves to these issues? What systematic treatment of the virtues is there in Scripture? We have already noted that the wisdom literature might be one such place. It is significant, I think, that by the time of the Wisdom of Solomon,[15] the links are being made explicit:

> If anyone loves righteousness,
> her [Wisdom's] labors are virtues;
> for she teaches self-control and prudence,
> justice and courage;
> nothing in life is more profitable for mortals than these.
>   (Wis. 8:7)

Here the four cardinal virtues of Aristotle are attributed to the work of Wisdom among her disciples. Similar concerns occupy 4 Maccabees, which defends the view that "reason is sovereign over the emotions" (1:1) and thus enables virtues to flourish. "Reason," we may observe, is carefully defined here in terms of a wisdom that consists of adherence to the law (1:15–18), the point being "to demonstrate to Jews that their own cultural and religious heritage already shows the surest way to attain the ideal of virtue that the Greeks claim to prize as honourable" (deSilva 1998: 44). Texts like these represent sustained reflection on the interrelationships between the two traditions, but in the process they perhaps highlight for us the absence of comparable reflection in the Hebrew Scriptures before them.

By the time of the New Testament, there clearly is a persistent habit of offering lists of virtues and vices as part of the ongoing moral argument.[16] Strikingly, the specific virtues listed differ even while the basic thrust remains clear. We recall the notion of a pre-theoretic idea of virtue to which such lists attest, and we can see

---

15. Between 100 BC and AD 30, according to Barclay 1996: 451.

16. For convenient summaries, see Fitzgerald 1992; Charles 1997: 119–27; Swartley 2007: 236–37. Charles 1997: 99–119 offers one of the most extensive explorations of such language as a framework for looking at 2 Peter 1 (see also Charles 2002).

that there is no "canonical" list of virtues in the New Testament tradition either. However, there is little that is comparable to this list-making tradition in the Old Testament (Charles 1997: 112n1). As noted by Fitzgerald, what comes closest is the listlike characterization of Yhwh in Exodus 34:6–7 and its parallels (Num. 14:18; Jon. 4:2) regarding the divine character as being merciful, gracious, slow to anger, abounding in steadfast love and faithfulness. As to human virtues, there is the description of Oholiab's skills in Exodus 31:1, 3: he is filled "with divine spirit, ability, intelligence, and knowledge in every kind of craft" (similarly 35:35–36:1). Slightly more general is the description of Job as blameless and upright, fearing God and turning away from evil (Job 1:1, 8), and—perhaps closest to the New Testament practice of list making—we have Ecclesiastes 2:26: "For to the one who pleases him God gives wisdom and knowledge and joy; but to the sinner he gives the work of gathering and heaping, only to give to one who pleases God" (cf. Fitzgerald 1992: 858). Perhaps one could add to this list Micah 6:8, with its requirement to practice justice and kindness and to walk humbly, described by Carroll R. as a verse designed to "promote the good and nurture the virtues" (2007: 113). Even so, this is not a long list.

The material in view could be broadened by going on to consider what we might term "character portraits" in the Old Testament, rather than just lists. Here we might consider passages such as Job 31, where Job offers a series of characterizations of his righteous behavior, or psalms such as Psalm 1 or 112, or the description of who is worthy of ascending the hill of Yhwh in Psalm 24:3–6. Once we start to consider these kinds of idealized character portraits, it becomes clear that actual character portraits, or more simply, descriptions offered of how various people do or did in fact comport themselves, can also serve as appropriate material for consideration if suitably handled.

A cogent analysis of precisely this hermeneutical possibility is offered in a short article by John Barton titled "Virtue in the Bible" (2003: 65–74; orig. 1999). Barton's piece provides probably the most helpful answer to the question of why, if there is so little explicit material with which to work in the Old Testament, one might pursue a virtue-oriented hermeneutic at all.[17] He argues that in terms of explicit ethical discussion or teaching, there is indeed basically a category mismatch between virtue ethics and the Old Testament. This is even the case, he argues, in the world of wisdom literature, where character may be important but is essentially fixed and unchanging (i.e., one is either wise or foolish, though one might note that "wise" characters elsewhere are anything but fixed and unchanging, such as, most obviously, Solomon). It may be that Barton assimilates the world of Proverbs a little too quickly to the world of Deuteronomy, since on a couple of occasions he clarifies his point with reference to the kind of divine-command model of moral obedience found in Deuteronomy (2003: 67, 69), which is perhaps not entirely a way of doing justice to the workings of the proverbial literature. Nevertheless, he presents a strong argument that the biblical texts most typically operate with a model he characterizes (anachronistically?) as one of *conversion* rather than moral progress: once one has turned to the Lord, one is rescued from the path that leads to destruction and transferred onto the way of the righteous (cf. Ps. 1:6). As Barton notes, such a model of moral transformation through the "disruptive" work of God is particularly valued in the Pauline/Lutheran tradition, which could see a virtue-ethic approach as actually opposed to the teaching of Scripture (2003: 68-69).

The way ahead then lies in seeing that "something like [a virtue] ethic may be implicit in places where morality is not directly under discussion" (Barton 2003: 71). In narratives concerning the trials and tribulations of specific people, Barton suggests, we find not a coded form of explicit ethical teaching, as has sometimes been supposed in various traditions, but examples of "the difficulties and merits of living a moral life or the problems of failing to do so" (2003: 72). The article goes on to discuss other possibilities that we need not consider here, though it is striking that it is the work of Martha Nussbaum to which Barton appeals as an illustration of what he has in mind

---

17. A related argument is offered by Thomasset 2005, whose conclusions lie if anything closer to the concerns of the present work but whose reasoning is driven by how narrative shapes ethical reflection on character—following Ricoeur (e.g., 2005: 80, 82–83); he thus does not consider the specific issues about the "unsuitability" of the biblical text for this project as considered by Barton above.

(2003: 72), specifically the way Nussbaum analyzes characters in Greek tragedies and modern novels.[18] Nussbaum's work (e.g., 1986; 1990), influential in the study of Aristotle, is actually one of the specific approaches critiqued by Gregory Jones as insufficiently *theological* in that it remains at the level of discussing autonomously conceived virtues such as "the proper estimation of one's own worth" (1990: 9–15), although this critique need not mean that Barton's appropriation of Nussbaum's interpretive approach to texts is invalidated on a methodological level.

We are now in a position to adapt this approach to our own specifically hermeneutical goals, looking for implied or implicit interpretive virtues. The goal is to build up a picture (or a character portrait) of the implied reader of the Old Testament. It must be admitted that the task would be considerably simplified if, by this point, we had secured a list of the particular virtues that one should consider, but as we have seen, not just in practice but in theory no such agreed-upon list may be found. However, a helpful way of proceeding will be simply to select some of the virtues most closely associated with interpretive (or sapiential) wisdom, and to ask the question of what is implied (or even said) about them in texts that in some manner or other occupy themselves with such virtues or shed light on them in some way—such as by portraying a person characterized by such virtues. The question of *how* such light is shed cannot be settled in a general way in advance of the examination of particular texts.

A Hermeneutical Focus: Virtue Ethics and the Implied Reader

The remainder of our introduction may be briefer. The project just described is irreducibly concerned with ethical evaluation. The very notion of an "interpretive virtue" is a moral one, and the kinds of

18. John Barton develops this approach along with particular examples in 1998: 19–57. A work that succeeds in approximately this vein is Wenham 2000, which looks for implicit virtues in the narratives of Genesis and Judges especially. Also of note is Whybray 2002, reading the Old Testament texts for what they can tell us about the presupposed values of "the good life" in Israel. An excellent summary of the issues at stake in such approaches is offered by Parry 2004: 48–69, and more generally 3–47.

discussion we have been considering about particular virtues and how they may be implied in the text of Scripture is typically one that oc-curs in areas demarcated with titles such as "Old Testament Ethics," or as the subtitle of Fowl and Jones's book (1991) has it, *Scripture and Ethics in Christian Life.*

The present study, while not disavowing such a focus, is primarily intended as a study in hermeneutics, or perhaps in "ethical interpre-tation." At least that is the generating idea behind it: consideration of one particular angle on the question of how one should read the Old Testament. It needs to be noted that there are many differing legitimate reasons for reading the Old Testament, and that varying estimates of the purposes and goals of reading it will lead to differ-ent considerations of what counts as an appropriate hermeneutic. The present study offers one approach that seems inherently worthy of exploration with regard to the question of the moral character of the reader of Scripture, without wishing to deny that many other ap-proaches will have their own parts to play in a range of engagements with the Old Testament texts.

Disciplined reflection on the multifaceted hermeneutical issues involved in engaging with Scripture is surely to be welcomed as a good thing, at least as opposed to any assumption that only one kind of question may be entertained as worthwhile, whether such a question is thought to be historical, ideological, or whatever. Equally, however, anyone abreast of the mass of hermeneutical discussion operating across the theological subdisciplines at the beginning of the twenty-first century will be aware of an odd feature of that dis-cussion: it is easy to allow the hermeneutical discussion to become a self-sustaining discourse increasingly distanced from the actual tasks and practices of reading the particular texts that go to make up the Christian Bible. Writing in the lead volume of this series of Studies in Theological Interpretation, Markus Bockmuehl suggests that "a turn to hermeneutics cannot by itself rescue New Testament studies from its current malaise; . . . many hermeneuts appear in practice to find it even more difficult than historical critics to escape the ever more complex intellectual maze of their discourse in order to bring home the interpretative fruits of their labors." Indeed, "some end up further from the . . . texts than they began" (2006: 60). Not all do

so, of course, but there is sufficient truth in this accusation to give
pause for thought. Perhaps the situation is not identical with the Old
Testament, but there are at least similarities, and we shall return to
some of the implications of this observation in chapter 6.

The foregoing discussion of virtues is important for our purposes
precisely because it allows us to discuss the notion of an *interpretive
virtue*. Now since we have explicitly followed Zagzebski's claim that
there is not a simple divide between moral and intellectual virtues,
it follows that discussion of interpretive virtues will leave us in some
of the same territory as various works of "Old Testament ethics."
Nevertheless, the goal is more focused: a consideration of interpretive virtues leaves us asking about the nature of the interpreter of
Scripture. Granted that this is not divorced from broader questions
of how to live a morally formed life, the point is perhaps moot, but
at least in principle this affords our study a sharper focus than an
attempt to harness a virtue-oriented hermeneutic to the full gamut
of ethical questions relating to the Old Testament.

In our consideration of John Barton's discussion of virtue in the
Bible (above), we concluded that the way to approach the topic was
in terms of the virtues implicit in the biblical text. For the circumscribed notion of ethical endeavor related to the reading of texts, this
draws us to consider that the moral agent we have in view is, in the
first instance, the implied reader of the text(s). A brief word, then,
about implied readers.

The implied reader is a literary-critical category relating to the notion of how a text "expects" to be read. In the light of Bockmuehl's
warning shot across the bows of hermeneutical theorists, I shall forsake
entering into a studied consideration of all the contentious issues
thereby raised and shall settle instead for some basic points about
implied readers, which I have in practice found useful.

The most straightforward definition of an "implied reader" remains, in my judgment, that offered by Wolfgang Iser: "This term
incorporates both the prestructuring of the potential meaning by
the text, and the reader's actualization of this potential through the
reading process. It refers to the active nature of this process—which
will vary historically from one age to another" (Iser 1974: xii). Implied
readers are not, therefore, real readers. How real readers match up

to the notion of the implied reader remains an interesting question, whether tackled historically (such as in analyses of the "reception history" of biblical texts) or ideologically (such as in the pursuit of "advocacy readings," which self-consciously posit an ideological position for the reader independent of whether such a view is germane to the conditions of production of the text being read). Some therefore adopt the terminology of a "perfect reader"—one who will notice only what is there to be noticed, who will never forget what has already been told, and who will not know in advance what is yet to be told. It follows, of course, that such a reader is only ever a first-time reader: a reader embarking on a text for a second or third time doubtless recalls the end from the beginning. In a later book, Iser actually suggests that the notion of an "ideal reader" is largely spurious. Such a reader either emerges "from the brain of the philologist or the critic himself" or must be identical with the author in that they operate with an identical set of values and presuppositions (1978: 28–29).

Sticking with "implied reader," then, two further characterizations may help. Seymour Chatman introduces the concept of "implied reader" as "the audience presupposed by the narrative itself" (1978: 150). He is following Wayne Booth here, who says, perhaps more by way of epigram than definition, "An author makes his readers . . . if he makes them well—that is, makes them see what they have never seen before" (1983: 397–98). Umberto Eco, on the other hand, has offered the notion of a "model reader": "A text is a device conceived in order to produce its model reader. . . . The empirical reader is only an actor who makes conjectures about the kind of model reader postulated by the text" (1992: 64). This is particularly noteworthy in the context of Eco's idea of the "intention of the work" (*intentio operis*) as an alternative to the endlessly problematic theoretical notion of authorial intention in interpretation.[19] I suggest that Iser, Chatman,

19. In this context, Eco says, "My idea of textual interpretation as the discovery of a strategy intended to produce a model reader conceived as the ideal counterpart of a model author (which appears only as a textual strategy) makes the notion of an empirical author's intention radically useless" (1992: 66). This thesis is then delightfully illustrated by his own experience of having his novel *The Name of the Rose* read in a way that attributed intentions to him that he did not have. Eco's model still has much to offer biblical studies. For a preliminary example, see Conrad 2003: 15–23.

Booth, and Eco are describing aspects of a model for understanding reading in a way that allows us to draw on the basic idea of a reader appropriate to a text without us being drawn into the finer points of the differences between their respective approaches.

All these notions and more have been appropriated in biblical studies, to greater or lesser effect.[20] My own interest lies in what we might term the moral character of the implied reader. Now in one sense this is a self-defeating notion since implied readers have no flesh and blood, and we shall defer consideration of how to relate the implied reader to actual readers, then or now, until our conclusion.

However, the sense in which we are interested in the implied reader of our biblical texts is the sense in which such texts presuppose certain interpretive virtues on the part of the reader they are aimed at. In this context, we may concur with the judgment of Walter Moberly regarding the work of Fowl and Jones discussed above: it "puts in a moral and theological form some of the valid insights of reader-response theory" (2000: 40).[21] The particular sense of the "implicit" approach to virtue ethics that we shall be following, therefore, is the sense in which such an implicit approach sheds light on the implicit reader. In other words, we are in pursuit of the virtues of the implied reader of the Old Testament.

One other hermeneutical point at this stage. The claim that hermeneutical reflection is essential, or perhaps inevitable, because intrinsic to all scriptural interpretation is not the same claim as saying that hermeneutical theory must come first. In general, and in line with the emphasis on the embodied practices of scriptural interpretation that we have had in view, we may say that hermeneutical reflection comes "in, with, and under" the actual practices of reading scriptural texts. To appropriate for hermeneutics an argument made by Richard Bauckham in another context, in his thought-provoking little book *Bible and Mission* (2003), the direction of inference within the bibli-

20. Most notable is Fowler's (1991) reader-response "commentary" on Mark's Gospel. See also Powell 2001. For an example in Old Testament studies, see Clines 1990.

21. Moberly's quote occurs in the context of a call for exactly the kind of project envisaged here: "Some attempts to reformulate the task of biblical interpretation should direct attention to the character of the interpreter and the question of how one develops wisdom" (2000: 40).

cal narrative is always, right from the Old Testament through to the book of Revelation, from the particular to the universal. One nation is chosen for all; one father (Abraham) is called on behalf of many; one man dies for the sins of the world. The "universal" claims of Scripture are best understood as accessed through the particular. This, it seems to me, is a wise word with regard to hermeneutics: attention to the specifics of a biblical text allows us to reflect on the appropriateness of hermeneutical models or paradigms for the consideration of further biblical texts.

This conviction underlies the approach of this book, the present introduction notwithstanding! By considering particular virtues as they are implied in particular passages, we shall make progress toward a generalized consideration of what makes a scripturally appropriate "virtuous reader."

One further topic requires brief (theoretical) consideration, however: the question of why such a project might appropriately work with the Old Testament as its primary frame of reference.

Working with the "Old Testament"

The Old Testament, so named, is a theological construct, and it is a construct that mainly makes sense when it is understood as being set alongside some other "Testament," which is not "Old" in the same sense. This is a traditional Christian statement about the two-Testament structure of Scripture. Debates in recent decades about the propriety of the term "Old Testament," and the search for some supposedly value-neutral label such as "Hebrew Bible" or "First Testament," do at least have this to commend them: they offer explicit recognition of some of the value judgments at stake in how one labels the collection of books under discussion. Such judgments have been thrown into sharp relief by the fragmentation of consensus regarding many of the standard, indeed fundamental, lexical terms of biblical studies: BC/BCE, God/god, which collection of books constitutes the canon (and even what "canon" means)—the list could go on. Faced with such possibilities, the simple heuristic device of starting with the Old Testament on the grounds of pressure of time or disciplinary expertise looks like it has a lot to commend it. Nevertheless, some brief points may be made here.

First, it is not just inevitable that value judgments encroach upon the terminology involved in biblical studies, but it is in fact an example of the kind of tradition-constituted discourses that MacIntyre himself has in mind when he discusses traditions of moral philosophy. If there were a metalanguage in which to couch such discussions, then life might be simpler, and life did perhaps have the appearance of being simpler when most scholars engaged in biblical studies were operating under a largely stable paradigm without necessarily acknowledging it. On a small scale or local level with respect to particular details of this or that Old Testament text, for instance, it seems quite likely that one can engage in fruitful reflection of many kinds without worrying overmuch about broader conceptual schemes. Simple examples may be offered, since the concerns do not lie here: What is the notion of "sin" understood in the book of Amos? What is the significance of temple worship in Chronicles?

However, such "fruitful reflection" is not of *all* kinds, since any interpretive line of inquiry will ramify into broader questions sooner or later (or at least, those kinds that do not are sufficiently small-scale not to occupy us here).[22] What is Isaiah's notion of justice? How far is it possible to go in responding to this question without engaging in a significant exploration of the notions of justice that occur in Isaiah, which in turn implicate myriad conceptions of human life and deity? All this is to say that almost any significant discussion of biblical texts has a *self-involving* dimension: the interpreter must interact with the subject matter of the text in ways that in turn shape or at least respond to the character of the interpreter.[23] In one sense, that of character understood as constituted by virtue, such a claim is precisely what is at stake in the present study.

The particular implication of this point arising here concerns the nature of any kind of interpretive inquiry that might be supposed to

22. Gregory Jones gives the example of the difference between debating the historicity of Jonah (flat, uninvolving) as against considering the message of Jonah concerning judgment (uncomfortable, leaving one's own character "at risk"; 2002: 20).

23. On self-involving biblical language, see Briggs 2001; 2008: 98–106. The example of justice in Isaiah was prompted by the fine study of Leclerc 2001.

fall somewhere under the rubric of "Old Testament theology." This category has been notoriously problematic in theory, though arguably less so in practice, at least if the number of weighty volumes of Old Testament theology appearing in recent years is anything to go by.[24] But the theological conundrum is simply stated: if "Old Testament" is a Christian theological label, then on what theological (rather than historical) grounds might one justify pursuing what is presumably meant to be a Christian theological account of one part of the Christian canon only? I am not aware of a satisfactory general answer to this question, at least on a conceptual level.[25] Perhaps there is no satisfactory general answer, and heuristic appeals to manageability and expertise will have to suffice. However, the move to "theological interpretation" in recent years suggests that the goal of such work can be understood as the interpretation of canonical scriptural texts with respect especially to their theological subject matter.[26] In this sense, the decision to work with the Old Testament occurs in the context of engaging with its theological subject matter from a range of perspectives that self-consciously move beyond those explicitly given in the Old Testament—that move in fact toward the wider range of Christian perspectives available.

The above account spoke indiscriminately of "one part of the Christian canon" in asking the question about why one would study some subset of the Bible. Yet it is not just any subset or part that is in view: it is the Old Testament, theologically tied in to the whole in a manner unique to itself. In general, the extent to which one expects (theological) continuity between the tasks of explicating the theology of Old Testament writers or texts on the one hand, and the articulation of Christian theological perspectives on those texts on the other, will depend on a prior judgment regarding the overall continuity or

24. I shall resist the temptation to survey or even list the literature, though the surveys offered in the two volumes by Perdue (1995; 2005) are of enormous value, regardless of how one estimates his own proposals.

25. The striking proposals of Seitz (1998; 2001) seem right, though part of their very point is that they problematize the notion of "Old Testament theology" anyway.

26. Vanhoozer et al. 2005 represents this as close to the heart of a wide-ranging network of practices of "theological interpretation." See also the focus of the *Journal of Theological Interpretation* (2007 to date) as well as volumes of the Studies in Theological Interpretation series, to which the present volume belongs.

discontinuity between the two Testaments. And this is a long-running central question in the study of biblical theology, never more ably framed than by von Rad, regarding how the "old" anticipated and looked for its fulfillment toward the "new," being "actualized" in it (1965: 319–35, esp. 323).[27]

However, in any specific case (or with respect to any particular topic or angle of approach), this "general" consideration still leaves us asking whether we expect continuity or discontinuity between the old and the new. At this point we must recall the nature of the present project: a description of the implied reader in the terms of virtue or character ethics. So the question becomes this: Is the implied "virtuous reader" of the Old Testament substantively different from the implied "virtuous reader" of the New Testament? If so, in what sorts of characteristics does the difference consist? In other words, would such differences be moral/ethical in nature?

My own implied reader will not be surprised to note that I do not think a generalized answer can be given to this question in advance of exploring specific cases, but it does seem to me, at least in terms of prima facie plausibility, that while the *theology* of the implied readers of the Old and New Testaments might well be distinguished in terms of how the identity of God or God's people is understood, the *character* of the reader, in terms of their moral virtues, will not necessarily be fundamentally affected.[28] Perhaps such a judgment presumes too quickly upon a view of the law as being taken up in Christ, its "righteous requirements" being met and newly embodied in the life of the Spirit. It is certainly possible that one would have to revise this provisional judgment of plausibility in the light of consideration of specific cases. We therefore shall return briefly to this question in the conclusion; but at this point we shall draw a veil over much else that could be said about the conceptuality and challenge of "Old Testament studies," in the hope that we have offered a sufficient rationale for proceeding.

27. And in turn, never more ably critiqued than by Seitz 2001: 35–47 (also Seitz 1998: 28–40; 2007: 155–87); cf. also Groves 1987: 7–62.

28. Note too Fowl and Jones's point about our moral and theological distance from the world of the "biblical" writers (1991: 61), which they address with examples from Paul and Jeremiah without regard to the significance of Old or New Testament location.

Plan of the Present Study

Perhaps the vindication of the approach will simply be in the sampling of it. We began this chapter with Gregory Jones's call for the virtues of "receptivity, humility, truthfulness, courage, charity, and imagination" in interpretation (2002: 32). Not all of these categories of virtue will serve as test cases for our explorations, though many of them will be incorporated as we proceed, from case to case. Here we list the virtues to which we shall address ourselves, with brief consideration of why they are appropriate candidates:

- *Humility*—an intriguing test case because, for all that it is more or less univocally praised in hermeneutical discussion today, it is the celebrated case of a virtue recognized in Christian tradition yet evaluated as a vice by Aristotle (cf. the comments of MacIntyre 1984: 182)

- *Wisdom*—probably the strongest candidate for a virtue greatly to be sought after by the reader of Scripture, and as we have seen, one of the categories most suited to the concerns of virtue ethics on its own terms anyway, where its appearance as *phronēsis* occupied the central place in Aristotle's scheme

- *Trust*—the virtue of hermeneutical trust is just beginning to reemerge in recent theological reflection after a lengthy period where suspicion has been so easily the default mode of biblical interpretation; but in what senses does suspicion remain appropriate to the reader of Scripture, and in the light of this, how should trust best be understood?

- *Love*—despite the all-too-common popular preconception that love represents the New Testament's trump card after the harsh rigors of the Old Testament, it is clear that love is a key characteristic in the Old Testament vision of the moral life, once we have tuned in to the various ways in which the Old Testament itself wishes to set the agenda for what constitutes love

- *Receptivity*—it is important to consider explicitly the ways in which human virtue is understood in "responsive" terms in the Old Testament, not as a self-sufficient moral category but as a way of life that is "summoned" by the presence of the God of Israel

The relevant passages of Scripture for each study will be introduced, and the choices will be explained, on a chapter-by-chapter basis. To some extent the discussions in each chapter will overlap, since obviously no one virtue flourishes in splendid isolation from others, but each chapter represents a focus on one part of the whole.

A conclusion will seek to draw together the threads of the inquiry, as well as considering some further questions concerning the overall project, questions that may have been raised along the way. In particular, the conclusion will be the point at which to reflect on the implications of our portrait of the implied reader for those real readers who actually engage in the practices of reading these texts. It is my hope that the succeeding studies will contribute to a broadening and deepening of our understanding of the kind of reader one should be in order to be best situated to receive, understand, and embody the life-transforming concerns of the Old Testament.

2

NEITHER MEEK
NOR MODEST

The Puzzling Hermeneutics of Humility

Few things are as well established in recent hermeneutical discussion as the maxim that hermeneutics should lead the biblical interpreter to an appropriate humility. Thus, in addition to Gregory Jones's listing of humility as one of the requisite "virtues for wise and faithful reading of Scripture" (2002: 32), we may find the following, more or less at random:

> An important lesson to learn from our survey [of interpretations] is that of exegetical and hermeneutical humility. (Wolters 2004: 283)

> The reliance on the Holy Spirit in interpretation effects interpretive humility. . . . [The Puritan John] Owen insists on the interpretive humility that should come with the Christian's belief in the power of God's word. (Zimmerman 2004: 115)

> The truth of our locatedness in interpretation should, however, encourage humility as we come to the biblical text. (J. Brown 2007: 126)

Perhaps the most thorough discussion of the area is that of Kevin Vanhoozer, who writes eloquently of hermeneutic humility at the climax of his epic plea for hermeneutical realism (Vanhoozer 1998: 462–68). He sees hermeneutic humility as an alternative to the two hermeneutic sins of pride (claiming "premature" knowledge of the text) and sloth (claiming that knowledge of the text is impossible). Thus:

> In recognizing real limits, humility is pride's defeat. In recognizing that interpreters are not makers but receivers of meaning, humility is realistic about the aims and objectives of hermeneutics. (Vanhoozer 1998: 463–64)

For Vanhoozer, humility is not a self-sufficient interpretive virtue; for it needs balancing with conviction, a view shared by Jeannine Brown: "In the end, conviction and humility are proper attitudes that reflect the incarnational nature of the Bible" (2007: 272). In a more recent article, though, Vanhoozer does describe humility as "the most important virtue," in a call for "self-effacing, humble-hearted readers, who do not consider equality with the author 'something to be grasped'" (Phil. 2:6; Vanhoozer 2006: 92).

In the face of such a crowd of witnesses, and conscious of humility's secure location on the moral high ground, what is there left to discuss? Who would wish to be proud rather than humble?

Nevertheless, there is good reason to pause at this point, and give some attention to the fact that humility has had an unusually colorful career as a candidate for virtue. As we have noted: as far as Aristotle was concerned, humility was not a virtue at all. It was not so much to be contrasted with pride or sloth as with courage, magnificence, and proper ambition, characteristics that would make for bold interpreters indeed.[1] Aquinas, on the other hand, thought humility was a virtue, indeed the specific virtue that "moderates and restrains moral virtue" from "tending to high things immoderately" (*ST* 2a2ae, 161, 1; cited in Hauerwas and Pinches 1997: 143).[2] Clearly, an alternative tradition

---

1. An engaging defense of the Aristotelian emphasis for some (though not all) Christian purposes is offered by Horner 1998.

2. Aquinas's discussion of humility, in dialogue particularly with Augustine, is found in the six articles of *ST* 2a2ae, 161, the last of which is a discussion of Benedict's "steps"

has been feeding into Aquinas's reflections, one that is already present in the Talmud, which tells us that the divine Spirit rests only on a person who is powerful, wealthy, wise, and humble (*b. Ned.* 38a). In the sixth century we find the Rule of Benedict, in its seventh chapter, "On Humility," describing a twelve-step ladder to the indwelling of this vital characteristic of the Christian life, a ladder predicated on the central importance of Luke 14:11: "For all who exalt themselves will be humbled [*tapeinōthēsetai*], and those who humble themselves will be exalted." From Aristotle onward, meanwhile, philosophers have labored long and hard to lay bare the nature and desirability of humility, none more so than Kant, who wrote at length on the significance of humility as "that meta-attitude which constitutes the moral agent's proper perspective on herself as a dependent and corrupt but capable and dignified rational agent" (Grenberg 2005: 133).

The concept of "humility" clearly covers a good deal of ground, not all of it either obviously or in practice desirable, as Dickens was able to demonstrate with his memorable portrait of Uriah Heep, the "very umble" clerk in *David Copperfield*, whose repeated protestations of being "the umblest person going" and "much too umble" for advancement were simply a cover for self-centered scheming (1966: 291–92). In a study of the development of the idea of humility in and beyond the Bible, Klaus Wengst (1988)[3] pinpoints a key shift in the range of meaning of the term to 1 Clement, where several examples from the history of Israel are marshaled to the cause of recommending humility in the face of the presumptuous actions that have occurred in Corinth (1 Clement being written in part to address the case of presbyters removed from office at the urging of some younger church members). Summarizing the examples, Clement writes, "The humility [*to tapeinophron*] and subordination of so many and such great men of renown have, through their obedience, improved not only us but also the generations before us" (1 Clem. 19.1). Wengst observes, "The category of obedience which is reintroduced here is in no way

---

(noted above). It would be another project again to consider Augustine's own view, which is helpfully reconstructed with relevance to interpretive charity by Schlabach 1994.

3. Wengst's own thesis—that humility has its roots in the experience of the humiliation of the poor, a humiliation critiqued by the prophets—has been rightly criticized by Dawes 1991b, but this does not affect my point here.

suggested by the examples given earlier. . . . [Humility] is made to serve the development and establishment of hierarchical structures" (1988: 55, 57). It is doubtless this notion of humility blurring between dignified respect and (potentially) abusive submission that provoked Nietzsche's famous aphoristic response: "When stepped on, a worm doubles up. That is clever. In that way he lessens the probability of being stepped on again. In the language of morality: humility" (Nietzsche 1968: 471). The inherent suspicion of humility as the legitimation of a will to power endures in some feminist critique too. Carolyn Osiek recounts with regard to the call for humility (*tapeinophrosynē*) in Philippians 2, for example: "It can sound like a patriarchal trap to the feminist reader. . . . This kind of rhetoric has been used perennially to control women and reinforce culturally induced feelings of inferiority" (1994: 243).[4] Even theologically constructive accounts of humility limit their horizons to such claims as "it would be better to try to conceive of humility as a matter of viewing everybody as basically equal" (Roberts 2007: 83; cf. 78–93).

The range of possible resonances of the term "humility" is thus so broad that unless we can give it some specific content, it seems too poorly defined as a moral category. This is all the more relevant when we consider its much-vaunted desirability in the area of biblical interpretation. It is interesting, in the light of this wider reflection, to note that in the kinds of claims quoted at the beginning of our chapter, humility is to a large extent being brought as a ready-made category to the text, with perhaps the assumption that all concerned can appreciate its self-evident merit. However, if our brief historical survey demonstrates anything, it must be that humility is something of a contested concept and that its status as an interpretive virtue appropriate to the reading of Scripture may require some deference to what Scripture itself has to say on the subject of humility. The goal of this chapter is therefore to ask whether the Bible itself might want us to conceive of humility in a certain way that might then in turn inform the kind of humility in view when it is embraced as an interpretive virtue. Or more simply, the goal is to ask what contribu-

---

4. Though Osiek is in fact determined to demonstrate that such a reading uses the text "the wrong way" (cf. also Osiek 2000: 51–55). Contrast this with, for example, Polaski 1999: 119, for whom Paul is guilty as charged.

tion Scripture itself makes to informing a hermeneutic of humility. And once phrased this way, it is evident that there is a great deal left to discuss.

The Most Humble Man on Earth

Of all the things the Old Testament wishes to say about humility, such as "The reward for humility and fear of Yhwh is riches and honor and life" (Prov. 22:4), or its claim that "humility goes before honor" (Prov. 15:33; also in 18:12), one in particular stands out: the claim made in Numbers 12:3, where we read: "Now the man Moses was very humble, more so than anyone else on the face of the earth." If there is a model of humility, in other words, Moses is it. Yet this verse does seem straightaway to contain an apparent oddity, given that humility is an interesting phenomenon, an elusive virtue that almost seems to defeat (or deconstruct) any attempt to strive for it. The old country-western song captured the joke, though admittedly without much musical merit: "O Lord, it's hard to be humble / when you're perfect in every way" (M. Davis 1980). Indeed, Numbers 12:3 seems at first glance to be almost a variation on this theme: is Moses to be understood as the one who excels most noticeably in the area of self-effacement?

Our discussion of the varying estimates of humility down through the ages should alert us to questions about what notion of "humble" is in view in this verse. We shall examine the text, explore three major avenues of approach to its surface-level oddity, and then argue that the kind of understanding of humility required to make sense of this verse relies on the primary importance of dependence upon God. Numbers 12, read this way, offers insight into the nature of a "hermeneutic of humility," or in other words, the virtue of humility appropriate to the reading of Scripture.

The Text of Numbers 12:3

The issue that detains commentators with regard to Numbers 12:3 is the unique singular form ʿānāw, meaning "humble" or "meek" or some similar word. The unique occurrence of this form is tied to the verse's affirmation of Moses as singularly humble, which is what suggests that here we have the prime candidate for a narrative portrayal of the virtue of humility in the Old Testament. But the matter of vocabulary and its range of meaning is not entirely straightforward and requires some comment first.

The plural form *'ānāwîm* occurs some twenty times in the Old Testament (e.g., Ps. 37:11: "The meek shall inherit the land") and is semantically related to *'ny* (poor), but the unique singular *'ānāw* can hardly mean "poor" in this context (cf. the review of options in Widmer 2004: 268–69). *'Ānāwâ*, the later term for humility in Rabbinic Hebrew, occurs six times in the Old Testament, including in the aforementioned verses from Proverbs, in Zephaniah 2:3 (the clearest parallel usage to the Numbers verse and usually the comparison cited in commentaries), and two slightly more complex uses of the term in Psalms 18:36 and 45:5 (where it is ascribed to God who "stoops down" and the king who governs with "righteous humility," though these additional resonances need not concern us here).[5]

The LXX translates Numbers 12:3 with *praüs* (meek, gentle), though it is debatable whether one can distinguish too strongly between LXX translations of various terms for poverty and humility by the pair of candidates *praüs* and *tapeinos* (cf. Bauder and Esser 1976). Nevertheless "meek" was the translation offered in the KJV, with the result that in general consideration, the Christian virtue of humility is often read as a form of meekness.[6] Since it will make a difference in due course, we might attempt to distinguish humility from meekness in terms of the latter's associated notions of gentleness or submissiveness, whereas humility has more to do with status, standing, or estimation. However, at least to some extent, for many centuries "meek" was simply a far more common word for the over-

5. Dawes 1991a offers a thorough survey, though his extension of later rabbinic meanings of *'ānāwâ* back into Old Testament contexts is sharply critiqued by Dickson and Rosner (2004), whose view we shall note after exploring Numbers 12.

6. One might note here the traditional phrase "as meek as Moses," such as is used by George Eliot, *Mill on the Floss*, I.1.xii.232 (1860).

lapping senses.[7] Most translations use "humble" today, though Levine offers "unassuming" (1993: 314).

The oddity of a comparative evaluation of the ultimate in non-competitive evaluative concepts—Moses is not just very humble but "more so than anyone else on the face of the earth"—is striking.[8] There are essentially three ways of dealing with it.

1. Moses Is Not in Fact Humble

The first line of approach is to suggest that *'ānāw* does not mean humble after all. This consideration comes from two different angles, the first of which may be dispensed with quickly.

In circles in which the authorship of the Pentateuch is attributed to Moses, the oddity of saying that Moses is the most humble person on the face of the earth is doubly compounded. If such were the case, then here would be the most humble person in the world ascribing unto himself an all-surpassing humility: "The self-commendatory nature of the statement occasioned difficulties to older commentators," as G. B. Gray noted a century ago (1903: 123). Thus Calvin seems uncharacteristically backed into a corner as he remarks, "Moreover, he does not praise his own virtue for the sake of boasting, but in order to exhort us by his example" (1855: 44), while Keil, who directly observes that this verse offers no leverage against Mosaic authorship of the Pentateuch, protests a little too strongly that it "is not an expression of vain self-display, or a glorification of his own gifts and excellences, . . . [but] is simply a statement, which was indispensable to a full and correct interpretation of all the circumstances, and which was made quite objectively" (1980: 77).

Most older commentators were actually more inclined to take this verse parenthetically in the sense that it is some form of editorial, or more commonly divine, comment on the character of Moses. Thus Origen comments: "Moses . . . was never so highly praised by God as on this occasion, . . . [where] it is said of him, in reference to this,

---

7. Cf. entries for "meek" and "humility" in the *Oxford English Dictionary*.
8. The oddity is not fundamentally different if one reads *mikkōl* as having the sense of "among" (as in Deut. 7:6: "*from all the* peoples of the earth" [AT]). The comparison becomes implicit: Moses is humble among everybody on the earth, but this is still worth saying of him!

'Moses was a man exceeding meek above all men that are upon earth'"
(Origen, *Commentary on the Song of Songs* 2.1; cited in Lienhard
2001: 220).

Today, those who hold to the notion that the "Torah of Moses"
requires an idea of Moses as "author" (whatever that may have meant)
tend to take a different tack: they suggest that *'ānāw* must mean
something else. When this concern is driven simply by the desire to
safeguard Mosaic authorship at all costs, it can have little to commend
it. One example shall suffice. Cleon Rogers, taking it as a given that one
must find a way around the "concern and consternation" caused by
Moses's apparently inappropriate statement, concludes, on the basis
of an etymological root meaning "to be bowed down; afflicted" (e.g.,
BDB 776), that the meaning in Numbers 12 must be "miserable." He
concludes, "Moses was saying that in the light of the burden of the
people and the complaint of his family he was the most 'miserable'
person in the world" (C. Rogers 1986: 263). The sheer implausibility
of this line of thought is highlighted by the one remaining sentence
in the article: "Who has not made this statement about himself at
some point in life?" whereby a text affirming a unique characteristic
of Moses has come to be a truism of every person.

However, concerns about authorship are not the only reason why
commentators propose that humility might not be in view in Numbers
12:3. A more helpful reason for raising the question about how to
translate *'ānāw* is articulated by George Coats: "What kind of virtue
. . . belongs to Moses more than to all the other persons who are on
the face of the earth? And how does that virtue relate to the description of Moses as responsible in v. 7?" (1993: 92). In other words, the
question of how the description of Moses as *'ānāw* functions in the
context of Numbers 12 is, with one significant caveat, a more plausible
line of approach for questioning whether some other characteristic
of Moses might be in view in verse 3.[9]

9. The caveat is that the tradition history lying behind Numbers 12 seems complicated.
The passage is notoriously difficult to fit into the standard categories of a J/E analysis.
It is, says Noth, "a complex which, from the literary point of view, can no longer be
disentangled" (1968: 93); a view that he would elsewhere express as its being "one of the
hopeless cases of Pentateuchal analysis" (cited in Coats 1988: 230). Arguably, the text as
we have it is not possessed of a literary unity (see the survey of studies, and defense of
a Deuteronomic redaction, in Römer 1997), though of course this does not mean it can-

Setting to one side, then, the imponderables of text sources and preliterary traditions, what happens if one pursues the sense of *'ānāw* by asking what it is in Numbers 12 that particularly singles out Moses as unique among the people of the earth? This is the question asked by Coats (1993) in his study of the passage, and by way of etymological association with "a root *'nw*, connoting responsibility or integrity," he argues that "the context highlights rather obedience within the context of personal responsibility." As a result, he concludes: "'To be 'meek' is to be responsible for the whole household of the master," and thus one might translate the relevant sentence as "The man Moses was the most honorable of all persons who are on the face of the earth" (Coats 1993: 92, 94).

Coats's aim in this article is to read Numbers 12 as a coherent literary unit.[10] The humility of Moses, he suggests, makes too odd a contribution to the narrative of the chapter, which instead affirms of him that he is honorable and by verse 13 sees his obedience emerging as "he stands face to face with God and defends his own" (1993: 98). For Coats, this is appropriately firm and decisive leadership, and it is this that is expressed by the description of Moses as *'ānāw* in verse 3.

Coats's approach is, I shall suggest, in the end unsatisfactory, but it will be illuminating to consider why this is so. There are three parts to the overall puzzle he is considering:

a. the meaning of the word *'ānāw* in Numbers 12:3

---

not be *read as* a literary unity. Certainly it is odd that the passage opens in v. 1 with the third-person feminine singular *wattĕdabbēr*, as if to say that Miriam spoke against Moses (concerning his marriage), only for Aaron's name to be added in v. 1 because the passage will proceed to consider the originally separate case of divine communication (prophecy). Hence, some commentators suggest that after Miriam and Aaron have been rebuked in vv. 6–9, only Miriam suffers the white-skinned affliction in v. 10 because two stories have here been woven together (e.g., Noth 1968: 92–94; E. Davies 1995: 113–14). On the other hand, all the details that at first sight seem odd could perhaps be accounted for either by noting that singular feminine verbs do on occasion serve to cover male and female subjects when the woman is the leader of the action (Milgrom 1990: 93; e.g., Judg. 5:1) or by judging that the two topics of contention (Moses's wife and his unique authority) are indeed intrinsically linked in the logic of the passage (a point we shall take up below).

10. This is explicit in the context of the article's original publication as a contribution to the project of Clines, Gunn, and Hauser 1982.

b. the question of whether Numbers 12 is a coherent literary narrative

c. what Numbers 12 overall tells us about the characteristics of Moses

The shape of the issue is, we must note, fundamentally dependent upon whether one wants to say yes in response to *b*. For as long as literary coherence has been denied or ignored in the passage, *a* and *c* simply function independently. Interestingly, one can still say yes to the question of literary coherence and think that *c* does not help much in answering *a*. The NIV operates with something like this view when it sets verse 3 aside in parentheses, marking it as tangential to the main thrust of the narrative. More commonly, however, once literary coherence is affirmed, there are then two ways to run the argument.

The first is the one followed by Coats. He uses his reading of *c* to drive his response to *a*, thus concluding from the overall portrait of Numbers 12 that *'ānāw* means "honorable." The etymological argument he advances, though it is presented as the first part of the evidence regarding how to read verse 3, in fact functions as supporting evidence for an argument that is predicated on *c*. The etymological argument is probably weak on its own. As noted in one review of his proposal, "If the point of the editorial comment is to emphasize Moses' honour, then there are far more direct and unambiguous ways of doing it than by using *'ānāw*" (Dawes 1990: 337).

The other way to run the argument, however, is to hold on to the likelihood that *'ānāw* means something in the area of humility and then ask, on the assumption of literary coherence, how what we read about Moses in Numbers 12 helps to shed light on what the text means us to understand by "humility." (In the terms we have been using, this is using *a* to drive a response to *c*, which can tell us about what constitutes humility.)

Once we phrase the matter this way, there seem to be two main possibilities to explore, corresponding to the two putatively separable concerns lying in (or behind?) the narrative as we have it. Either Moses's humility is defined in some way relevant to the matter of his wife, or it is defined in some way relevant to the question of his unique status before God.

2. Moses's Humility Is Related to His Actions toward His Wife

When Numbers 12 garners critical attention these days, it is often because of the story of Miriam (cf. Trible 1994; the several essays gathered in Brenner 2000: 104–73; Pimpinella 2006). In many ways, Miriam functions as a symbol for an alternative to reading the Torah "with the grain": here she stands in opposition to Moses, arguing that he inappropriately arrogates to himself the voice of the Lord. What better symbol could there be of the range of options open to the interpreter? Walter Brueggemann captures the point: "Well beyond her historical significance, Miriam is clearly a generative metaphor for ongoing interpretative work that precludes any simple, settled patriarchal closure. She is a durable presence that attracts interpretation, which in turn refuses to let her be silenced" (2002: 133). It is no coincidence that a prominent women's commentary on the Torah was titled *The Five Books of Miriam* (Frankel 1997).

Numbers 12, however, is doubly implicated in the hermeneutical concerns of so-called advocacy reading (i.e., reading that self-consciously privileges a particular interpretive viewpoint regardless of whether it captures the text's own inherent flow and agenda). As well as the gender-relative concerns of Miriam and her being singled out for punishment in response to a protest undertaken alongside Aaron, verse 1 raises the famous conundrum of Moses's Cushite wife: a reported action in most translations, although the JPS's *Tanakh* translation follows Ibn Ezra, reading *kî-* as a way of introducing direct speech and thus bringing the charge in the words of Miriam (and Aaron): "He married a Cushite woman!" (v. 1c; cf. Milgrom 1990: 91).

The issues raised here are well known. Is this Zipporah? Zipporah, as readers of Exodus 2:21 are aware, was a daughter of the priest of Midian and not a black woman from Cush, so such a suggestion requires emending "Cush" to Cushan, located, according to Habakkuk 3:7, as being in (or near) the land of Midian. As Eryl Davies points out, this fits poorly with the whole point of Numbers 12:1, since Miriam's complaint seems to presume that Moses's Cushite wife is a new arrival (1995: 118). Levine thus affirms that "the woman in question was most certainly not Zipporah" (1993: 328). So if this is a second (or at least a subsequent) wife for Moses, what has happened to Zipporah? According to Exodus 18:2, Jethro, Moses's father-in-law, took back Zipporah "after she had been sent home [*šillûḥeyhā*]"[11] and received her two sons as well.

The most insistent recent treatment of this topic, by Fischer, suggests that the Piel of "sending away" "is a common technical term for 'get a divorce' (cf., e.g., Deut. 21:14; 22:19, 29)," in the light of which we might read "divorce" here in Exodus 18 (2000: 164). Fischer suggests that failure to translate this way "insinuates" a temporary dismissal, but startlingly she does not pause to reflect that one reason such an "insinuation" remains in translations is because of verse 5 in the same passage, where Jethro brings "his sons and his wife" to Moses. Admittedly the Hebrew "his" is vague here, but the context strongly suggests that this is Zipporah and (her) sons. Clearly one way to read the passage is that Moses's family has simply been spending time with Jethro. On the other hand, a modern reader might see in verse 7 a certain lack of marital engagement between Moses and Zipporah, since all we are told is that Moses and Jethro "each ask after the other's welfare."

In the end, Exodus 18 will not yield a full answer to the question of the state of Moses's marriage because it is not about that, and what hints we do have are simply hints of a background that the story is not telling. The result, then, is that Numbers 12:1 is underdetermined as to whether we know where Zipporah has gone. However, given the dynamic of Miriam's new complaint, we may conclude that Moses has either divorced Zipporah or at least taken advantage in some way of her absence and has taken a new wife. Consideration of what the complaint against this new wife was is another pursuit of a silence in the text: proposals tend to focus either on some aspect of her race and/or skin color, perhaps to be contrasted to the whiteness of Miriam's punishment (e.g., Felder 1991: 135–37), or some aspect of family jealousy (e.g., Weems 1988: 72–74). Perhaps the complaint is not fundamentally about her at all but might be seen as a displaced expression of Miriam's frustration about the issues described in chapter 11 (noted below), which seem to be the precise issues that then come back into focus as chapter

11. Following here the JPS *Tanakh* translation.

12 progresses. In any case, it would take us too far afield to pursue this question further.[12]

According to the narrative of Numbers 12, Miriam's complaint against Moses causes Yhwh to "break ominous silence" (Trible 1994: 176) and summon Moses, Aaron, and Miriam to hear the divine response at the tent of meeting (vv. 6–8). In outline, Moses's unique status as a prophet before God is reaffirmed, and Miriam and Aaron are rebuked for supposing that their own status as recipients of prophetic dreams and visions could equate them with Moses, who receives from Yhwh *peh 'el-peh* (literally "mouth to mouth," or "face to face," as most translations render it).

In this context, what can make the affirmation of Moses's unique humility relevant? The only possibility relevant to the vexed question of Moses's marriage must be that somehow, in connection with his wife, Moses has done something to which no one else could aspire.

For this proposal to sound anything more than far-fetched, it would first be necessary to establish an interpretive framework for the passage in which some aspect of the question of marriage could be assumed

---

12. For the sheer intrinsic interest of the matter, not because it affects the present argument, what do the rabbis say about Moses's possible divorce? It is surprising, after all, how such a topic seems to be passed over in silence so often. Perhaps it is less surprising that the rabbinic tradition can be appealed to for both alternatives. More interestingly, the argument that Moses had divorced Zipporah has to contend with a series of factors germane to the rabbis: Moses cannot have divorced after the giving of Torah, and therefore the divorce must have occurred in Exod. 18 (or earlier); Miriam's complaint assumes something new in the situation, and therefore what is new must be the state of Miriam's knowledge of the matter rather than the divorce itself; the occasion of Miriam finding out about the divorce must be related to the context of Num. 12:1 and is thus to be found in the argument about prophecy in 11:26–30, where Eldad and Medad begin to prophesy. Joshua asks Moses to stop them, and Moses replies, "Would that all Yhwh's people were prophets" (v. 29). According to some of the midrashim, at this point Zipporah tells Miriam that Moses has separated from her. According to others, Miriam deduces it from reflecting on Moses's status as one prophet among many and yet still not spending time with his wife, a characteristic heretofore hidden by his unique status and workload. (I am indebted here to the summary of various rabbinic opinions on this matter by Reb Chaim HaQoton 2007, citing, among others, *Sifre* on Num. 12:1.) According to *Exod. Rab.* (1.13), Zipporah (the estranged and still only wife) tells Miriam at this point that Moses has stopped sleeping with her; hence Miriam's concern that Moses's prophetic status has driven him to neglect his wife. In any case, the rabbinic predisposition to work with a supposition of literary unity and to look for clues as to Miriam's complaint in the context of the surrounding passage leads us on to consider the particular matter before us.

to lie in the foreground. This is the proposal of Fischer (2000), alluded to earlier, who reads the chapter in terms of the political realities of postexilic Israel, hosting a confrontation between differing traditions of Torah interpretation. For Fischer, the "texts favouring the dissolution of mixed marriages by divorce" (Ezra 10; Neh. 13) offer the voice represented in the story by Moses, whereby prophecy simply is the interpretation of Torah, whereas Aaron represents the priesthood and Miriam represents the prophetic groups working on prophetic books (2000: 165–66).

What then does Moses's unique humility signify? Simply this: "As the meekest of all humans on the face of the earth, Moses has more than richly fulfilled the divine instruction by letting go of his foreign wife" (Fischer 2000: 168, reading the wife of 12:1 as Zipporah). But the text of Numbers 12, in Fischer's scheme, has thereby set aside the practical possibility of enforcing divorce by showing that only Moses was capable of this; it is a standard too high for others to reach. In sum, Miriam is right about mixed marriages, though wrong in failing to acknowledge Moses's position. Her punishment, so long a particular cause of concern to feminist interpretation, is to be taken (says Fischer) as the counterpart to the punishment of Moses and Aaron in Numbers 20:2–13, and the key requirement of the narrative is that all three are shown, at some point, to be guilty of a sin that precludes their entering the land. The theological payoff follows: a woman's voice can be right, even in the midst of its provoking punishment.

On a general level, Fischer makes a strong case for saying that the significance of Numbers 12 may be discernible in the midst of taking it as part of a longer narrative whole. Moses's marriage is thereby tied to the question of prophecy, in narrative terms, while being attached to the question of the politics of marriage by way of a historical reconstruction of the function of the finished (or nearly finished) Torah. In this way of thinking, Fischer joins a long line of critics who have seen the text of the Torah as only fully interpretable in terms of its ongoing role as a living tradition in the later life of Israel (e.g., Sanders 1972). On one level this is clearly plausible. With regard to this chapter's "affirmation of the legitimacy of the Mushite priesthood," for example, no less a critic than Frank Moore Cross suggests that "some such function must be asserted for the formation and preservation of the traditions" (Cross 1973: 204; though most think it is prophecy and not priesthood that is in discussion here; e.g., R. R. Wilson 1980: 155–56).

Nevertheless, granting the non-impossibility of such a thesis, one must finally conclude that Fischer's proposal is unlikely. First, if it is indeed more likely that Moses has now taken a second, Cushite wife, this can hardly recommend him as the voice of Ezra-Nehemiah against mixed marriages. Second, reading Torah texts in terms of later politics is fraught with questions of how to weight probabilities and plausibilities. A simple way to see this is to stand Fischer's thesis alongside an alternative view, such as that of Levine, who reads chapters 11–12 as helping to lay "the foundation for the legitimacy of the Davidic monarchy," partly on the basis of parallels between 1 Samuel 22:14 and Numbers 12:7 (1993: 342–43). While one could say that the legitimation of subsequent views of prophetic activity is at least a topic anchored in the surface level of the text of Numbers 12, and arguably divorce and remarriage is too; mixed marriage is much more of a framework brought to the text than deduced from it. Finally, the fundamental thesis that humility could equate to unique ability to divorce raises problematic questions about the virtues to which the humble might aspire elsewhere in Scripture, which might simply be the interpreter's lot if the point were well grounded in the text before us, but which perhaps weighs against a relatively speculative proposal.

We have dwelt on this proposal at length because, for all its problems, it does represent a serious attempt to read Numbers 12:3 in its context as relating to the presenting issue in 12:1. The fruit of this inquiry lies not in its exegetical results but in the framework it forces us to develop for reading the verse about Moses's humility in terms of the dynamic of the passage.

3. Moses's Humility before God

As we have noted above, what is unique about Moses in the developing narrative of Numbers 12 is that he meets "face to face" with God, in contrast to the mediated way in which Miriam and Aaron receive their prophetic gift.[13] This unique role, directly present before God, is what sets him apart from all other people, and therefore it is in this that we should look for an understanding of the contextual reference to humility. I want to suggest that what sets Moses apart as the most humble person on the earth is defined in this passage as his unique status as a recipient of God's spoken word "face to face." In other words, humility, as it is depicted in this narrative, is dependence upon God, and in particular, it is dependence upon God for any speaking of a divinely authorized word.

Once humility is defined in this passage as dependence upon the presence of God, light is shed upon several details of the text. First, the reason for the assertion about humility in verse 3 can be seen as linked to Miriam's complaint as developed in verse 2: "Has Yhwh spoken only through Moses? Has he not spoken through us also?" Verse 3 affirms that though it may indeed be true that he has spoken through Miriam (and Aaron) also, there is something unique about his presence to Moses that may be properly compared with others: "more so than anyone else on the face of the earth." This is not the self-deconstructing category of "modesty," in which it seems paradoxical to excel, but it is a category of relatedness to (or perhaps dependence upon) Yhwh, a category already illustrated in two diverse ways in Numbers 11 with respect to daily manna and the outpouring of the spirit of prophecy. Israel has not done well with accepting the provision of manna (11:4–6); nor has it done well, apart from Moses, in rejoicing about the outpouring of the spirit (11:26–30). Ellen Davis has pointed out the link in Numbers 11 between greed and prophecy, suggesting that the spirit of prophecy challenges Israel here "to focus on God's faithfulness instead of their wants" and to learn that God's provision is sufficient (2001: 202–8). To practice, indeed, the virtue of humility, as exemplified only by Moses in this story.

Second, if Moses has this unique ability to stand before God and live, then does this indicate some unique state of Moses's being that separates him (or singles him out) from the human race? Some have suggested that there is a broad range of evidence of such views in Jew-

13. Levine (1993: 342) is right to note that "face to face" here means "direct communication, with nothing intervening," given that—in the light of Exod. 33:20–21—it does not mean Moses *meets* God face to face.

ish tradition (cf. the survey of Lierman 2004: 226–47). For example, 1 Enoch 89.36 has been read as an "angelization" of Moses: a sheep representing Moses in Enoch's allegory "was transformed into a man and built a house for the Lord of the sheep" (Lierman cites Fletcher-Louis 1996: 243). Sirach 45:2, in praising famous men, says that Moses was made "equal in glory to the holy ones" (hagiōn, possibly translating 'elōhîm). Acts 6:11 sees the charge being brought against Stephen that he had spoken "blasphemously" against Moses. Philo, on the basis of Exodus 7:1, also locates Moses somewhere in a category between God and humanity, in a divine state (Life of Moses 1.158; cf. also evidence cited in Lierman 2004: 193–94). Against such traditions, whether or not by way of conscious interaction with them at some stage of development, it is noteworthy that Numbers 12:3 starts with the description of Moses as hā'îš Mōšeh (the man Moses) before going on to elevate him above any other person on the face of the earth.[14]

Third, humility understood in the way we have suggested does not connote meekness (as some older translations had suggested). Thus in response to Miriam's punishment, Moses "cries out [wayyiṣ'aq]" to Yhwh: 'ēl nā' rĕpā' nā' lāh (12:13), rendered by Fox (1995: 721) as "O God, pray, heal her, pray." If the passage is working as a coherent whole, this is the action of the most humble man on earth, and it is a vigorous action engaging with God in the confidence of one who knows God face-to-face. In this it is characteristic of several key moments in prayer in the tradition of Moses (and Abraham before him): Exodus 33:12–16 is the most obvious example (cf. Widmer 2004: 162–68). Arguably, too, Moses's decisive act of striking the rock at Meribah (Num. 20:11) should be seen as reminding us that his unique humility did not lead to his being unusually submissive or meek. Having said that, there is no record of Moses's response to Yhwh's fairly blunt reply to his cry (12:14), so one might suppose that after arguing his best, Moses nevertheless accepts the final judgment. Humility,

14. The main defender of an "angelomorphic Moses" is Fletcher-Louis (e.g., 2002: esp. 137–49). For unconvinced response, in the first instance with regard to Qumran but also with wider application, see van Peursen 2007; Makiello 2007. Makiello (2007: 127) concludes that one can be described as "exalted" without implying either angelomorphic or theomorphic categories. Perhaps Numbers 12:3 itself should serve as a textual anchor weighing against such a trajectory.

then, replaces meekness not so much with stubbornness as with an appropriate, vigorous, yet still respectful engagement with God.

This reading of humility seems to shed a certain amount of light on the passage. One may then briefly consider the vexed question of how the passage, thus understood, might have played out in postexilic politics. The obvious problem, on any account, is that where Numbers 12:6–8 seems easily designed to set apart Moses's prophetic status from the claims of any other prophetic voice, Moses has himself wished in 11:29 that all Yhwh's people would be prophets. The interpreter must maintain a balance here. As Olson writes, "The legitimacy of other prophetic voices is here affirmed but also subordinated to Moses' voice" (2007: 57).

The discussion of this matter generally becomes tied up with the question of the closing of Torah in Deuteronomy 34:10 and following: "Never since has there arisen a prophet in Israel like Moses, whom Yhwh knew face to face [pānîm 'el-pānîm]." If Numbers 12:6–8 (which, we have seen, does not use the phrase "face to face," contra NRSV and others) is designed to indicate the uniqueness of Moses, does this relate to any attempt to situate the prophetic writings as of secondary status with respect to the Torah, in the light of Deuteronomy 34? In the current burgeoning field of studies of the canon, opinion on this question is split far and wide, and one might have sympathy with John Barton's understated comment on how Numbers 12:6–8 separates Moses from all other prophets: "What is meant by this distinction is not entirely clear" (1986: 117).

Nevertheless, to proceed to a tentative conclusion with indecent haste, the position of Stephen Chapman has merit, taking on board as it does an important point with regard to so-called incomparability formulas (i.e., sayings of the kind "no one like him before/since"), which he takes to indicate preeminence rather than uniqueness. Thus, allowing that Numbers 12 uses different vocabulary, its point with regard to the ongoing tradition stands in continuity with Deuteronomy 34:10–12, which indicates that "Moses attained pre-eminent status as God's *prophetic* servant. However, . . . [it] also makes clear that Moses was succeeded by faithful prophets who—more than anyone else—*continued* his work of mediating and interceding with God on Israel's behalf" (Chapman 2000: 131).

In the context in which humility is introduced into the discussion, then, there is a continuity between Moses and those who come after him, a continuity that allows us to say that a reader of Numbers in the time of Ezra and Nehemiah might see Moses as a model to which one should aspire. In particular, such a reader is asked to aspire to the rooting of any ability to speak for God in the humility of receiving any prophetic message from God. One might suggest, in the midst of claim and counterclaim concerning the reception and transmission of Torah, that Numbers 12 asks for dependence upon God, in continuity with the Mosaic Torah, as the requirement of speaking for God. Or to put the matter differently: humility, as it pertains to Moses in Numbers 12, is the root of faithful handling of the word of God.

Such a claim is not so very far from the point being made in Deuteronomy 8:2–3:

> Remember the long way that Yhwh your God has led you these forty years in the wilderness, in order to humble you, testing you to know what was in your heart, whether or not you would keep his commandments. He humbled you by letting you hunger, then by feeding you with manna, with which neither you nor your ancestors were acquainted, in order to make you understand that one does not live by bread alone, but by every word that comes from the mouth of Yhwh.

The point being made by reflecting on the role of the Numbers text in subsequent debates about prophetic legitimation is that with the passing of time this requirement of humility in order to speak for God becomes a requirement for the handing on of the word of God already spoken. Thus the virtue of humility becomes a virtue required for the tasks of ongoing interpretation of the word of God. This leads us to a final consideration of humility in its specific role as an interpretive virtue.

The Hermeneutics of Humility

My claim is that Numbers 12:3, read in context, offers a resource for understanding the virtue of humility as it is appropriate to the practice(s) of biblical interpretation. Thus we may affirm the importance of humility as an interpretive virtue along with the crowd of witnesses with which we began, while at the same time suggesting that Scripture envisages a specific theological turn to the content we give to the virtue. As such, humility offers our first example of the general project of reading the Old Testament for its implied interpretive virtues. We may make one or two points about the larger project in the light of this first test case before concluding by reflecting on how the virtue of humility may be understood as part of the interpretive virtues appropriate to the reading of Scripture.

First, there is a sense in which the concerns of virtue or character ethics, as they inform interpretation, bring the governing interpretive paradigm into more of a relationship with the long tradition of the church's interpretation of Scripture. Such a general move in biblical studies today is widely, though by no means universally, acknowledged and is seen as an asset at least as often as a step backward. Nevertheless, such a recovery of this wider frame of reference neither necessitates nor even supports the rejection of the critical traditions of more recent centuries. Our reading of Numbers 12 has benefited from insights drawn across a wide range of reference, and arguably it is the traditio-historical paradigm of James Sanders's canonical criticism (Sanders 1972) that feeds most naturally into working with the posthistory of the text from within the canon itself. If there is a general lesson, it is perhaps that while critical method does not resolve interpretive dispute, it does at least frame the relevant areas of dispute with an appropriate clarity. The more voices at the table the better, as long as one recalls that having more voices at the table is not an end in itself, and that the table was for a meal rather than a seminar.

Second, a full study of humility would obviously need to go a good deal further. There is a trajectory concerning humility in Scripture, and a proper hermeneutic of humility suited to biblical interpretation would need to go on to engage with it. This is perhaps the place to offer a brief comment on the famous statement of Yhwh's requirements found in Micah 6:8, sometimes seen in rabbinic circles as nothing less than a summary of all the commandments (*b. Mak.* 23b–24a), and described by Dawes as "a statement of the major virtues to be cultivated by those who would seek to be faithful to the God of Israel" (1988: 336). Its final injunction is traditionally translated "to walk humbly with your God [*wĕhasnēaʿ leket ʿim-ĕlōhêkā*]," but there has been some dispute over how best to render *haṣnēaʿ*, functioning here as an adverb: "wisely," "modestly," or indeed "humbly" (Dawes's own preference), in a range of active and passive shades of meaning (Jenson 2008: 173–74). Suffice it to say here that it is difficult from the context of this verse to use Micah 6:8 to fill out our notion of humility, since it serves in itself to draw upon a preestablished (and somewhat elusive) sense of the term. Rather, the verse might indicate that, once we have established what humility is, we are to estimate it very highly indeed. More generally, Dickson and Rosner (2004) offer a fairly full study of the vocabulary of humility in the Old Testament, observing that while Numbers 12:3 stands alone in some respects, it is nevertheless "a *locus classicus* in the discussion of humility in the Hebrew Bible" (2004: 470) and accords well with the general thrust of humility language. Their own view is that *ʿānāw* here should be understood as meaning "lowly/submissive toward God," a virtue they describe as "theological humility" (2004: 472–73). Their argument is explicitly addressing the earlier work of Dawes (1991a; 1991b) and contesting his claim that humility is a "social virtue" in the Old Testament (i.e., a virtue relating to how one might humble oneself before another person). This they see as the new feature introduced by Paul in Philippians 2:3: "In humility [*tapeinophrosynē*] regard others as better than yourselves"—an injunction every bit as culturally out of place in the Greco-Roman world as it is, they say, against the background of the Old Testament. To clarify, the difference between my own conclusions and those of Dickson and Rosner is not whether humility is a social virtue, for here their theological emphasis seems just right. Rather, it is that their notion of humility to some extent maintains its linkage with meekness in being a condition of lowly submission before God, whereas I am proposing that Moses's humility is not really a form of meekness at all, but *dependence* upon God.

Numbers 12:3 seems to capture something very specific about the nature of humility, even though it is an unusual occurrence of the word. The *ʿānāwîm* (traditionally "the meek") will go on to inherit the land and then the earth, and in the end they will be exalted. There is more to say about humility, but it lies on the other side of the careful critical consideration of any given instance of it.[15] However, a narrative that allows us to capture something of the implied virtue as it relates to a main character arguably offers us more of what we are after than the explicit teaching of the wisdom literature regarding the humble, for the reasons explored in the previous chapter. It is the way in which Numbers 12 lends itself to hermeneutical considerations as a result of its own possible role in postexilic debates about legitimation and authorization that allows the text to feed quite neatly into our own concerns with interpretive virtues.

Finally, in this more circumscribed context than a full-scale biblical theology of humility, it is appropriate to reflect on the way in which humility may serve as an interpretive virtue. Clifton Black, in an article that bears the striking title "Exegesis as Prayer," makes a point about humility that draws at least in part on a reflection derived from the text of Genesis: "Humility is not self-degradation, which is a sin. To surrender one's self before Scripture is to become like the soil from which we were created (Gen 2:7), *humus* that is fertile and needs mulching. Humble reading is hospitable to another's voice, patient, wholly attentive, still" (2002: 140). Here Black models the kind of dialogical consideration of the nature of the interpretive virtues alongside the contribution of specific biblical texts that we are envisaging.

How then might one further explore the practical value of suggesting that speaking for God requires "dependence" on God, a word that I am aware operates with a certain fuzziness regarding specifics? To put the matter in as focused a way as possible, if the prophetic criterion at work in the case of Moses is that he speaks because he has been spoken to ("mouth to mouth"), then what is the would-be prophet to do when God does not speak? Transposed into the hermeneutical categories we have in view, does our proposal say that an interpreter of Scripture must await "mouth-to-mouth" communication from God before being able to speak forth a word from the biblical text? This, I suggest, is a conundrum long known to preachers, at least

15. See the preliminary remarks on how the New Testament develops the model of Moses in this passage in Olson 1996: 72–73.

those aware of the responsibility of trying to speak within the remit of the text. To explore it, one would need to develop a theology of a God who speaks, who indeed desires to speak, through the words of Scripture already given for this purpose. This hermeneutical situation is not identical to the question of whether and when a prophet ever has anything to say, since in the case of interpreting Scripture, the point is that God has already spoken, and the presenting task is to know how to speak today.[16] Nevertheless there are obviously going to be points of congruence between how one discerns the work of God in and through the voices of biblical interpreters and the question of discerning the work of God in connection with prophecy. Indeed, on the subject of prophecy, an analysis not dissimilar to the present one has been offered by Walter Moberly, who writes of prophecy that "it is the content of the encounter with the divine that is determinative of its validity" (2006: 10).

The contribution of Numbers 12:3 suggests that humility before the text translates as saying that spiritual life is one key to faithful handling of Scripture. What, practically, can the interpreter *do* in order to understand the scriptural text handed down in the tradition? One answer, our argument suggests, is to pursue God, through all the range of spiritual disciplines available, including but not limited to the unique discipline of exegesis, if one wishes to see how the text speaks in the wider world of life before God.

In his fascinating study of "the virtues of an interpreter," an account that interestingly enough takes as its test case Aquinas's interpretation of the ceremony of the red heifer in Numbers 19, Eugene Rogers says that Aquinas "makes prayer the highest of secondary causes, that is, the highest among human efforts. . . . It is therefore to prayer that Thomas would turn the interpreter who seeks to achieve some purpose by the most effective means" (1996: 81). At an altogether different point on the theological spectrum, Barth suggests that "in its totality it is peculiar and characteristic of theology that it can be performed only in the act of prayer" (1963: 160; cited also in Black

---

16. One recalls Barth's striking characterization of the task of dogmatics: in contrast to exegetical theology, "dogmatics as such does not inquire what the Apostles and Prophets have said, but what we ourselves must say 'on the basis of the Apostles and Prophets'" (1936: 16).

2002: 145n40). Granted that Rogers may perhaps overemphasize the distinction between hermeneutics and prayer as different modes for addressing worries about interpretation—I have tried to suggest that there is scope for both in the pursuit of the text—and Barth does arguably tend to raise every helpful observation to the level of "a theory of everything"; yet in both these sets of observations lies an important clue to the practices of biblical interpretation. If one is interpreting the text in any sort of connection with the question of discerning how God is at work in the world, then prayer, not least as a way of seeing, makes a relevant contribution. Humility, moreover, especially when understood as it is in Numbers 12:3, turns out indeed to be a virtue greatly to be sought after in one's interpretive work.

"The man Moses was very humble, more so than anyone else on the face of the earth." God spoke to him face to face. A hermeneutic of humility will seek to be informed by Moses's example in this passage.

This chapter has begun our pursuit of interpretive virtues with a deliberately circumscribed example: one key verse, which offers one key perspective, on one key virtue. Part of the rationale for such an approach was to illustrate just how much can and must be said regarding specifics in order to handle the Old Testament's moral categories carefully enough to allow us to transpose their concerns appropriately to today. It has not proved possible to read Numbers 12:3 without reference to far wider concerns about the narrative not just of Numbers but also of much of the Old Testament. Subsequent chapters will likewise seek to situate specific narratives in their wider contexts. Likewise, each virtue that we consider could be discussed on its own terms at far greater length than is possible here. Our analysis of humility, for example, would have implications for some of the ways in which much avowedly postmodern thinking appeals to a vague notion of humility as a bulwark against making any sort of definite claims about knowledge: an "epistemology of humility," which can in turn be somewhat intolerant of other perspectives but is fundamentally in need of much greater clarity as to what humility actually is. But the study offered in this chapter is hopefully enough to indicate that the project of this book can make sense in practice, offers insight into the moral character of the Old Testament's implied reader, and has begun to sketch out some of the ways that this has implications for our own situations as readers today. Thus encouraged, we turn in subsequent chapters to consider hermeneutical categories that require more wide-ranging engagement with scriptural narratives in order to see their specifics more clearly.

3

WISDOM TO DISCERN THE LIVING INTERPRETATION FROM THE DEAD

U nlike humility, wisdom has always been considered a virtue. Practical wisdom (*phronēsis*) served as the organizing principle of Aristotle's approach, and right through to contemporary discussions of hermeneutics, both philosophical and theological, wisdom has always been understood as a virtue entirely appropriate to responsible handling of texts. Indeed, one can even find explicit discussion of the interpretive virtue of *phronēsis* in some recent hermeneutical literature, such as Daniel Treier's "*Phronēsis* and Theological Interpretation of Scripture" (2006: 129–62).[1]

David Ford in particular has made wisdom a constructive focus for theological thinking. When he set about "redescribing theology" in his inaugural lecture of that name at Cambridge, he said of churches today that "I see the most important item on their theological agenda at present being the education of their general membership for living in truth and wisdom" (1992: 14). Elsewhere he describes wisdom as "the

1. Cf. also Fowl 1998: 188–202; Vanhoozer 2002: 337–73; and esp. 2005a: 324–44; Zagzebski 1997; Allen 1989.

most satisfactory overall 'interest' for a theologian to have, embracing truth, beauty, and practice in relation to the whole ecology of reality before God" (1999: 178). His recent book *Christian Wisdom* draws together many of the threads of contemporary theological reflection on wisdom. It includes a lengthy chapter on "a wisdom interpretation of scripture" (2007: 52–89), although in terms of specifics this is in large part concerned with taking up and reaffirming the nine theses for theological interpretation offered in *The Art of Reading Scripture* (E. Davis and R. Hays 2003: 1–5).

The Davis and Hays volume represents the fruit of the "Scripture Project" at Princeton's Center of Theological Inquiry, which ran from 1998 to 2002. It brings together some fifteen essays and half a dozen sermons with the aim of nothing less than "proposing a quiet revolution in the way the Bible is taught in theological seminaries" (2003: xx). For this ambitious aim, it is, I think, a strikingly successful manifesto. Of some interest for our own concerns is the fact that virtue plays little part in the Princeton group's conception of what it means to cultivate the art of scriptural interpretation, albeit that this might be a difference in terminology rather than substance. Indeed, Gregory Jones's essay in this volume (Jones 2003) overlaps a little with his plea for interpretive virtues in his contribution to the SBL *Character and Scripture* book (Jones 2002), and in general, one has the impression that much of the content of what is said in the Davis and Hays collection could be rearticulated without loss (and perhaps even with gain) in the language of virtue.

Wisdom, though, as one can see from this volume and other attempts to co-opt it as a framework for biblical interpretation, remains something of a banner headline category too easily thin on content. After all, who is going to object to a project such as "Reading the Bible Wisely" (what are the alternatives?), and yet how is content to be given to this concept of wisdom?[2] The question in view here is a more focused version of the discussion of the virtuous reader in chapter 1, a question of how to articulate criteria for what is desired in biblical interpretation. And the approach of this chapter, in line

---

2. I write in partial reference to my own brief foray in this area (Briggs 2003), which bears the title *Reading the Bible Wisely* but only very briefly attempts to say what wisdom is.

with that discussion, is to seek to allow the biblical text to fill out our idea of wisdom by way of looking at the notion of wisdom implied in some narrative within Scripture itself.

In this case, there is an obvious candidate: the narrative of Solomon's arrival on the scene as a wise king in 1 Kings 3. It contains two parts: a dream, wherein he asks for wisdom, and a "test case," where two prostitutes come before him, quarreling over which of them is mother to a living baby and which has discovered her baby dead. First Kings 3 is obviously a thematic statement of Solomon's wisdom (which as a result is perceived by "all Israel"; v. 28), and Solomon's wisdom goes on to be legendary in international terms (witness the visit of the Queen of Sheba in 1 Kings 10) and then in Israel's own tradition (hence the ascription of so many writings to him; cf. 1 Kings 4:32 as well as, traditionally, the Wisdom books—Proverbs, Ecclesiastes, Song of Solomon—and as pseudepigraphic witness to such a tradition, the Wisdom of Solomon). If we can discern the supposed nature of wisdom from this passage, then we shall have made some progress in describing the interpretive virtue of wisdom germane to reading Scripture. Indeed, there is a further point of congruence here since dreams represent paradigm cases of interpretable phenomena in the Old Testament, as we shall see later. The paradigmatic status of 1 Kings 3 as a text concerned with hermeneutical wisdom, in other words, is secured by recognizing the hermeneutical function of dream interpretation in the Old Testament.

There is one brief but significant angle to consider before turning to 1 Kings 3. In seeking to illustrate the virtue of wisdom from the canonical narrative, one might be drawn to reflect on whether such an illustration already embodies the virtue(s) of wisdom to be discerned in the text. And on pursuing this line of thought, might it be the case that one already has to be wise in order to discern the virtue of wisdom for which one is looking? Perhaps this is just a special case of the (in some ways) circular nature of virtue ethics: one can tell the good by seeing if it contributes to the good.[3] First Kings 3 will actually have something interesting to say on the question of whether wisdom is humanly conceived or divinely given, or—better—in what

3. See the discussion of "the good" and *eudaimonia* in chapter 1, pp. 21–23.

sense these two modes of wisdom are interrelated. In any case, we can hardly propose that one must plod flat-footedly through the text while handicapped by an allegiance to one method or another (whether a historicizing pursuit of original context, or textual redaction, or perhaps a rhetorical analysis of dream narratives) in order to see if such an approach might yield the fruit of wisdom on its own untroubled terms. If wisdom involves some reconceptualization of the categories of biblical interpretation, then we must try them out to see what is at stake: the gains and losses as we explore the text from a wide range of angles. Such a recognition of the cart-and-horse dilemma of text and approach can be understood as a virtuous application of the notion of the hermeneutical circle, rather than a "vicious" one. In the light of which, let us turn as wisely as possible to 1 Kings 3.

Reading 1 Kings 3

First Kings 3 is a multipart narrative section of a larger whole and plays its own complex role(s) in constructing a rich narrative portrait of King Solomon.[4] For reasons largely derivative upon the perception that 2 Samuel 9–20 and 1 Kings 1–2 constitute a so-called "succession narrative" (Rost 1982), or as it is now sometimes called, a "court history,"[5] and can therefore be considered as a separate unit, it has been common in recent decades to read the narrative of Solomon's kingship as basically a lengthy positive account (1 Kings 3–10) followed by a chapter that accumulates in short order his failings and the resultant woes (chap. 11). As is widely recognized, there are details of the text that do not sit easily with this picture, and the picture is strained considerably by allowing chapters 1–2 to stand as part of the whole Solomon narrative (so Provan 1999), given that Solomon

---

4. The historical accuracy or otherwise of the portrait is largely irrelevant to our project, except arguably to the extent that details of the narrative are constrained by attention to what happened, although even here one needs only to allow a certain literary flair to the author(s) to avoid being detained by such considerations. The example of 1 Kings 3:1 is considered briefly below. A range of recent opinion on these matters is summarized in Handy 1997: esp. 1–105. We return to this question in more general terms at the end of the chapter (at note 33, below).

5. Thus Flanagan 1972; cf. Whybray 1968, who seems to prefer the term "political novel."

in 1 Kings 2 is something of a godfather-type figure, rooting out and destroying other claimants to the throne. The relevance of such observations is the extent to which they might (or might not) provoke a more complex evaluation of chapter 3 than just "wise king—installed and exemplified."

We shall consider the chapter in three stages, reserving the focus of our attention for the third and longest section: the case of the two women before Solomon. Before we reach that point, it is interesting to ask to what extent the chapter sets up that story as a model of wise judgment, and to what extent it offers destabilizing hints that something more complex is going on. In terms of the overall development of 1 Kings 1–11, commentators need to find some way of navigating between the emphasis on wisdom in parts of the Solomon narrative and its disappearance from the scene as the book progresses: "After Solomon, wisdom simply disappears from 1–2 Kings. . . . Royal wisdom, touted so heavily at the opening of the book, fails to deliver" (Leithart 2006: 18–19). The question is how to discern whether there are pointers in this direction in some of the odder features of chapter 3.

Conflicting Signals: The Problems of Tuning In to 1 Kings 3

The opening verse of the chapter raises an immediate question: "Solomon made a marriage alliance with Pharaoh king of Egypt; he took Pharaoh's daughter and brought her into the city of David." Commentators cannot agree on whether this is a neutral observation (perhaps on the basis that it is simply a record of what happened) or a deliberately negative comment given that in due course Solomon's downfall will be attributed to his attachment to foreign wives (cf. 1 Kings 11:1–8 and following). For one thing, it is difficult to know what the implied reader of this text is supposed to know already, especially (at least from a historical point of view) if this verse is a late redaction and thus was only ever intended to function as the introduction to a story that was known to conclude with the marriage to foreign wives. One can at least note that any reader of this text as it now stands in the Old Testament will have plenty of reason to suspect, long before reaching 1 Kings 11, that marriage alliance with Pharaoh is not to be construed positively with respect to the king of a people who were led out of slavery in Egypt into their own promised land.[6] The import of 1 Kings 3:1 is complicated still further by its relocation in the LXX to 5:14a, where it is combined with some of the other brief notices concerning Pharaoh from 9:16.[7] Pharaoh's daughter remains unnamed in the book—her main role in the remainder of the narrative seems to be to have Solomon build a large house for her (1 Kings 7:8), perhaps prompting the reader to wonder whether fundamentally it is her existence as a prototypical foreign wife that is the point of 3:1. The estimation of the various lengths of time it took Solomon to build the different houses mentioned in 1 Kings is another cause of differing evaluations of him, as to whether one should hear a negative judgment implicit in the juxtaposition of 6:38 (seven years building the temple) and 7:1 (thirteen years building his own house).

One begins to see that the Solomon narratives raise interesting questions regarding how to discern the extent or nature of moral evaluation present in the text. Does such evaluation take place in a subtle or understated way, or indeed is it there at all, an interpretive construct best located in the reader's mind's eye? Such questions are raised already in 3:1 and will continue to be raised in surprising ways throughout the chapter.

There are enough understated moments in the incidental framing sentences of the first half of chapter 3 to leave the reader somewhat alert to the various narrative possibilities as they progress. As well as questions concerning Pharaoh's daughter becoming Solomon's wife, we have the listing of building projects in the latter half of verse 1 as "his own house and the house of Yhwh"—is the order significant? And then, what sort of judgment is implicit in the note that the people "were sacrificing at the high places" (v. 2)? Solomon does this too in verse 3 (at the high places) and in verse 4 (at Gibeon), and it is often claimed that the comment of verse 15 is then deliberately designed to

6. Some (e.g., Seow 1999: 37) detect implicit reference here to Deut. 17:16, that the king should not "return the people to Egypt," though the questions raised by reading the portrait of Solomon in 1 Kings in the light of the warnings in Deut. 17 about kingship are familiar, wide-ranging, and cannot be addressed here.

7. For details, see van Keulen 2005: 62–81; cf. Na'aman 1997: 61–62. Variant LXX traditions complicate the matter still further (including the numbering of 1 Kings 5:14a) but need not detain us here (cf. Mulder 1998: 130–31; and more generally, 2–10).

show that Solomon, newly possessed of wisdom, goes to Jerusalem to stand before the ark of the covenant, in conscious distinction from his sacrifices at Gibeon. This makes for an awkward final narrative: the excuse offered for the people in verse 2 is that the high places are at this time the best available option, but clearly Solomon demonstrates a better one twelve verses later. Perhaps no judgment was implied at all.

The opening verses of this chapter, as it now stands, are doubtless the result of complex redactional processes, remaining opaque perhaps even to the LXX. Carr (1991: 7–30) offers a full analysis and is convincing at least with regard to verse 2 being a gloss to soften verse 3, appropriating verse 3's opening *raq*, "only/however," but thus reading oddly in its final location. Whatever the historical explanations for the current form of the text, reading it now on its own (finished) terms turns out to be a difficult and indeed underdetermined project. Brueggemann's book-length exploration of irony in these texts regards 3:1–2 "as a plunge into interpretive disputation, . . . signs of a major critique of Solomon" (2005: 85–86). It is hard to contest a claim for interpretive dispute: the very act of doing so witnesses to the dispute in question—an irony Brueggemann would probably be happy to embrace.

The Dream at Gibeon: It Pleased the Lord

This opening interpretive instability, though, is barely present in the dream narrative itself, which occupies verses 5–14. Setting to one side the questions regarding Solomon's choice of location for sacrifice, the reader of the dream account is propelled consistently to a straightforward interpretation: God offers Solomon whatever he would like (v. 5), in the manner of being willing to outfit the new king for his responsibilities. When Solomon chooses a discerning heart (*lēb šōmēaʿ*) to distinguish good from evil, in order to govern the people (v. 9), this pleases the Lord, who as a result throws in the very things Solomon had not asked for (riches and honor, v. 13) as well as what he had—a wise and discerning heart (*lēb ḥākām wĕnābôn*, v. 12).[8] Another thing Solomon didn't ask for was long life

---

8. Moberly 1999: 3–6 explores the wider significance of some of this terminology.

(v. 11), and this too is offered, with the provision that he keep the Lord's "statutes and commandments" (v. 14), though most likely the way this condition comes at the end of the divine speech suggests not that it is a requirement for the long-life part of the arrangement only, but that it is an assumed framework within which all of this gift is given.[9]

Dream narratives have a variety of functions in the Old Testament.[10] On the whole, however, they are the source of "reliable" information concerning how the narrator would have the reader understand and evaluate the action, especially with respect to theophanic dreams or renderings of the divine voice. As noted by Husser, "The dream account is a simple compositional technique whereby authors can introduce a dialogue between God and a human being" (1999: 104). He goes on to observe that such accounts have pedagogical functions in the narrative: they can provide "the opportunity to underline certain theological principles at a key point in the story, as in Solomon's dream at Gibeon, for example" (1999: 104).[11]

Upon awakening, Solomon immediately exchanges Gibeon for Jerusalem as his place of sacrifice (v. 15), and thus the reader anticipates that we now have before us a wise king, divinely bestowed with discernment and the knowledge of good and evil. In this sense, the succeeding judgment narrative is clearly set up as a chance for the king to shine, and arguably the narrative indeterminacies of the opening verses have been laid aside or at least left to do their longer-term work for when the reader arrives at chapter 11.

Of course, in biblical interpretation, little is ever that straightforward, and it is only fair to note the striking reading offered by Iain

9. Carr 1991: 69–70 offers redactional reasons for thinking this, too, though he is also quick to dispense with the view that 1 Kings 3:14 anticipates Solomon's later apostasy by subtle indication of the conditionality of the original promise (cf. his note 131).

10. Husser (1999: 99–103, with elaboration at 106–66) considers symbolic dreams, message dreams, varieties of prophetic dreams concerning judgment or premonition, and wisdom dreams. Note also Fidler 2005 (in Hebrew) and Seow 1984, who helpfully highlights the importance of reading 1 Kings 3 in terms of parallels within the Bible itself rather than elsewhere.

11. Cf. Fidler (1994; 2005: 243–71), who presents this as a matter of "propaganda." For a subtle treatment of propaganda here, see Seibert 2006, who defines it fairly neutrally as "a form of persuasion consciously deployed with the intention of convincing others to see things from the point of view of the propagator" (2006: 13).

Provan in his commentary, where he argues that despite the outward appearance of Solomon's dream being a triumph of wisdom over greed and self-centeredness, the narrator has found ways to undermine the estimation of Solomon implied here (1995: 43–49). Provan points to the specific language of "love" (*'hb*) for Yhwh (v. 3), the same word used in 11:1–2 with respect to foreign wives, which is uniquely used of Solomon among the kings of the book—perhaps to indicate a relationship not unlike his love for women rather than one predicated on covenant faithfulness. He also cites Solomon's poor grasp of the dynamics of David's relationship with Yhwh (cf. 3:6), and the strange self-evaluation of verse 7: "I am only a little child." Undeniably this is data in the text, but the question is how to interpret that data wisely, and here one wonders whether Provan's insightful critique of the distorting effect of the "succession narrative" on readings of 1 Kings 1–11 (cf. Provan 1999 especially) has spilled over into an unnecessarily suspicious reading of the Gibeon dream narrative. Several factors indicate caution. Love for Yhwh, after all, is enjoined in precisely these terms in the Shema (Deut. 6:5). As Brueggemann notes, "The term 'love' does not refer to romantic sentimentality, but rather to the practice of singular and obedient loyalty"; so this is a vision of Solomon "determinedly obedient" to Yhwh and the torah (Brueggemann 2000: 46). And though 1 Kings 3:7 reads oddly against the bloodshed of chapter 2, it seems clear from a comparison of 11:42 with 14:21—which at face value suggests that Solomon was a father at or around the time of chapter 3—both that numbers in the narrative have symbolic functions not to be pressed too hard for historical or logical detail, and that this consideration probably extends to the language of being "a little child" too, which need not be pressed literally. Even so, it is salutary to recognize that such questions as Provan's can at least be asked, even by someone whose overall aim is certainly not to critique the biblical text into a baffled silence.

The main question raised by others who are suspicious of this narrative has to do with God's decision to give Solomon the very things that, in his not asking for them, qualified him as wise in the first place according to the logic of the dream. Is this a kind of divine trap, given that riches and incomparability will in the end work their way into a life somewhat removed from obedience to the statutes and commandments? The logic of Deuteronomy 8:11–12 is germane here: eating one's fill in some future prosperity raises the prospect of too easily forgetting the commandments, ordinances, and statutes of Yhwh. Lasine's version of this complaint is a good deal less cynical than some and in fact comes as part of a penetrating analysis of how different scholars read the ideology of the Solomon narrative's "golden age" as variously positive (and typical of the ancient world) or implicitly negative, indeed tyrannical:

> The fact that Yahweh gives Solomon riches "because . . . you have not asked for yourself long life; nor have you asked riches for yourself" (1 Kgs 3:11) would seem to accord with the values expressed in Deut 17:16–17. However, if Yahweh is assuming that an older, wealthy King Solomon will not desire more riches for himself because the young Solomon did not do so, Deut 8 and Hos 13 suggest that this assumption is unwarranted. (Lasine 2001: 150)

How the opinions of Yhwh in the text as well as those of the narrator and the implied reader relate to opinions held by scholars today raises questions about the status of the narrator, to which we shall have to return below. In one sense, this question of appropriate discernment of the textual data anticipates important questions regarding the modes of trust and suspicion in interpretation that will occupy us in the next chapter. For now we shall simply note this approach in the literature and return to it later when we have wisdom in clearer focus. We turn instead to a reading of Solomon with two prostitute mothers, alert to the point that how to weigh the significance of specific details will be an important interpretive factor.

Two Women before Solomon

1. *Discerning which woman is which.* The outline of this story is familiar; its complexities less so. I shall offer an analytical sketch of the narrative, to be explained below.[12]

12. The basic setting out of the reading that follows is indebted to the crystal-clear narratological analysis of van Wolde (1995) along with the perceptive study of Lasine 1989: esp. 79–80n9.

Verse	Action
16	Two women (prostitutes) stand before the king
17–21	C: story + "child is mine"
22	R: "no, child is mine"
23–25	Solomon: recaps, calls for sword, orders to divide living child in two
26a	L: "give the living boy to the other"
26b	D: "divide the child"
27	Solomon's judgment: "give her (H) the living boy; she is the mother"
28	All Israel heard, and perceived that "the wisdom of God was in him"

This schematic representation of the narrative employs a labeling designed to highlight its two notable indeterminacies. It should be read as follows:

C = the Complainant, who brings the case in the first instance, with the story that while she was asleep the other woman switched the babies

R = the Respondent, who simply contradicts C's account

L = the mother of the living child (identified, we note, by the narrator in v. 26)

D = the mother of the other (i.e., dead) child

H = "her," to whom Solomon awards the living child (v. 27: "Give her . . .")

The indeterminacies are two:

I^1 Does H = C or does H = R?
I^2 Does H = L or does H = D?

In the first case, the question is whether the woman who is finally awarded the living child is the one who first brought the case or the one who says, in simple contradiction in verse 22, "No, the dead son is yours, and the living son is mine." For reasons that (justifiably) appear entirely unclear to commentators, it is the near consensus of English translations that the solution to this question is that H = C (i.e., the complainant is vindicated). Verse 27 is translated with a consistency bordering on zeal as "Give the first woman the living boy" even though the Hebrew simply says, "Give her the living boy." In actual fact, readers of the narrative not only do not know which "her" Solomon has in mind (or perhaps which one he pointed to at the time); they also cannot possibly work it out. This is a narrative gap, and those who note this usually leave it at that: "The readers do not yet know whether the first or the second woman is this mother, and they never will" (van Wolde 1995: 638).

In the second case, something more central to the narrative is at stake: Solomon makes his judgment, which, verse 28 tells us, is resoundingly viewed as demonstrating the "wisdom of God." And here something a little more complex happens, because although the narrator can label the first speaker this time around as L (the mother of the living boy), for Solomon this identification is precisely what is at stake. Van Wolde offers a convincing argument for saying the narrator thinks that the vindicated woman (i.e., H) is L: justice is done in the sense that Solomon judges correctly at the end. The key, she notes (following Beuken 1989), is that the woman's cry from the heart (with warmed "compassions," *raḥămêhā*, v. 26) breaks through the impasse. The narrator then allies Solomon's view with L by having him repeat her wording (v. 27: "give her the living boy," with only these two instances in the whole story replacing the generic *yeled* [child] with the description of him as "the living child"—*hayyālûd haḥay*). Thus, although there is nothing in the text that says it explicitly, just a barrage of pronouns referring to "she" and "her," the logic of the narrator's judgment, as van Wolde demonstrates, is that H = L.[13]

Solomon also concludes that H = L, though the logic of how this is shown in and by the text is the narrator's and not his. Solomon's logic concerns the merits of the case in the world of the story and relies on the argument that only the true mother would value the life of the child at all costs, even if it meant losing the child to the other

13. Rendsburg 1998 suggests that one may go further than van Wolde and identify H as R on the basis of a consistent use of "and this one says [*wĕzō't 'ōmeret*]" on three occasions in the passage (vv. 22, 23, 26). It is not clear that his key distinction between this phrase and the phrase "this one says" (without the "and," the *wāw* prefix) is not simply a feature of the progression of the narrative, and in my view the first indeterminacy (I[1]) remains unresolved (and unresolvable). Garsiel 2002 also claims to identify H, though for him it is C (who is "mannerly") as against R ("crass"). Further examples could be given.

woman. In other words, by changing the frame of reference, he shifts the debate to a level where the right distinction can be made. Where C and R are debating what happened, L and D (though which is which is not known to Solomon at this point) are debating what will happen. One is a debate about past life and death; the other is a debate about future life and death. For Solomon, the second unlocks the key to the first, thus revealing which mother is which (and we note that Solomon, or indeed any actual observer, would thereby know whether C or R was vindicated; it is simply the reader who never finds this out). Justice is done to the past by orienting the case to the future, transforming the nature of the women's involvement in the case. According to 3:28, justice is done, at least as perceived by all Israel: here is the wisdom of God embodied in Solomon.

2. *Critiques of Solomon's wisdom.* Thus far Solomon's judgment in the story. It has not been as well received as 3:28 might lead one to expect. Though it is true that a great many commentators have come to a conclusion similar to the above ("Here is the wisdom of God embodied in Solomon"), it is also true that the majority do not trouble to consider the indeterminacies laid out above. Indeed, one notes that Brueggemann, a scholar consistently attuned to narrative irony and underdetermination, can say of this text that "this well-known story is straightforward and not difficult to understand," before spending all of one page on it in his more than 600-page commentary on Kings (Brueggemann 2000: 49). In contrast, when scholars do begin to reflect on how much is left unsaid here, the result is that a certain suspicious momentum is built up, perhaps with the belief that if only the reader would stay long enough to raise some questions in the narrative gaps, then all manner of interpretive appreciation of Solomon's judgment will vanish rather like his covenant faithfulness in chapter 11. Complaints against the supposition that this is a paradigm of wise judgment have come thick and fast from various quarters, including the rabbis, some feminist critics, and most memorably, Mark Twain. We shall take our cue from Mark Twain, if only because he is generally more fun than most scholars.

Twain had a troubled relationship with the Bible, and indeed with Christian faith in many forms. He exerted a great deal of his prodigious imaginative energy on rewriting it in such a way as to draw out what he found to be its various absurdities and problems.[14] His treatment of Solomon's wisdom occurs in *The Adventures of Huckleberry Finn* (1958; orig. 1884), chapter 14, where Huck is discoursing with Jim, whom Twain describes as Huck's "negro" friend. Many of the points of critical engagement with 1 Kings 3 are present here, and we may as well enjoy them in Twain's inimitable style. Huck has been describing the life of a king, which he thinks mainly consists of hanging around the harem, which drew from Jim the comment that "Mos' likely dey had rackety times in de nussery." Huck goes on:

> "Well, but he *was* the wisest man, anyway. . . ."
>
> ". . . He *warn't* no wise man nuther. He had some er de dad-fetchedes' ways I ever see. Does you know 'bout dat chile dat he 'uz gwyne to chop in two? . . . Warn' dat de beatenes' notion in de worl'? You jes' take en look at it a minute. Dah's de stump, dah—dat's one er de women; heah's you—dat's de yuther one; I's Sollermun; and dish yer dollar bill's de chile. Bofe un you claims it. What does I do? Does I shin aroun' mongs' de neighbors en fine out which un you de bill *do* b'long to, en han' it over to de right one, all safe en soun', de way dat anybody dat had any gumption would? No; I take en whack de bill in *two*, en give half un it to you, en de yuther half to do yuther woman. Dat's de way Sollermun was gwyne to do wid de chile. Now I want to ask you: what's de use er dat half a bill?—can't buy noth'n wid it. En what use is a half a chile? I wouldn' give a dern for a million un um."
>
> "But hang it, Jim, you've clean missed the point—blame it, you've missed it a thousand mile."
>
> "Who? Me? Go 'long. Doan' talk to *me* 'bout yo' pints. I reck'n I knows sense when I sees it; en dey ain' no sense in sich's doin's as dat. De 'spute warn't 'bout a half a chile, de 'spute was 'bout a whole chile' en de man dat think he kin settle a 'spute 'bout a whole chile wid a half a chile doan' know enough to come in out'n de rain." (Twain 1958: 69–70)

Jim goes on to suggest that the "deeper" reason for what happened lay in Solomon's having "'bout five millin chillen runnin' roun' de

---

14. Primary source material is most easily available in Baetzhold and McCullough 1995, mainly on Genesis. I am indebted to the study of T. R. Wright 2007: 27–50 and the literature cited there.

house. *He* as soon chop a chile in two as a cat. Dey's plenty mo'. A chile er two, mo' or less, warn't no consekens to Sollermun" (Twain 1958: 70).

At the risk of sounding somewhat po-faced, our analysis might draw three points from Twain's midrash-like whimsy: Solomon is at fault for failing to explore a wider range of evidence relating to the case; cutting the child in half doesn't solve anything anyway; and the problem in Solomon's lack of judgment can be traced to his bizarre family circumstances of having such a large number of children, and thus, indirectly, to his excesses in marriage. Whether or not he knew it, Twain was tapping in to a range of problems found by many with this text. The lack of cross-examination, which in Jim's memorable phrase is the failure to "shin aroun' mongs' de neighbors," is a particular concern of some feminist interpretation, as, of course, is Solomon's summary decision to call for a sword (e.g., Hens-Piazza 2006: 46).[15] Furthermore, in a study of "the criticism of the sages regarding Solomon's trial," Gilad Sasson notes three points of critique in rabbinic literature, which partially overlap with the ones just noted: there were no witnesses in the trial; Solomon should not have directed them to cut up the child; and the final decision was not, in important ways, Solomon's, since it required the intervention of the Holy Spirit, a view most commonly traced to *Midrash Tehillim* 72.2, which attributes Solomon's insight to a *bat qôl*, a "heavenly voice," at the key moment (Sasson 2004).[16] None of these lines of consideration has raised what remains one of the obvious surface-level conundrums in the biblical text: the complainant who broaches the topic in verses 17–21 gives an account of what happened in the

15. Lasine's (1989) fascinating study of this passage even cites expert opinion regarding medical evidence that might have been taken into account (Levin 1983), though he is rightly suspicious that this is the right line of approach here (Lasine 1989: 64; cf. 79n4). Garsiel (2002: 233), though, finds similar reasoning as far back as Rabbi Joseph Kara (AD 1065–1135).

16. Sasson's article (in Hebrew) also cites *b. Roš Haš.* 21b as well as *Tg. Qoh.* 12:10; *Midr. Qoh. Rab.* 10.17; *Midr. Gen. Rab.* 85.12; and *b. Mak.* 23b. The title of Sasson's article, "Woe to You, O Land, When Your King Is a Child," echoes the rabbinic use of Eccles. 10:16 to pass judgment on the Solomon story. For further reflection along this line, see Seow 1999: 44–46.

night when, according to her own account, there are no witnesses and she herself was asleep.

As the book of Proverbs suggests, "The one who first states a case seems right, until the other comes and cross-examines" (18:17). And faced with such a formidable array of those who have dwelled with the text to discern its problems, must we in the end dissent from 3:28 and follow Hens-Piazza with her claim that "with our purview of history we may be more reticent than 'all Israel' to unresistantly claim that 'wisdom' has prevailed here" (2006: 46)? Was all Israel then sadly mistaken? And have we been fooled after all?

I argue that the answer to these questions is no—a simplifying summary that will be worth holding on to in the barrage of critique with which we are about to engage. The argument will proceed in three rather distinct stages: first with respect to specific points of detail in the text, then with regard to what I perceive to be an important underlying hermeneutical issue—the status of the narrator of the text—and finally with an eye on questions of wider canonical setting and the various intertexts that help to illuminate this passage. This will then clear the way for a concluding section regarding the interpretive virtue of wisdom as it is modeled in this passage in its context in 1 Kings 1–11.

Evaluating Solomon's Wisdom

1. *Specific points of interpretation.* This is an exercise in point-by-point engagement with specifics, for which there is perhaps no obvious order in which to take the issues, so we shall simply consider a nonsymbolic seven of them in turn.

First, it may be that 3:28 is a redacted red herring. Perhaps one could disentangle the evaluation of all Israel from the narrative we have been reading by tracing precanonical layers of redaction and isolating 3:28 as a reflection on some simpler prior text. Mulder thinks it functions in connection with verses 4–15 too (1998: 160), and John Gray is happy to speak of "unskilful insertions in the [Solomon] text" that render even coherent narrative blocks unclear (1963: 114); yet overall the second half of 1 Kings 3 seems to stand as a unity, in contrast to the jigsaw puzzle–like approaches to 3:1–15, where there does at least appear to be some evidence of layers of redaction.[17] In any case, verse 28 functions now to complete the story, so at best all this approach would do is shift the putative misunderstanding from the author to the redactor, which is not a great deal of comfort for our pursuit of wisdom.

Second, regarding the failure to consult other witnesses, the way the tale has been set up is dependent upon precisely the point that there are no other witnesses; at least in part, that is what makes it the prototypical hard case. For some, this is one explanation of the unusual detail that both women were prostitutes, unusual in the sense that comparable narratives of judgment by a wise man between competing claims exist in other cultures (and indeed it is worth noting that Solomon is not identified by name in this narrative, suggesting to some a generic tale), but only here are the women specified to be prostitutes.[18] There are no extended family members, no other prostitutes or even children (v. 18), and perhaps even the notion of char acter witness is deliberately problematized by this setting. For Phyllis Bird, part of the point of the tale lies here: can Solomon see past the stereotype of the woman as prostitute and understand the woman as mother, finding truthful testimony beyond the unreliability? Yes, says the narrative, wisdom can be found in this (cf. 1997: 216–18).[19] This is not designed as a story of woman wisdom and woman folly: it is two women primarily characterized as being away from the path of wisdom, and Solomon must judge.[20] Thus removed from the standard

17. Kenik 1983; and most strikingly, Carr 1991: 7–87, though his self-confessedly "relatively confident" approach (1991: 173) is aided by the fact that his part of the chapter is indeed taken up in demonstrably different recensions elsewhere in the canon.

18. A useful review is offered by G. H. Jones 1984: 130–31; cf. Lasine 1989: 70. Both authors cite Gressman 1907. Ipsen 2007 is suspicious that the "prostitution" aspect of the story can be dealt with so quickly, seeing it as part of the focus of what's wrong in Solomon's Israel.

19. This point is not always seen positively, though; thus Camp 2000: 166: "Solomon demonstrates his ability to bring social order by dividing from the chaos of female sexuality before him the 'true speech' of the mother, the woman whose sexuality is (stereotypically, if not actually) controlled, and thus acceptable."

20. Camp (2000: 165–68) does read 1 Kings 3 in terms of woman wisdom and woman folly. For her, the story resolves around the management of sexuality, a theme picked up in the story of the Queen of Sheba later on. Camp's study of "Reading Solomon as a Woman" (2000: 144–86) is a fascinating account of female strangeness construed in a va-

wisdom framework, the criteria for judgment are considerably more elusive, and hence perhaps comes the tradition of the *bat qôl* (the heavenly voice) sorting it out for him, though we shall come to this claim presently and have reason to be suspicious of it.

Third, violence and the sword. What if Solomon's gambit had not worked? In other words, what if the second round of discussions had not separated the true from the false mother? Would Solomon have cut the child? Such counterfactual musings in narrative worlds are ultimately imponderable, but the threat of violence is often noted by scholars, and indeed it is the one point of critique offered by Brueggemann on this passage that, despite all the positives, "his way to a solution was by way of a sword" (2000: 54). Ipsen even writes of Solomon's "violent judicial scare tactics" (2007: 8). Yet it seems a peculiar lack of imagination to insist that Solomon's words in verse 25 ("Divide in two . . .") must be construed as a statement of intent to divide rather than some other performative utterance, an act of provocation, indeed, which is what they turn out to be.[21] For some there are even narrative echoes here of Genesis 22, with its command to slay the son as a test: here the test involves losing the son not to death but to the other woman (cf. Seow 1999: 47).

Fourth, the question of whether C's account is contradictory in claiming to know what happened all unwitnessed in the night as she slept. This is another issue that provokes various judgments in the literature: for some, it is a self-incriminating inconsistency on the part of C (Seow 1999: 44) and perhaps good circumstantial evidence that R is the true mother, stunned into flat contradiction with no embellishment in verse 22.[22] For others, it is merely narrative color, intending to say little more than that C has deduced what happened, from the experience of waking from her sleep and finding the dead child of the other woman at her side (De Vries 2003: 59). Either way, the LXX noticed the problem: it omits the detail of C's being asleep

riety of ways, though perhaps it is not on the whole dependent on seeing woman wisdom and woman folly in 1 Kings 3.

21. On construing texts as performative acts other than straightforward assertions, see Briggs 2001: 119–37.

22. Van Wolde (1995: 630) cites scholars who see Solomon finding the key to the case here (cf. Garsiel 2002: 238). Long (1984: 68–69), on the other hand, thinks that R's brevity is itself a sign of guilt.

in verse 20, "presumably to make the facts fit the theory that she is the true mother," says Lasine (1989: 67), though as we have seen, one does not need to identify C to grasp the story in the Hebrew text, and it is a bold critic who knows the heart of the LXX in cases like this.

And then, fifth, what if in the end a woman capable of spinning a false story in the first place was capable of keeping one step ahead of Solomon's gambit and spotting that willingness to give away the child would be construed as indication of true motherhood? This is of course not impossible (for what is ever impossible in interpretation?), but it has to reckon with the statement of the other woman to ask for death (from the true mother, it would have to be supposed), and it would require the construction of a framework where no amount of emotional self-involvement can break through the lie. In the next chapter we shall return to the questions this raises about trust and suspicion.

Sixth, what if motherly compassion is constructed in fundamentally different ways across time and culture? Is it plausible to suppose that what might sound like profound wisdom with regard to human nature in the twenty-first century would represent the actual embodied values of mothers in the ancient world? In some ways, this is a good and appropriate question to ask, especially given the evidence that some forms of child sacrifice were indeed practiced in Israel and were clearly required in other cultures and faiths (Stavrakopoulou 2004: esp. 283–99). The comparative material gathered by Gressman (1907) with respect to 1 Kings 3 also turns up some interesting case studies here, such as the power of jealousy to drive a woman to kill her own child and blame the other woman if it makes a difference to how the king will perceive her.[23] However, the narrator in effect sidesteps such questions for us here by saying that the mother of the living child was provoked to speak "because compassion for her son burned within her" (v. 26). Either this tells us that the social world of the time had a value system such as we can indeed comprehend, because her compassion is as we might expect it, or it tells us that this was an unusual characteristic worth noting of this particular woman (as against, say, the norm of the time), but that in the end it proved to

---

23. This Indian variation on the story is reported by Gressman 1907: 222–23; cf. Lasine 1989: 81n13.

be the decisive one. Either way, the point is that in this particular case the motherly compassion is along the lines that today's constructions of motherhood might praise as suitably compassionate, and presumably the interpreter does not need to be able to say more than this for the analysis of this particular text.

And finally, some critiques of Solomon's judgment seem to me to blur into simple appeal to the various indeterminacies that we have been noting, leaving the impression that the puzzle over which woman gets the child somehow compounds the problems perceived with Solomon's action.[24] Indeed, the point of expending all this energy on engaging so many specific points of critique is in part to show that complex, puzzling, and sometimes underdetermined features of the text do not in themselves necessarily draw the reader to the conclusion that something suspicious is going on or that the narrator has basically tripped up by thinking themselves to be telling one sort of story when it turns out that they have succeeded in doing something quite different. Read this way, those in the tradition who find 1 Kings 3 charmingly straightforward might simply be right, for there is a fine line between teasing out subtleties from the text and teasing the text to interpretive distraction. I have been trying to show that wisdom need not necessarily consist in finding ever more things to wonder about, rather as if hermeneutics were a strange parody of the Jewish lawcourt, and the one who could raise most interpretive questions wins. Instead, I suggest that wisdom lies with knowing when an underdetermined detail is significant or when it is underdetermined because we do not need to know it. That leads us to the next issue, the question of how we estimate the status of the narrator.

2. *The status of the narrator.* Earlier in this chapter I suggested that how the narrator indicates that justice is done—by way of the techniques of narration present, such as repetition and echo (as per van Wolde 1995)—is not the same as how Solomon reasoned his way to seeing that justice was done, which was a matter of the judgment about which kind of mother would choose the life of the child over possession of the child. And in 3:26, identifying the speaker as L

---

24. Eslinger 1989: 129–40 is a particular example of this, though, as Lasine (2001: 160) points out, he is strangely determinate about how all the indeterminacies count against Solomon.

(the woman whose son was alive), the narrator says something that Solomon could not know at that point, setting up, if only briefly, a distinction between how they each relate to the unfolding narrative. But it is difficult to see how one might by the end sustain a reading that wants to posit a fundamental difference between Solomon's view and the narrator's, given the narrator's identification of L, and the view of all Israel that Solomon must have gotten it right (or else, to bend over backward, that the wisdom of God was perceived to be just even if mistaken, by which time some of Mark Twain's words come back to mind: anyone who thinks this doesn't know enough about the Old Testament to come in out of the rain).

The status of narrators is a familiar issue in biblical poetics. In his landmark study of the area, Meir Sternberg famously equates the narrator's literary-critical omniscience (i.e., narrators in the nature of the case know everything, even if they pretend not to for the sake of narrative effect) with the divine perspective of deity on the stage of human drama (1985: 84–99; e.g., 89: "the very choice to devise an omniscient narrator serves the purpose of staging and glorifying an omniscient God"). That translates as saying the narrator is basically always right, if one wishes to side with the God of Israel, a view that has sometimes been critiqued solely on the basis of not wishing to side with the God of Israel rather than on its merits as a feature of narrative analysis (cf. some of the views explored in Gunn and Fewell 1993).

I do not intend to try to argue that the narrator is always right, if indeed such a thing were possible. More modestly, though, one can at least explore the logic of interpreting Scripture on the assumption that the narrator is to be trusted, and it seems to me that this forecloses a good deal less on how to interpret Scripture than some critics seem to think. A good case study of precisely this phenomenon might be had with respect to 1 Kings 3:16–28, where the analyses of Sternberg (1985: 166–70) and Herbert Chanan Brichto (1992: 47–61), in explicit dialogue with Sternberg and dissenting from several of his conclusions, indicate that a great deal still hangs, even within this high estimation of the narrator, on the "differing estimate of the level of the audience that the biblical author had in mind in constructing his narrative" (Brichto 1992: 56). One example must suffice: Brichto thinks it unlikely that Solomon was taken by surprise, as it were, by the case, but he must have planned to hear it and therefore considered in advance what sorts of legal (i.e., torah-related) issues would be raised by it. The call for the sword, he concludes, is the decision to raise the stakes from a case of theft to kidnapping (a capital offense; cf. Deut. 24:7), and he then shows the narrator to be carefully indicating the various stages of raised tension and realization of the seriousness of the charge (1992: 51–54). This reading diverges quite markedly from Sternberg's analysis of how the narrator has guided the reader through contrasting points of view, but the only point I wish to draw out of this is that this quite spirited disagreement with respect to how to construe the significance of the data in the text all takes place within the basic supposition of the narrator's competence to tell the story that results in the response of 3:28.[25]

It is interesting, then, to reflect on how many of the points of contested detail considered in the previous section turned on stepping outside of the narrator's frame of reference and asking instead whether "we" see it that way (in contrast to readings that seek their purchase in such details as 3:1 and construe them as key to the succeeding narrative). Now this extrinsic (or "etic") reflection is also an important thing to do in dialogue with texts worth taking seriously, but it is clear that it will often tell us more about ourselves than the text. Or to come back to the overall purpose of this study: it will tell us more about our own conception of interpretive virtues than that held by the text, and the danger then is that in prematurely foreclosing on what the narrator would have us understand, we fail to hear it properly in the first place.

3. *Wider canonical resonances*. Strikingly, Brichto's pursuit of the narrative art of 1 Kings 3 leads him into an expanding range of intertextual witnesses, which are drawn into the discussion of how the text is rightly understood. We have suggested earlier that the wisdom displayed by Solomon in this passage involves discerning the difference between the impulse that leads to life and the impulse that leads to death. So, as a theologian might put it, human wisdom here is a

---

25. Brichto (1992: 59) offers reasons for the attribution to Israel of "awe of the king" rather than "rejoicing to have so wise a ruler," pursuing his reading through yet further details of the text.

divine gift that enables discernment between a wisdom from above and a wisdom from below.

James, in the New Testament, was such a theologian, contrasting a "wisdom from above" (3:17) with a wisdom "not come down from above" (3:13–16; indeed "earthly" and "devilish," v. 15). And the test that James offers for such wisdom is that it is characterized in certain ways in the life of the wise person; it is first of all pure (3:17) and then characterized by a sevenfold fruit: "peaceable, gentle, willing to yield, full of mercy and good fruits, without a trace of partiality or hypocrisy." A similar bifurcation in wisdom is evident in Paul's critique of the church in Corinth (1 Cor. 1:18–3:23; cf. R. Hays 1999). For Paul, faith rests "not on human wisdom but on the power of God" (2:5), and to the delight of those who love a paradox, he argues against rhetorical sophistication and "plausible words of wisdom" (2:4) with "quite considerable rhetorical skill" (so R. Hays 1999: 118). This may be all that one should expect for a paradoxical maneuver such as a human being seeking to demonstrate that wisdom comes from God.

Having considered briefly two New Testament intertexts, it is worth noting the nearest Old Testament narrative to shed light on the call for wisdom that Solomon faces: the narrative of two cannibal mothers fighting famine in Samaria (2 Kings 6:24–31).[26] In a striking inversion of the case of the two prostitute mothers, here the first woman recounts how, at the prompting of the second woman, they have cooked and eaten her own son, and she now demands the justice of cooking and eating the other woman's son, who is hidden. In this case, the narrative assumes that the wronged woman's son is already dead (in contrast to the wronged prostitute's son, still alive) and that she now seeks a second death as justice (in contrast to the prostitute mother's cry of "give the living boy to the other"). Everything seems deliberately inverted (see Lasine 1991; 1993; Pyper 1993). The king, meanwhile, offers no judgment: he tears his clothes and vows to behead Elisha, holding the prophet responsible for this terrible situation.

Does wisdom fail here? Is this narrative designed to show that 1 Kings 3 offers no program for wisdom such that it can be depended upon to rightly divide the living from the dead? Does the juxtaposi

---

26. I am indebted here to the thorough study of Hens-Piazza 2003 on this passage.

tion of these two texts from Kings depict, in Hugh Pyper's words, "the monarchy . . . not as something either bad or good, but as something that failed as all human enterprise must fail" (1993: 35)? Well, something fails here, but I think it is not wisdom or monarchy *tout court*. As Lasine points out, 2 Kings 6 serves an intertextual purpose of problematizing 1 Kings 3 only if one recognizes some of the inherently destabilizing factors within the earlier narrative in the first place (Lasine 1993: 45–46), and since we have been cautious about extending such destabilization as far as the notions of wisdom or monarchy themselves, it seems slightly ambitious to reckon on such wide-scale judgments about them as a result of 2 Kings 6. The specific point of inversion is rather, I suggest, that the king does not know what to say, and that this represents the failure to embody divine wisdom in human form, which Solomon modeled in 1 Kings 3.

A further point follows here, which concerns the earlier discussion of the *bat qôl* as the mechanism whereby Solomon's judgment is ensured to be effective. In the final analysis, this seems to miss the point about the king's embodying wisdom. If the king's judgment is saved only by miraculous divine intervention at the key moment, then he is not as such a wise king. Though arguably such a line of reasoning might work for a prophet in any particular case (i.e., the heavenly voice providing the word of prophetic pronouncement), it seems stretched to correlate this to the category of wisdom or the judgments of "the just king" (cf., though with different emphasis, Whitelam 1979: 155–65).

The portrait of Solomon in 1 Kings is complex and contains unnerving indicators such as are present in 3:1–2. Yet for all the questions that this appropriately raises about the extent of Solomon's wisdom as he is portrayed in the succeeding chapters, he is nevertheless still a king who exemplifies the wisdom of God to execute justice (3:28), and his failings, though in due course spectacular, do not expunge his wisdom from the record. It is perhaps too easy to construe some of the details of the Kings narrative in unduly cynical terms. In my judgment, this tendency is compounded by the high-profile failure of Gerhard von Rad's celebrated hypothesis about the so-called Solomonic Enlightenment, the tenth-century sociocultural "coming of age" that he suggested gave birth to the noble achievements of majestic building schemes, wisdom literature, and indeed the epic history of the Yahwist.[27] Given the collapse of this thesis, it then becomes easy to find fault with its face-value reading of 1 Kings 4:20—"Judah and Israel were as numerous as the sand by the sea; they ate and drank and were happy"—and to suggest in turn that it is one thing for the writer of 1 Kings to celebrate the conscription of 30,000 men to work shifts in the Lebanon, "quarrying out great, costly stones" (5:17), but altogether another to have had to be there doing it (cf. Jobling 1991, in different terms). Well, I don't mind saying that I personally would be happier writing about it than doing it, but once again that is an insight about me rather than the world of the text, where it seems distinctly possible that it would have been considered an honor to contribute to something so grand and lasting.[28] Fleeing from von Rad's hypothesis, Brueggemann finds "important hints that the final form of the text [of Kings] intends to recast Solomon as Pharaoh, albeit a homegrown pharaoh" (2005: 155). Perhaps in part, here or there—but this is a strangely unidimensional evaluation of a complex narrative, a reading that seems attuned to only one aspect of the text, a feature that occurs in only a few scattered places.[29] By way of contrast, the extracanonical tradition that grew up around the figure of Solomon indicates some of the quite extraordinary lengths to which later thinkers would go in their appreciation of him.[30] In comparison to that, the figuration of Solomon in the New Testament, while undeniably positive, seems relatively circumspect.

The interpretive tradition developing from 1 Kings 3:4–15 leads to Jesus's statement in the Sermon on the Mount that the glory of

27. See von Rad 1962: 48–56; and his description of J as "redolent of the untrammeled days of Solomon" (2005: 51). In contrast, note the oft-cited refutation by Scott 1955.

28. We have records that say as much, indeed, about much more recent projects. See, for example, K. Clark (1969: 56) on the "old chronicles" recording that "enthusiasm spread throughout France" for people of all social levels to "harness themselves" to the building of Chartres Cathedral in the Middle Ages. I am indebted to Walter Moberly for this reference and the point made here.

29. It is an oddity of Brueggemann's reading of Solomon explicitly as, in his book's subtitle, *Israel's Ironic Icon of Human Achievement* (2005), that he offers little by way of evidence that irony is more than just a partial and very occasional key to some aspects of the multifaceted biblical picture.

30. Brueggemann (2005: 225–44) offers some highlights, while a thorough study by Torijano 2002 is an eye-opener, focusing on Solomon as exorcist, magician, and astrologer.

Solomon could not be compared to God's providential care for all
creation, and thus just as Solomon sought wisdom and not riches, so
Jesus's disciples should "strive first for the kingdom of God, and all
these things will be given to you as well" (Matt. 6:33//Luke 12:31).[31]
And the point of the Gospels' reference to the Queen of Sheba story
is straightforward: "Something greater than Solomon is here!" (Matt.
12:42//Luke 11:31)—a point that would lose its impact somewhat if
readers of 1 Kings in the time of Jesus could see Solomon simply as
a failed exemplar of embodied wisdom.

In sum, the wisdom of Solomon is the wisdom of God (1 Kings
3:28), exemplified in the just judgments of the king, yet embodied
within the human sphere and not removed from it. In the canonical
picture at least, Solomon is not thereby removed to some exalted
status; nor is his wisdom the result of a co-opted divine voice that
arrives at key moments to tell him what to do. It is a divine gift, generously given, but that, like all the other gifts that God adds to it in
1 Kings 3, does not serve as a form of insurance against ever going
wrong again.

1 Kings 3 and the Interpretive Virtue of Wisdom

It is time to ask after the implied interpretive virtue of wisdom
as it is found in this narrative. The kind of wisdom modeled here
is fundamentally concerned with finding the right practical way
ahead, especially in the face of some of the various puzzles and
indeterminacies that we have been considering. It is striking how
many of the concerns of today's reflection on wisdom in theological
interpretation are issues that are found right here in 1 Kings 3. The
main questions raised, both in our text and in contemporary discussion, are:

• How to judge between competing claims (or texts)
• How to hear testimony rightly and to distinguish between what
  can and what cannot be known

31. The link between this passage and the Solomon narrative is convincingly explored
by Carr 1991: 164–70, though he is concerned with the "Q" version of it.

- How to assess the truthfulness of testimony when there is no access to any historical world "behind" the text
- How to find a way forward, a practical course of action that satisfies the demands of justice before God

The kind of wisdom displayed by Solomon, then, speaks directly to the nature of the interpretive virtue of wisdom sought after by the reader of the Old Testament. In the light of our reading of Solomon's judgment, we may offer the following reflections on interpretive wisdom, corresponding to the points just noted.

First, wisdom involves facing the competing claims of the texts before us. No purpose is served by refusing to recognize the diversity of Scripture, but its recognition is a first word rather than a last. In this narrative, it is the presenting issue: two women in the same house disagreeing over whose baby is dead. It is clearly absurd to suppose that some higher conceptualization will reveal them to each have partial insights into some transcendental whole, a kind of hermeneutical *Aufhebung* (taking up)[32] where all shall be well and all manner of texts shall be well. What is required is the willingness to press on past the presenting conflict and seek ways of discerning how, for example, each claim might make sense of the other, and then ultimately which has greater claim to be trusted. As Paul Ricoeur has demonstrated in many different situations, this "conflict of interpretations" (1974) is fundamental to the hermeneutical scenario facing the patient reader. In his essay "Hermeneutics and the Critique of Ideology" (1991: 270–307), he explicitly addresses the need to make progress in interpretive dispute by first of all doing justice to each competing claim on its own terms, and in particular seeing how each account might succeed in offering a way of understanding the other. One might suggest that Ricoeur's hermeneut is today's version of Solomon sitting in judgment, pressing on until the point where the irreducible difference between the two cases is finally laid bare, and discernment becomes possible.

32. I owe this use of the term to Shults 1999: 159, who writes of Pannenberg's theological method, noting that "Aufhebung" is "sublation": "We have here the idea of something being negated, yet preserved, as it is elevated into something else." It is a useful term even if (perhaps especially if) one is not persuaded by this idea.

Second, wisdom involves the patience to hear the testimony rightly and to discern what is and what is not said. As we have seen, the narrative of 1 Kings 3 claims only a little, not as much as one might have first thought. Interpretive wisdom discerns how much one needs to know in order to reach required judgments, and often, indeed, how little one actually does need to know (except that in advance we do not know which features will turn out to be the significant ones). Our study of 1 Kings 3 has paid careful attention to the somewhat underdetermined nature of much of what can be interpreted in this passage. Perhaps a case could be made that the author of this text deliberately left much unsaid, knowing that it would provoke thoughtful reflection and thus promote wisdom. To some extent, it is fruitless to speculate, although it does seem to be the case that the underdetermined nature of this text can be discerned as a result of a careful reading of it, rather than being asserted as a form of hermeneutical presupposition regarding all forms of interpretation equally (thus *pace* Fowl 1998: 56–61).

On a general level, the traditions of biblical scholarship are littered with hypotheses large and small relating to background issues and concerns with what one needs to know regarding the relevant texts. We have already considered the example of von Rad's "Solomonic Enlightenment," and if most scholarly hypotheses do not suffer the same fall from grace as that one, it is doubtless at least in part because they do not attain to such prominence in the first place. But to many of the historical conjectures of contemporary interpretation of the books of Kings, the wise interpreter might perhaps say that we shall never know, but then maybe we shall never need to.

Such considerations lead us on to our third reflection. Granted that one might learn to be agnostic with respect to this or that historical reconstruction, how far does such interpretive ease extend? Can it go all the way to denying any sort of historical backing to the text at all? This brings us back to such basic questions as whether or not there ever was a historical Solomon, given the conspicuous lack of impression left on the historical-archaeological record by such a reportedly impressive empire.[33] Is the absence of evidence to be construed as a

---

33. Here we revisit the point made in note 4 above and the literature noted there.

form of evidence or not? How far does any of the accrued wisdom the narrative desires to impart actually depend on whether any of it happened? Or does the wisdom of historiographically sensitive interpretation consign such questions to the standoff between the complainant and respondent (C and R) and instead seek a way forward to questions of the living and the dead? Just as Solomon's judgment seeks a justice oriented to the life of the future, is concerning oneself with the present and future effects of these texts the way to do justice to the text(s) before us? We have seen, in Brichto's approach to the texts especially, that the world behind the text plays a significant role in terms of helping to frame the appropriate questions to ask about the purposes and goals of the text for the reader then and now, but that such questions might be multiplied indefinitely without necessarily helping to clarify the subject matter (the *Sache*) of the text. So perhaps the third characterization of interpretive wisdom is that it discerns the difference between questions that lead us forward (toward life, away from death) and questions that amount to the anxiety or futility of shouldering impossible interpretive burdens.

Finally, the interpretive virtue of wisdom is concerned with finding a way forward. This is Aristotelian *phronēsis* transposed into an Old Testament key, or indeed a New Testament one, where believers are enjoined to have the same mind (*phroneite*) in them as is in Christ Jesus (Phil. 2:5)—a sense that the people of God are to set themselves to go through life while making the same kinds of practical and ad hoc judgments as Christ their exemplar. And Solomon before him, indeed, for here we see the real point about taking care to understand the overall portrait of Solomon in 1 Kings appropriately, as a man who in this paradigmatic test of his ability to see the way forward found the key: to frame the matter in hand in such a way that everyone's real commitments and desires were laid bare. The virtue in question is a matter of knowing how to proceed—or as the well-known Wittgensteinian aphorism has it, "Now I know how to go on" (1953: §179). Solomon's ability to navigate forward stands in striking contrast to the unresponsive king rending his garments before the two cannibal mothers in 2 Kings 6:30, leaving their dispute unresolved and instead heading off in pursuit of the prophet (6:31–32).

In all of this, interpretive wisdom is fundamentally occupied with the details of the texts before us. A good deal of broader theological and hermeneutical reflection on the need for interpretive wisdom seems strangely at ease in remaining at some distance from the specifics of the biblical text. The problem with this is that wisdom does not exist as an abstract virtue in interpretation, as if Solomon could tell who would make a trustworthy mother in the abstract without attention to the specifics of a particular case before him. Interpretive wisdom, then, is like a king who is confronted with two interpretations of a text. This one says that one view leads to life and the other to death, while that view simply contradicts the first. Well, says the king, preparing to bury the only copy of the manuscript in the basement of a large library, then we may as well stop reading the text altogether if all it does is cause dispute. No! says one voice. Even if it will be misread, better to have it in the full view of public scrutiny. Meanwhile the other says that indeed burial in the library would sort it all out nicely. The parable could be told in various keys—perhaps with a variety of ways of invoking the transfer of the conflict of interpretations to the level of compassion, or life over death. The point is simply that texts themselves are given over to interpretations that lead in various directions, and the chance of generalizing a series of interpretive procedures as being what constitutes wisdom is slim.[34]

These, then, are some pointers to the interpretive virtue of wisdom as it pertains to grappling with biblical texts. Such wisdom is valued highly in the biblical world itself, perhaps most notably in Proverbs 4:7: *rē'šît ḥokmâ qĕnēh ḥokmâ*, translated variously as "Wisdom is supreme; therefore get wisdom" (NIV) or "The beginning of wisdom is this: Get wisdom" (NRSV). And whatever else you get (or "in all your gettings," hence "though it cost all you have" NIV), get understanding. The place of wisdom *bĕrē'šît*, in the beginning, has long exercised readers of Proverbs 8 and Genesis 1:1, suggesting to many that wisdom is foundational to the way the world is seen in Old Testament terms. And likewise, in matters of interpretation, right from

---

34. This is clearly related to the standard question of the relationship between special and general hermeneutics, on which see the masterly discussion by Ricoeur 1991: 89–101.

the very beginning, hermeneutical wisdom is supreme; so however else you read, read wisely.

At various points in this chapter we have had occasion to touch on issues concerning the role that trust and suspicion play in the exercise of wisdom. Clearly, a full account of interpretive wisdom needs to consider these somewhat contrasting virtues, and it is to this task that we now turn.

4

LIKE A HERMENEUTIC IN A CAGE

The Eclipse of Biblical Trust

D oes the wise reader always agree with the text? Stated this way, the question is too broad and should be refined immediately.

One way to do this might be to talk, as do many hermeneutical theorists, of the difference between reading "with the grain" of the text and reading "against the grain" (after Eagleton 1986). The question could be: does any reading *with* the grain require the assent of the wise? Certainly one needs to get past the various cases of flat misreading of multilayered tropes, or the appeal to empirical effects of texts far removed from their originating or canonical function, in order to arrive at a well-defined question about the link between wise readers and the purposes of Scripture. At the risk of being misunderstood, it is this more carefully refined and well-defined question I have in mind when asking: does wisdom consist in always assenting to the communicative purpose of biblical texts?

A quick way with this question could be to take up a typical "problem text" and, upon rehearsing its problems, announce, "And one cannot agree with that." Instances of commentators doing just this would not be hard to find. However, for reasons that we shall explore in this chapter, this procedure would prompt some important questions about interpretive frameworks and the exercise of certain interpretive virtues. I shall eventually return to the claim that this is not a simple way to answer our question, for reasons not unrelated to our discussion in chapter 1 concerning the nature of academic inquiry as tradition constituted rather than consisting of a series of freestanding "problems."

In the previous chapter we have suggested that, among other things, the interpretive virtue of wisdom involves patient attention to the details and the gaps of the text, and the ability to navigate between them. Wise judgments, we proposed, are oriented to the desire to do justice not just "to the text" but also to how the text will continue to have effects on its readers to come. But as we have seen, this can involve a wide range of judgments that vary in the extent to which they read this or that detail as either supporting or subverting whatever substantive point is at issue, and at times it is not possible to resolve details at all.[1] Even within generally "assenting" analyses of biblical texts, one may be called upon to exercise dissenting judgments at some level or another (and indeed, and quite interestingly, vice versa, whereby negative evaluations of texts often depend on construing certain details positively or reliably). Such considerations bring us to the prominent hermeneutical mode of suspicion and to questions about how to exercise it rightly. One way to articulate our subject matter in this chapter would be that we are concerned with the question of how to evaluate the exercise of suspicion in interpretation, and the extent to which it cuts across (or possibly works alongside) the interpretive virtue of trust.[2]

Trust is not one of Aristotle's cardinal virtues, but presently I shall suggest that there are reasons for this, reasons that have only become

1. For wider reflection on "choosing between competing plausible interpretations of Scripture," as his subtitle has it, see Cosgrove 2004.

2. See Briggs 2009a, an earlier version of some aspects of the present chapter that offers more of an overview of key issues rather than the detailed analysis undertaken here.

clear under the long, slow influence of suspicion in the modern world. And clearly, it is too simplistic to say that trust is a virtue and leave it at that. Trust can extend into credulity too easily, as a simple example from the book of Joshua might demonstrate (in addition to any number of instances in our world, and indeed in our religious practices, where unquestioning obedience to a self-serving leader is inculcated under cover of supposing that this constitutes a virtuous form of trust). In Joshua 9 the inhabitants of Gibeon hear what Joshua has done to Jericho and Ai and "on their part acted with cunning," as the NRSV puts it (v. 4), packing up worn-out sacks, sandals, and dry and moldy bread to deceive Joshua into believing that they have "come from a far country" (v. 6). "Here is our bread," they say, "still warm when we took it from our houses . . . but now . . . dry and moldy" (v. 12). As a result they negotiate a treaty with Joshua that saves their lives, though when Joshua learns what has happened, he curses them and consigns them to various forms of perpetual slavery. The logic of the book of Joshua within which this counts as a result for the Gibeonites is not our concern here. Rather, the point is that, on Joshua's part, it might be said that suspicion would have been the appropriate mode of engagement.

Having said this, I actually want to suggest that focusing on the question of suspicion does not enable us to start in the right place. Our concern with interpretive virtues suggests that our real goal is the question of what constitutes appropriate trust. And in line with our approach in this book, the goal is to consider the virtue of trust as it is implied in an Old Testament narrative, before asking how such a virtue can be understood as playing a role in interpretation. Again a particular narrative suggests itself for consideration, one that is strikingly attuned to questions of trust: the account of Hezekiah and his men hearing the speech of the Assyrian Rabshakeh (the "chief cup-bearer" [i.e., the adjutant] or perhaps "communications officer") at the wall during the siege of Jerusalem, as portrayed in 2 Kings 18. This will offer us a provocative portrait of the nature of trust, which in turn can find remarkable resonance in our quest for the interpretive virtue of trust, as the goal and final section of this chapter.

However, before turning to 2 Kings, it seems worthwhile to explore a little further the key question of how to frame our interpretive cat-

egories around trust rather than suspicion. For reasons that will in turn
have something to offer our analysis of 2 Kings, we shall pursue this
question by way of asking how it is that hermeneutical suspicion has
become so prominent in our day, at least in the academy.[3] This excur-
sus into a little of the historical development of biblical interpretation,
I suggest, will be of particular use in framing our understanding of
how 2 Kings helps us to grasp the interpretive virtue of trust.

The Eclipse of Biblical Trust

The hermeneutics of suspicion are almost certainly better known
than the hermeneutics of trust. Why is this? Upon reflection, it seems
that trust occupies a certain type of default position in the act of
reading, so that for as long as one reads without overt accompanying
theorizing, one defaults to trust. It is precisely the problematizing
of this assumption that is the key shift recasting traditional hermeneutical questions in new ways. Although she is writing more about
postmodern philosophy, Patricia Sayre has the right insight about
the modern world: "Both trust and suspicion have a role to play.
. . . The important question is whether suspicion is to provide the
attitudinal context for trust or *vice versa*" (1993: 580). The rise of
hermeneutical theory, in turn, has been driven more by the need to
explore the issues surrounding suspicion than those surrounding trust.
The result is that one rarely thinks explicitly in terms of "a hermeneutic of trust," and those rare attempts to articulate such a thing
end up presupposing a prior notion of suspicion as too frequently
exercised for anyone's good. Thus Richard Hays states: "While the
hermeneutics of suspicion—rightly employed—occupies a proper
place in any attempt to interpret the Bible for our time, I want to
argue that a *hermeneutic of trust* is both necessary and primary"
(2005: 192).[4]

3. It would be a fascinating but altogether different study to explore hermeneutical
credulity as it may or may not exist outside of the academy, though its presence in at least
some churches is surely a factor motivating certain forms of suspicion in academic theological circles.

4. Cf. also Stuhlmacher 1977, cited below; and Richard Burnett (2001: 197), who writes,
"Karl Barth's answer to the hermeneutics of suspicion, in short, was a hermeneutic of

I want to explore, briefly, the significance of noting that trust was indeed the presupposed mode of hermeneutical engagement with Scripture prior to the "modern" age. In his probing study of this very issue, Garrett Green makes this point by arguing that suspicion, in effect, is what is characteristic of the rise of modernity. He cites Nietzsche (from 1887) as marking a turn of the ages of enormous hermeneutical significance:

> The greatest recent event—that "God is dead," that the belief in the Christian god has become unbelievable—is already beginning to cast its first shadows over Europe. For the few at least, whose eyes—the *suspicion* in whose eyes is strong and subtle enough for this spectacle, some sun seems to have set and some ancient and profound trust has been turned into doubt. (Nietzsche 1974: 279 [§343]; cited in G. Green 2000: 190–91)

Garrett Green's own project is to pursue "a Christian theology of suspicion and trust" (2000: 21) by way of reconceiving what he calls the hermeneutical imperative (i.e., the requirement of interpretation), not as a back-foot response to suspicion but as the space wherein the "faithful imagination" might flourish (2000: 183). He argues that the theological resources for appropriate suspicion are found in the cross, with its inherent critique of all claims to knowledge. Proper suspicion, for Green, must be based on some underlying trust. Though various liberal and conservative projects have sought such trust in the realm of history or fact or morality, a Christian theological approach "require[s] a hermeneutics whose suspicion stems from an underlying trust in the crucified Messiah" (2000: 203). In the end, Green offers an apologia for something like the mirror-image project of this chapter: "There is indeed a valid, even necessary, Christian suspicion; it will be discovered, though, not by the application of secular hermeneutics but rather theologically—that is, by attending to the sources and norms implicit in Christian faith itself" (2000: 190). His emphasis on suspicion rather than trust marks a point of significant divergence from what is undertaken here, and in fact his

---

trust." Burnett's analysis of Barth's handling of trust is tied up with a broader discussion about love, which we shall explore in the next chapter.

appeal to "sources and norms" does not extend as far as exegesis, but in principle this is our goal.[5]

Green's analysis is in turn notably indebted to Hans Frei, whose magnum opus on the history of eighteenth- and nineteenth-century hermeneutics defended the thesis that with the rise of modern critical inquiry had come the "eclipse" of biblical narrative (Frei 1974). In essence, Frei's argument was that the arrival of historical consciousness had had a profound and negative effect on our understanding of the narrative portrayal of reality in the biblical texts, because it shifted the default interpretive framework to questions of whether the biblical narrative was historically accurate. This, in Frei's view, subsumed the biblical category of "realistic narrative" into the essentially modern category of "historical narrative" and bequeathed to the troubled interpreter a whole raft of questions that had no real reference points in Christian tradition and that therefore threatened forever to distort the reading of biblical narrative. The reconstructive part of Frei's later hermeneutical work is perhaps more tendentious than his profound analysis of what had gone wrong, relying as it does on something like a theological hermeneutic uniquely specific to the biblical narratives and an attempt to read the traditional framework of biblical narrative as the "literal sense of scripture."[6]

Nevertheless, with regard to the thesis that the traditional framework of interpretation has been lost, it is interesting to ask whether the issue has to do not so much with narrative per se as with trust

5. Westphal 1998 offers an account of suspicion with many points of contact with Garrett Green's work. See also R. Hays 2005, a brief New Testament–oriented project parallel to our own, including the idea of shaping the notion of "trust" in terms of Paul's language in Romans. It may be appropriate to note here that general reflection on the notion of trust in other disciplines (such as Hollis 1998 in philosophy or Barber 1983 in sociology) offers relatively little help in negotiating the specific virtue in view with regard to the "sources and norms" of Christian faith.

6. The thesis of *The Eclipse of Biblical Narrative* is basically set out in its entirety in the introduction to the book (Frei 1974: 1–16). An excellent account is offered by Higton 2004: 136–50; cf. esp. G. Green 2000: 167–73. Frei's turn to the literal sense as the focus of attention in reading Scripture is evident in Frei 1986 (cf. Bowald 2007: 95–107; and appreciative but different disagreements in Hunsinger 1993: esp. 257–59; and Lee 1999: 76–98). Higton (2004: 177–220) tries to argue that Frei's turn to the literal is not a substantive change of direction, though his argument depends on a thesis about the point of Frei's earlier work that we shall encounter below (see note 10). My reading of Frei is also indebted to the various contributions to G. Green 1987 and Olegovich 1999.

in the narrative world. The moment of asking whether perhaps this text leads us astray is a moment of profound distanciation in the economy of human reading of the sacred text, as it is in the individual reader's spiritual life. This need not mean that asking is to be feared or altogether avoided in a world where suspicion is something of a lingua franca, but neither is it to be entered into lightly. Whereas it is not unknown for accounts of the history of biblical interpretation to arrive at the modern period and offer a narrative of essentially a "happy fall," a "fall upward" into a critical impulse that consists of opened eyes and the knowledge of good and evil (so, most famously, Farrar 1886, though there are more recent examples too), the striking insight of Frei's analysis is that something considerably more complex is at stake in this turn to criticism. It is (to extend the metaphor) a real fall that, like the narrative of Genesis 3, accounts for the state of the world as we presently find it: in interpretation, as in life, the impulses to good and evil wrestle side by side, and the critical spirit of humankind leads now to life, now away from life, with a range of moral and spiritual shadings that far outreach reductive attempts to characterize criticism as merely a "method."[7] But equally, as readers of Genesis 3 and the following narrative come to see, the response to a fall is not to recover the lost (garden) territory and reconquer Eden, because what is lost is not so much territory (i.e., physical location in Genesis 3; temporal location in Frei's narrative) as the nature of the relationship with the one heretofore trusted: Yhwh Elohim in the one account, biblical narrative in the other. The transformation of self effected by the fall allows no way to unmake the transformation or even to believe that one would be better off, having now known good and evil, to not know it again. Although Genesis 3 is surely not intended as a narrative of maturation, the irreversible dynamic of self-involved transformation is very much comparable to such a life change (which may be, after all, why such a reading commends itself to so many patient readers; e.g., van Wolde 1996: 34–73; Bechtel 1993). And so, just as human living requires a complex range of skills and practices to negotiate a world of good and evil and in it to

---

7. By way of contrast, Stuhlmacher's (1977: 22–60) masterly historical survey is very much aware that every gain brought with it considerable cost.

find the God we no longer know face-to-face, so the interpretation of Scripture is cast into equally complex questions of how to discern the ways in which this text moves among us, rendering the stories of creation, Israel, Christ, and the church for "as long as it is called today" (cf. Heb. 3:13).

As I have suggested, Frei's analysis of the problem, while brilliant, is not matched by his attempts at reconstruction. These, for one thing, are fairly rare, evidenced in the main by his treatment of the passion narratives in *The Identity of Jesus Christ* (1975), where he seemed to end up proposing that these narratives select themselves out of the general category of "realistic narrative" and end up in fact historical, by virtue of their subject matter.[8] Whatever its theological merits (on which see Higton 2004: 93–121), this work is, ironically, a failure of extraordinary proportions as a work of biblical interpretation since it "actually works with an abstracted and idealized 'common story.' Astonishingly . . . Frei's analysis simply *fails to engage with the New Testament texts*" (so Lee 1999: 66, emphasis original).[9]

But even if his 1975 work had succeeded on some exegetical level, this would still be a long way from securing insight into a way of reading Scripture in general. The reason why Frei's analysis does not in practice follow through to the concerns of, say, interpreting the Old Testament, it seems to me, is that he presents in formal terms (i.e., as a thesis about narrative) what is actually better understood as a thesis of material substance (i.e., one concerned with the practices of human reading). My proposal for the material substance actually in view in Frei's *Eclipse* is that it concerns the willingness to *trust* the narrative world with which the reader engages.[10] A similar proposal

8. His argument here is consciously modeled after Anselm: the identity of Jesus cannot be conceived without his being the risen one; thus, if he is not in fact risen, he is not Jesus Christ (cf. Stout 1999).

9. Lee's comment comes in the midst of a particularly acute discussion of Frei's book from the perspective of its relevance to biblical interpretation (1999: 64–75).

10. Higton takes the view that the fundamental issue in all of Frei's work is God's providential ordering of history, and that what is at stake in the sacrifice of the Bible's realistic narrative for any form of "mediating theology" (i.e., with respect to any other conceptual scheme) is the "eclipse of providence" (2004: esp. 143, 147). On this account, there is indeed less reason to distinguish an "early" and a "late" Frei. I suspect that my claim about an "eclipse of trust" could be construed as the hermeneutical component of the

is put forward by Garrett Green: "The rise of the hermeneutics of suspicion, then, was the complement to the eclipse of biblical narrative, the other side of the coin" (2000: 171). I want to suggest, further than that: it is actually the side of the coin that has currency. Failure to make this distinction leaves the reader treating the resurrection narratives as sui generis on account of the defining characteristics of these particular texts as text; whereas if we take Frei's argument as a claim about the eclipse of modes of human reading, then it becomes generally applicable to all forms of relating human interests to scriptural texts.

This, I suggest, is the eclipse of a suitably "biblical" form of trust as it relates to interpretation in the modern world. In particular, trust in the narrative world of Scripture has become eclipsed by shoring up the appeal to the narrative world by way of locating the reality of this world in the extratextual world of historical events. As this relates to Old Testament interpretation, it leads us to the claim that though it may or may not be true that events occurred in line with the witness of the Old Testament texts, such a coincidence of testimony is not the basis on which one trusts the texts. It will be clear at once that this is markedly different from two well-known lines of approach in contemporary Old Testament scholarship. On the one hand, the well-known conservative argument is to secure trust in the text precisely by demonstrating its historical reliability (cf. such projects as Kitchen 2003). This position is one with which Frei engaged somewhat reluctantly when it was forced upon him in an exchange with the evangelical statesman Carl Henry (Frei 1993: 207–12), reluctantly perhaps because he sensed that there is interpretive goodwill behind it, but it is mistaken nonetheless, not just in practice (where it is certainly difficult to carry out), but also conceptually. Perhaps he was reluctant too because a common alternative to it is the second response, that of unmasking historical inaccuracy as a way to call trust into question. This approach might perhaps seek to redefine trust into categories of moral import, usually of a general or existential nature, a project every bit as insecure as the search for historical

___

human ("responsive") side of Higton's thesis, which, with some merit, somewhat relegates the significance of hermeneutics as such in Frei's overall work.

fact—witness Stuhlmacher's characterization of eighteenth-century exegesis as assuming "almost without question that the spirit of the rational, enlightened, and morally engaged religion of the time was also the Spirit of the New Testament, and of Jesus above all" (1977: 38). In both these approaches, hermeneutics appears rather like a bird shut up in a cage of its tradition's own making, and Frei's goal was perhaps to show the bird the way out of the cage.[11] Arguably, at least, the bird has forgotten how to fly, a point suggested by the bizarre profusion of hermeneutical analyses urging something like Frei's recovery of Scripture, analyses that themselves do not get as far as reading it (including, of course, Frei himself; 1974: vii).

To draw this hermeneutical detour to a close, then, biblical interpretation today struggles to articulate appropriate modes of trust and suspicion, but two routes are blocked off by Frei's analysis: a return to the forms of trust that predated the arrival of suspicion, or a surrender to suspicion as the simple given of critical inquiry. Some form of interaction between the two is characteristic of our present place in the history of thought, and as Stuhlmacher pointed out, "no historical-critical interpretation can avoid being embedded in its time" (1977: 42). Stuhlmacher's probing call for a "hermeneutics of consent" resists most strongly any attempt to turn the clock back, commenting of Gerhard Maier's proposal to abandon critical method (Maier 1977) that it represented "the requirement of a spiritual, self-evident Bible exposition within the circle of the reborn, a requirement which came to grief a hundred times in church history from Christian Gnosticism to every shade of fanaticism" (1977: 70). Such caution must be in place if one is to hear his constructive proposal rightly: "We consciously begin from the basic principle of consent and of hearing" (1977: 88).

We may also thus rightly hear Paul Ricoeur's famous aphorism about interpretation in the shadow of the "three masters . . . [who] dominate the school of suspicion: Marx, Nietzsche, and Freud" (1970: 32),[12] in his still unsurpassed analysis of suspicion, *Freud and*

11. Just as Wittgenstein's aim in philosophy was "to show the fly the way out of the fly-bottle" (1958: §309).
12. Westphal 1998 explores "the religious uses of modern atheism" through the lens of these same three thinkers.

Philosophy, whose subtitle, *An Essay on Interpretation*, is from its original French title (*De l'interprétation*, 1965). In Ricoeur's terms: "Hermeneutics seems to me to be animated by this double motivation: willingness to suspect, willingness to listen; vow of rigor, vow of obedience" (1970: 27).[13] On our way to an analysis of the interpretive virtue of trust as it is modeled in 2 Kings 18, we shall endeavor to demonstrate just how relevant this double motivation is at almost every turn.

Trusting in 2 Kings 18–19

"Like a Bird in a Cage": Approaching 2 Kings 18–19

On any account, plenty of Old Testament texts expect their readers to see that trust is a virtue that will lead the reader on straight paths:

> Trust [*beṭaḥ*] in Yhwh with all your heart,
>   and do not rely on your own insight.
> In all your ways acknowledge him,
>   and he will make straight your paths. (Prov. 3:5–6)

The vocabulary of trust suffuses the Psalms as well as being common in the book of Isaiah. Elsewhere there is the broader question of how best to understand the similarities and differences between the *bṭḥ* root and words derived from the semantically overlapping root *'mn* (often translated in terms of trust or reliability, or in certain celebrated cases "faith" or "belief": cf. Gen. 15:6; Hab. 2:4), though this wide-ranging issue does not need to be sorted out for our purposes since the passage on which we will be focusing consistently uses *bṭḥ*.[14]

The Old Testament's great narrative "portrayal of trust" (cf. the title of Bostock 2006) occurs in 2 Kings 18–19, the story of Hezekiah

13. Ricoeur's point is taken up and explored by Rowan Williams (1988) in his probing analysis of "the suspicion of suspicion."

14. For a useful review of the data and its significance, see Bostock 2006: 13–14. See further the two *TDOT* articles of Jepsen (1974; 1975), where he highlights the ambiguity of *bṭḥ* with respect to "false security" and "complete security in God alone" (1975: 89); also the wisdom regarding semantics in the two *NIDOTTE* articles of Moberly (1997a; 1997b).

and his men being challenged by the Assyrian envoys during the Assyrian assault on Jerusalem. If ever a narrator wanted to pin readers against the wall and ask where they place their trust, this is it. The Rabshakeh reports the urgent query that Sennacherib, the king of Assyria, is making of Hezekiah:

> What is this *trust* in which you are *trusting*? Do you think that mere words are strategy and power for war? On whom do you now *trust*, that you have rebelled against me? See, you are *trusting* now on Egypt, that broken reed of a staff, which will pierce the hand of anyone who leans on it. Such is Pharaoh king of Egypt to all who *trust* on him. But if you say to me, "We *trust* on Yhwh our God . . ." (2 Kings 18:19–22 AT)[15]

Six times in four verses the word "trust" occurs in one form or another—one can hardly miss it, though it is sometimes obscured in English translations. And thus commentators routinely open their discussions with reference to this theme: "At one basic level, this narrative is about trust. Whom will you trust?" (Fretheim 1999: 206). "In both obvious and subtle ways, this lengthy report addresses the issue of trust . . ." (Seow 1999: 273). What commentators often do not stop to consider is the rhetorical function of placing this extraordinary emphasis on trust in the mouth of the Rabshakeh, representative of Assyria. In what follows I want to suggest several ways in which some important aspects of the virtue of trust are highlighted by the way in which the narrative is told.

But to get there we have to navigate, however briefly, through several levels of interpretive inquiry, for this is a text that raises notoriously complex questions regarding matters of history behind the narrative, textual history, and even canonical repetition (since it reappears, or is at least paralleled, in Isa. 36–39). Or perhaps one should say, in the light of our reading of Frei above, that we shall have to discern how far and in what sense to explore these issues. These various "hermeneutical cages" have proved strikingly difficult to unlock in the past. They have had the combined effect of somewhat shutting up this text, both in the sense of hemming it in under a critical siege of

---

15. The NRSV translation is adjusted here to bring out the repetition of the *bṭḥ* root; cf. Moberly 1997b: 647.

sorts, and in the sense of silencing its voice with respect to how trust might best be understood. On the rarer occasions when scholars have chosen the rhetorical route and engaged in final-form readings of the text (notably Bostock 2006, and others cited below, including Provan 2002: 188–92), the voice is clearer, although we shall suggest ways in which appropriate discernment of relevant background details may help us to understand the virtue of trust more clearly. Nevertheless, wisdom in this case will at least in part involve knowing what sort of historical detail to press for and why.

701 BC and All That: The Eclipse of the 2 Kings Narrative

Few Old Testament texts present as complex a raft of critical issues as the Hezekiah narratives of the second book of Kings, and the multiplication of secondary literature amply demonstrates this. As Childs observed many years ago, "It has become a classic issue on which each new generation of biblical scholars seems constrained to test its mettle" (1967: 11). Four main complicating factors may easily be enumerated, adapting a comparable list offered by Grabbe (2003a: 20):[16]

1. "the literary and source analysis of the account in 2 Kings 18:13–19:37
2. the relationship of 2 Kings 18:13–16 to the rest of the account
3. how many invasions of Palestine were carried out by Sennacherib [and other related historical questions]
4. the question of the Rabshakeh's mission and speech"

Brief comment is in order for the first three points, by way of orientation (and in some respects, reasons not to pursue such matters too far), before we turn to substantive consideration of the final point.

Literary analyses of the passage usually derive from the work of Stade (1886: esp. 172–83), who, typically for his time and perspective,

---

16. Grabbe's list of six issues heads his invaluable survey of "Two Centuries of Sennacherib Study" (2003a: 20–36) and, owing to its historical focus, expands point 3 by way of extra questions about Hezekiah's fourteenth year (2 Kings 18:13) and the character of King Tirhakah (19:9), neither of which are particularly relevant to our inquiry, though 18:13 is a notorious crux in discussions of historical reliability.

applied confident criteria to the supposedly fragile text and succeeded
in cracking it into component parts that then, as is the way of these
things, were shown to have been added together to create the finished
whole of Kings. He posited a variety of sources, and for better or
worse, his labels have become the standard terminology:

> source A—now present in 2 Kings 18:13–16, and of historical
> worth
>
> source B—a single narrative occurring in two variations:
> B1—most usually assigned to 18:17–19:9a (or thereabouts)
> B2—running from approximately 19:9b to 19:37

B1 and B2 are understood as two variations of the same basic narrative, on the grounds that in each of them a threat from the king of
Assyria is mediated by some messenger, to which Hezekiah (or his
representatives) responds with the aid of the prophet Isaiah, who
brings Yhwh's perspective on events. B2 reaches its climax with what
appears also to be the required ending for B1, a resolution to the tale
that involves, famously, the angel of Yhwh slaughtering 185,000 Assyrians in the night, never more memorably translated than in the
KJV: "And when they arose early in the morning, behold, they were
all dead corpses" (19:35).

With regard to Grabbe's second matter, account A does appear to
represent an altogether different dynamic from B1/B2, with only A
telling the story of Hezekiah paying tribute to Sennacherib, a point
confirmed in the surviving annals of Sennacherib (cf. the text in Cogan
2000: 302–3), even if the amounts of the tribute differ. In 2 Kings 18:14
it is set at 300 talents of silver and 30 talents of gold, while Sennacherib has the first figure at 800 and adds a veritable superstore of other
valuable goods as well as Hezekiah's daughters and other "palace
women." Account A differs from B in tone (A being "terse, factual
. . . without moral judgement"), substance (with regard to the matter
of tribute), and vocabulary (for instance, uniquely using the phrase
"Hezekiah King of Judah," *ḥizqîyâ melek-yĕhûdâ*, as in 18:14, rather
than B's "King Hezekiah," *hammelek ḥizqîyāhû*, as in 18:17; cf. Cogan
and Tadmor 1988: 241). The place of A in 2 Kings 18 also leads to a
certain roughness in the reading of the finished chapter's narrative,

with Hezekiah apparently capitulating up front before entering into
a lengthy resistance when Sennacherib sends messengers, although
one can read the issue of tribute and the issue of actual conquering
as different matters. It is often noted that A alone in Kings seems to
bear relationship to the Assyrian account, and also that most of A
is omitted from the parallel passage in Isaiah 36, which matches B
quite closely. Nevertheless, Seitz's study of A in conjunction with the
annals of Sennacherib (AS) makes the striking point that "the lack
of agreement between the two accounts would be immediately noted
were they both found in the biblical record, and were a formal analysis
to be as rigorously applied to AS as to Account A" (Seitz 1991: 65).[17]
Overall, the source-critical account seems to highlight some key issues
but falls short of actually explaining them. However, whatever may be
said historically, the literary flair of AS has at least given us the phrase
that characterizes this whole event, as Sennacherib records that he
"locked up [Hezekiah] within Jerusalem, his royal city, like a bird in a
cage," though it is clear from AS and other comparable accounts that
this maneuver is better described as a "blockade" of Jerusalem rather
than a "siege" (cf. Mayer 2003: 179–81; Knauf 2003: 145).

This leads us on to the third point: the historical reconstruction
of what happened in (approximately) 701 BC, although this is not
really our main interest, except insofar as one cannot gain interpretive
purchase on the texts without at least some plausible reconstruction
in mind. While it was popular for much of the twentieth century to
read B1 and B2 as pertaining to two different invasions, with only
the first in 701 BC (so, e.g., Bright 1960: 282–87), this view is largely
discarded now as an improbable hermeneutical expediency (though
a version of it lives on in Becking's redating, which leaves 701 BC as
the second of the two invasions; 2003: 58). It is important to note that
the kinds of historical questions that occupy much scholarship these
days have little tradition behind them for the simple and contingent
reason that the relevant Assyrian cuneiform texts were not translated
and published until the mid-nineteenth century (in Rawlinson 1852).
This relates to our foregoing discussion of the "eclipse" of biblical

---

17. Seitz's analysis is part of a full-scale update of the analysis of Childs 1967: 69–103,
and he is drawing here on Geyer 1971.

narrative as Frei saw it: the default assumption that the world of the scriptural narratives was the real world was in part so compelling because it was not substantially relativized by having other accounts at hand. Given the arrival of competing accounts,[18] it is no longer possible to recover the state of ignorance—our eyes having been opened, as one might say. To read the narrative of 2 Kings 18–19 *now* as one continuous narrative and postulate a historical reconstruction based on taking it all at more-or-less face value is not the same move as it would have been before other sources came to light, and thus it may be that such a reading (as that by Provan 2002: 188–92, noted above) can be understood to *construct* a version of history just as much as those readings that operate with a less trusting impulse.[19]

History is not our prime concern here, but we need to understand in what sense it is not, so a simple example may clarify matters, especially since we alluded to it earlier: the striking verse in 2 Kings 19:35, with its account of the activities of the angel of Yhwh destroying the Assyrian army. It has long been noted that in his account of Sennacherib's exploits, full though this is of details that do not fit the story of 2 Kings, Herodotus (in the fifth century BC) writes that when the Assyrian armies were encamped against Egypt in Pelusium, "a number of field-mice, pouring in upon their enemies, devoured their quivers and bows, and moreover, the handles of their shields; so that, on the next day, when they fled bereft of their arms, many of them fell" (Herodotus, *Hist.* 2.141).[20] The context and general import of this account actually has markedly little to do with the Kings account, as noted by Grabbe: "There is no element in Herodotus's story that could be said to show remarkable agreement with 2 Kgs 19 or Isa. 37. The only resemblance between the two is that Sennacherib is defeated" (Grabbe 2003b: 136–37). As to the possibility of reconstructing a his-

18. Now transliterated and translated in Mayer 2003: 186–200 and conveniently set out and summarized in Childs 1967: 11–12; cf. the wide-ranging study of these texts in Gallagher 1999: 91–142.

19. This view is complicated, though not completely, by the parallel accounts of 2 Chron. 28–32, which are sufficiently different to raise another set of questions again, familiar to interpreters of Chronicles, but which need not be resolved for our analysis. Here note especially Vaughan 1999.

20. Cited in Gallagher 1999: 248, with discussion (1999: 248–51) of the various elements of the text that do not fit the Kings story.

torical event here, it has often been mooted that the mice as carriers of some form of plague struck down the Assyrian army overnight. This is "surely too conjectural" says Gallagher (1999: 250), even though he is keen to find some sort of historical plausibility here and indeed goes on to say that all this is "evidence that something unexpected happened to Sennacherib which made him turn back" (1999: 251).

The issue being raised for us is the relative status of textual accounts vis-à-vis historical reconstruction. And the question that concerns us is not, or at least not primarily, which account is historical over against which account offers only ideology or apology. Rather, it is what each account wishes us to deduce about the ways of the divine in the world of humans. In the age before suspicion, Sirach 48:21 offers us the simple thought that "the Lord struck down the camp of the Assyrians, and his angel wiped them out" (for, says the next verse, "Hezekiah did what was pleasing to the Lord"). This is a world away from the version of events discussed in Boswell's *Life of Johnson* (1791):

> (Mr. Erskin) seemed to object to a passage in scripture where we are told that the angel of the Lord smote in one night forty thousand (sic!) Assyrians. "Sir, (said Johnson,) you should recollect that there was a supernatural interposition; they were destroyed by pestilence. You are not to suppose that the angel of the Lord went about and stabbed each of them with a dagger, or knocked them on the head, man by man." (Boswell 1979: 159–60; cited in Gallagher 1999: 243)

But equally, it is a world away from Boswell's near-contemporary Lord Byron, whose celebrated poem "The Destruction of Sennacherib" offers to all intents and purposes a realistic narrative drawn straight from Kings and reinscribed in the real world of human history. For Byron, when "the Assyrian came down like the wolf on the fold," this was like the blue wave rolling nightly on Galilee; and the result of the Angel of Death spreading "his wings on the blast" was that "the widows of Ashur are loud in their wail / And the idols are broke in the temple of Baal" (Byron 1812; "Ashur" = Assyria). The "event" described is here cast in terms of its wider ramifications in human and social history, moving outside the perspective of the biblical narrative (e.g., to the weeping of the Assyrian widows) and thus mapping the tale into a historically reconstructed notion of space and time, or reality. That Byron's reality fits almost perfectly the world projected by 2 Kings 19 should not lead us to suppose that the function of the two texts could be the same. After all, 2 Kings 19 operates before the "eclipse" of which we spoke earlier, and Byron's poem, emerging into the new world rendered possible by the eclipse, makes claims about the nature of divine action in a reality full of alternative possibilities. In the past two centuries, biblical scholarship has tended to find it easier to side with either Boswell or Byron, and think that in so doing it is either critical of or voting with Ben Sira. But as we have seen, questions of history and hermeneutics cannot bypass questions of trust and suspicion so simply, as if these did not have profound epistemological consequences of almost every sort.

Childs's own 1967 analysis of these narratives concludes on one level by saying that "the historical problems have not been solved. . . . It seems unlikely that a satisfactory historical solution will be forthcoming without fresh extra-biblical evidence" (1967: 120). But he then proceeds to "the theological problem" and says, "One of the most consistent theological problems which arises in connection with biblical diversity is the application of norms for establishing some order of relative value among the many testimonies" (1967: 123). This is nothing other than the refusal to let historical reconstruction be the norm for theological work and may be seen now, looking back, as a nascent exploration of his later, paradigm-shifting "canonical" approach. If nothing else, Childs's 1967 book *The Assyrian Crisis* admirably demonstrates that his canonical approach is not an end run around historical questions but is in principle the willingness to look further and deeper than the framework within which they are presented.[21]

Such matters need only detain us because the fourth and final point listed above, the question of the Rabshakeh's mission and speech, is crucial to the function of the narrative about trust cited earlier. On this occasion we need to probe questions of the status and function of this text that can only be addressed satisfactorily from the midst of the discussions we have been considering.

---

21. Seitz 1991 is noteworthy for taking this line of thought even to the point of saying that 2 Kings 18–19 and Isa. 36–37, while formally parallel texts in many ways, are irreducibly different theological constructs.

The Rabshakeh's Speech: 2 Kings 18:19–25

The presenting critical issue with respect to the Rabshakeh's speech in 2 Kings 18 concerns its origin: to what extent does it intend to be (or serve as) a historical report of the Assyrian's words, and to what extent is it a reflection of Israelite thinking? Its phraseology is notably Israelite: disavowing reliance on Egypt, and in particular claiming to come against Jerusalem as Yhwh's agent, a thought not unrelated to Isaiah's claim about Assyria being the rod of Yhwh's anger in Isaiah 10:5. A turning point in the study of this passage is Ben Zvi's succinct rhetorical analysis (1990), followed by Rudman's study with the perceptive title "Is the Rabshakeh Also among the Prophets?" (2000).

Ben Zvi analyzes the terminology of the speech to explore the question of its provenance as a literary text. On the basis of its heavy borrowing from Deuteronomistic and Isaianic characteristics, he concludes that it is actually "a piece of biblical literature and neither a transcription nor a closely related version of an actual Assyrian speech" (1990: 91). Two features of the passage under discussion prompt this view. First is the Rabshakeh's suggestion that Hezekiah has erred by removing the Yahwistic cult centers (v. 22), when the reader is expected to grasp that Hezekiah has actually done right, which places the reader at or after the time of the Josianic-era Deuteronomistic centralization view. Second is the claim that Jerusalem will fall, which is designed to invoke in the reader the notion of the inviolability of Zion in response, in true Isaianic fashion (1990: 86).

Now one could argue that this analysis is entirely back to front, reading the text's details into a certain historical reconstruction rather than letting the content of the text determine the reconstruction. Indeed, Ben Zvi does somewhat disarmingly note that one way to account for the various issues raised by the text of the speech is that it "could be explained as 'natural discourse' . . . closely related to Rabshakeh's actual words" (1990: 83). But it is one thing to suppose that this speech had some historical backing, and another to suppose that its delivery in the midst of fraught negotiations on the highway to the fuller's field, in the hearing of the men on the wall, would have enabled some form of memorization or transcription of the actual words. So on this occasion the historical plausibility of Ben Zvi's approach seems secured. At the end of his article he does note that, all in all, it would have made more sense from a literary point of view to have the Rabshakeh's points made by a higher-ranking Assyrian officer than just the chief cupbearer: "If the writer were a free narrator, Rabshakeh's role would have been played by someone else. However it seems that the narrator was not entirely free" but was "restricted" by some "collective memory" of an event something like the one described (1990: 92). This admixture of narrative art and historical constraint is one we have encountered before, in our discussion of Solomon, and Ben Zvi handles it wisely. In sum: the "historical Rabshakeh's speech" is lost, but into his mouth comes the gist of his words, carefully phrased in Israel's own idiom.

What such an approach opens up, then, is the question of how the Israelite author (or at least the narrator) of 2 Kings is seeking to draw out the claims being put to Israel in the narrative person of the Rabshakeh. This is Rudman's focus, observing that "one of the most remarkable features of the Rabshakeh's speech in Account B1 is that it is full of prophetisms" (2000: 101). For Rudman, "the Rabshakeh is to be considered as an 'anti-Isaiah' and the passage as a whole construed not just as a confrontation between Sennacherib and Yahweh, but also as a prophetic duel between the Rabshakeh and Isaiah" (2000: 103). This takes further the earlier literary analysis of Fewell, who noted that the tale presents Yhwh and Sennacherib both as "distant" characters, whose words are mediated by messengers, engaged in a war of words (1986: 82–83).

The move to something like Ben Zvi's historically sensitive rhetorical analysis is significant: it allows us to assess the text in the terms of "realistic narrative" such as Frei was concerned with, and to locate the genuine insight of this narrative as presented by way of the construct, the Rabshakeh's speech. In other words, 2 Kings 18:19–25 represents a claim about trust that Israel is asked to consider by one of its own "prophets"— the author(s) of 2 Kings. The intractable questions regarding how to locate genuine Assyrian ideology or rhetorical technique in the history behind this text may be sidestepped, but this is not by way of adopting a "literary reading" (such as Fewell 1986). Rather, it is because on its own terms, the text presents the challenge regarding trust as a question that Israel must ask of itself. Seen in this way, four points may emerge that shed light on the nature of the virtue of trust involved.

Trust in This Text

First, and in line with our earlier discussion concerning trust being articulated only as a response to suspicion, we must recognize that the question of where Hezekiah is to put his trust is presented to him as a question coming from Assyria. The foregrounding of trust in this narrative thus derives from the onslaught of suspicion presented by the Rabshakeh, who is the one who asks, "What is this trust in which you are trusting?" (2 Kings 18:19).

The key point here is that trust is "provoked." Many references to trust in Yhwh in the Psalms, though they may look like straightforward assertions of a relationship marked by confidence, are explicitly presented in terms of self-involving claims of trust in the face of alternatives. To borrow Brueggemann's felicitous terminology, there is a world of difference between a claim to trust in Yhwh in a world of "orientation" and a claim to trust in a mode of "reorientation" (1980). This is obvious in cases where the trust is compared in the text with other pulls on the believer's life; thus, "Do not put your trust in princes" (Ps. 146:3) or "I hear the whispering of many—terror all around! . . . But I trust in you, O Yhwh" (Ps. 31:13–14). But it is equally true in cases where the alternative claims lie unvoiced in the text. Texts with this dynamic include Psalm 125:1, which looks as solid as the mountain it celebrates: "Those who trust in Yhwh are like Mount Zion." This psalm of ascent may be read in the shadow of the hills to which the pilgrims lift their eyes in 121:1, asking where the believer's help comes from, perhaps in the face of a skyline populated by alien gods, high places, and other claims to allegiance. Even the notoriously problematic "orientation" Psalm 37 (with its psalmist who has never in all his long years seen the righteous forsaken or their children hungry; v. 25) twice urges trust in Yhwh early on (vv. 3, 5), in terms that do perhaps simplify the rewards involved ("so you will live in the land, and enjoy security"; v. 3), but that are at least predicated on the opening empirical observation that the wicked and evildoers seem to be doing rather well (v. 1), in the light of which, "Trust in Yhwh." In all these cases and more, the verb is *bṭḥ*: this kind of trust is provoked. And if one had interviewed Hezekiah prior to the assault on Jerusalem and asked him whether he would say that he trusted in Yhwh, the hypothetical answer would doubtless have been yes (cf.

2 Kings 18:5, written, one may be sure, with the benefit of the long view), and yet the king is not provoked to grasp what this means until the enemy is at the gate.

Could it be any other way? If our analysis of what is at stake in Frei's reading of divine providence and the history of thought is right, then trust is the mode of thinking and living that forms the basic "bedrock" of human activity, such that it will only be articulated in response to the accusation of suspicion. Once again, a Wittgensteinian aphorism serves us well here. In his discussion of construal at the end of the *Philosophical Investigations*, Wittgenstein suggests that taking something *as* something else (e.g., a picture of a duck-rabbit as either a duck or a rabbit) is predicated upon realizing that it can be taken other ways, and then he says, "One doesn't *take* what one knows to be cutlery at a meal *for* cutlery" (1958: 195).[22] Thus, one does not assert trust when there are no alternatives, and to do so, indeed, is somewhat self-undermining.[23]

To bring together the various lines of our inquiry: the Rabshakeh's speech represents a startling way for Israel to articulate its own trust in Yhwh, highlighting the fact that one typically affirms trust only when provoked to contrast it with other possibilities. The narrator of 2 Kings, perhaps historically constrained, as Ben Zvi suggests, has in any case found a way to bring forth the key issue as forcefully as possible. He does so by placing in the Rabshakeh's mouth a speech heavily indebted to Israel's own prophetic idiom. As Nelson declares, "Rabshakeh's interpretation of events is not unreasonable," building as it does on the notion already underlined in verses 9–12 earlier in 2 Kings 18 that foreign armies can do Yhwh's will (1987: 238). On various levels, then, doubts would be raised: in the minds of those trapped in Jerusalem in 701 BC, and in the minds of readers of 2 Kings pondering the reality of subsequent exile. The narrator, we might say, knows that the requisite affirmation of trust can only be found on the

22. Elsewhere (Briggs 2001: 118–31) I have discussed the significance of this notion of construal for the idea of self-involvement in biblical interpretation, including this specific example (2001: 127).

23. For a more contemporary example, in May 1994, film and fashion stars Richard Gere and Cindy Crawford took out a full-page ad in *The Times* of London to publicize the fact that they were happily married, which had the singular effect of provoking a wide range of rumors and speculation. They divorced in 1995.

far side of articulating the doubt that perhaps the Assyrians are in the right and have annexed the will of Yhwh to themselves; or as the speech has it in its rhetorical climax, perhaps it is in fact Yhwh who has sent them (v. 25). By articulating this doubt in the repeated and deliberate language of trust, the narrator draws the reader through the process of fear, doubt, and (very reasonable) wondering, thus handing the reader the language of trust in which to formulate the appropriate response.

Notice what this argument does and does not claim historically. That the Rabshakeh's speech is an Israelite construction seems historically plausible, while the notion that some argument at the front line of whatever took place in 701 BC constrains the narrator seems equally likely. But the implied reader of 2 Kings 18 is not expected to push beyond this to historical reconstruction. Indeed, on the face of it (i.e., to read this narrative "realistically," in Frei's terms, without judgment as to whether it is in fact historical), the point being made about trust is rooted in the historical events of the Assyrian siege without necessarily being a point anyone in the siege ever made. Nelson again formulates the issue helpfully. First, he deftly sidesteps the entirety of the historical discussion in his commentary: "This narrative is a call to trust God in the face of inevitable disaster, even when all evidence and logic point the other way" (1987: 241). Then he goes on to remark, "The major interpretive problem with this narrative is that most of its modern readers will simply be unable to believe that it actually happened" (1987: 242). Nelson deals with this issue by appealing to story as the key hermeneutical category, but Frei helps us to go further: the question as to whether it actually happened is the question that rises when the trust in the text's ability to speak truthfully about what it wants to talk about is eclipsed. In the light of Nelson's comment about evidence and logic, it is then an interesting hermeneutical move to suggest that the lack of evidence and logic perceived with regard to this text might count against the point the text wants to make. But we shall return to this thought below.

Second, it is worth dwelling a little on 18:20a. The drive to translate this text into smooth English perhaps loses its striking import. For example, the NIV misleadingly offers, "You say you have strategy and military strength—but you speak only empty words." One could tackle the sentence more literally with a somewhat halting "You say, but it is a word of lips [*'āmartā 'ak-dĕbar-śĕpātayim*]," followed by the content of what is claimed to be possessed: "counsel and power for war" [*'ēṣâ ûgĕbûrâ lammilḥāmâ*]" (cf. Rudman 2000: 104); or one could follow the NRSV: "Do you think that mere words are strategy and power for war?" For the Rabshakeh as prophetic voice to Israel, this is rather more than a rhetorical question. His speech will go on to make the point that even if Hezekiah were given two thousand horses, he would not be able to find riders for them (v. 23), so the point is not that the Rabshakeh's speech is to provoke Israel to greater efforts to improve its military might. The irony is that "mere words" are precisely what constitute strategy and power, an insight that one can trace through history's long testimony to the effective force of words in rhetoric, speeches, and self-description, all the way back to the Old Testament notion that the word of the prophet is effective and that the word of Yhwh will achieve its purposes (cf. Isa. 55:11). As is often noted, the message of Isaiah in response to the Rabshakeh's taunting, as narrated in 2 Kings 19:6–7, says that it will be on hearing "a certain report" (NIV) that the Assyrian king will return home, and that Hezekiah in his turn is not to be afraid of the words of Sennacherib. The conflict will turn, one could say, on words. Here Fewell is exactly right: "The story as it now stands is an ironic story about words, offensive words and words of rebuke, blasphemous words and words of judgment" (1986: 87). In short, the Rabshakeh is presented as one who clearly thinks that the notion of trusting in words in the time of war is ridiculous, but the narrative portrait shows that Israel knows better—if it can hold fast to the God whose word is trustworthy.

A third observation may be made with respect to 18:23: "Come now, make a bargain [or wager; *'ārab*] with my master, the king of Assyria." Here is the question of existential allegiance put most forcefully. With this uncanny foreshadowing of Pascal, Kierkegaard, Ricoeur, and so many others down through the centuries, the Assyrian envoy urges the people of Israel not to listen to Hezekiah when he "misleads" them by saying, "Yhwh will deliver us" (v. 32). Again, the terminology of the Rabshakeh's speech offers Israel the conceptuality for articulating its own appropriate response: even when evidence and logic all seem to point away from trusting Yhwh, the wager of faith pulls Israel back to the God whose claims did indeed seem clearer before the present crisis. The wager asks us to consider how we construct our world in terms of divine action and trustworthiness. It is Ricoeur who translates Pascal's basic insight into hermeneutical terms: the symbol (in the text) gives rise to thought, as he urges at the end of *The Symbolism of Evil*, and as such "I wager that I shall have a better understanding of man and of the bond between the being of man and the being of all beings if I follow the *indication* of symbolic thought" (1967: 355; cf. 347–57). In his discussion of Ricoeur's version of this wager, Alan Jacobs suggests that "it is a valuable and necessary wager . . . because without it understanding is impossible. . . . The charitable reader offers the gift of constant and loving attention—faithfulness—to a story, to a poem, to an argument, in hope that it will be rewarded." The alternative, as Jacobs puts it in his striking work on "a theology of reading," is the despair of absolute suspicion (2001: 89).

Finally, we should note that the discussion following the Rabshakeh's speech, if understood as a continuation of the narrator's own challenge to his readers, takes on an interesting aspect. On the surface, the worried representatives of Hezekiah ask the Rabshakeh to speak to them in Aramaic so that the Hebrew-speaking people on the wall will not understand the threats (18:26). The Rabshakeh promptly seizes what he perceives to be an opportunity and calls out "in a loud voice in the language of Judah" to whoever can hear (v. 28). But perhaps the narrator who has known how to frame the question of trust so ably in the words of the Rabshakeh is ahead of his Assyrian character here too, since arguably at least this is a deliberate ploy to provoke the Rabshakeh into spreading his accusation further afield, thereby actually rallying the people of Jerusalem to greater resolve in their resistance (this possibility is interestingly explored by Bostock 2006: 56, drawing on Botha 2000). If this is so, and perhaps one can find it only a possible reading, then nevertheless this says something powerful about the role of trust in liberating from fear and suspicion. Trust, we might say, allows suspicion to be broadcast, confident that it will not have the last word.

Suspicion: A Brief Foray

The focus of this chapter is the virtue of trust. As discussed at the beginning of our analysis, we have deliberately chosen to attempt to pursue trust head on, as it were, rather than as what is left when suspicion has been either accounted for or dealt with, which from a historical perspective at least would be the wrong way around to frame the issue. But the last two points above, and other points made through this chapter, have demonstrated that suspicion has never been far from our focus. In line with the project of allowing biblical narratives to portray the nature of the relevant virtues and characteristics that we are discussing, it would be interesting to pursue a narrative of suspicion for the same project. Indeed, we have considered briefly Joshua 9 and its moldy bread, and noted Garrett Green's claim (2000: 190) that suspicion is rooted in a proper understanding of the cross, resourced by the texts of the Christian tradition.

Yet few Old Testament narratives explicitly foreground issues of suspicion. The most striking exception is the so-called *sotah* (woman suspected of adultery) narrative of Numbers 5:11–31, an extraordinary procedure for the suspicious husband to ascertain whether his wife has been unfaithful to him. If the spirit of jealousy (the *rûaḥ-qin'â*, the "rushing wind" perhaps; v. 14) comes upon the husband, he may, with no proof whatsoever, take his wife to the priest, who will make her swear an oath, which he will then write down and wash the letters off into a liquid mixed with the dust of the tabernacle floor. This "water of bitterness" (vv. 18, 24) will then test the woman, who is made to drink it: if she is guilty of unfaithfulness, then what sounds rather like a forced abortion will occur (v. 27), but if not, "then she shall be immune and be able to conceive children" (v. 28).

What is one to make of this startling, abrasive, and deeply problematic text?[24] Much of what is made of it is made on gender-sensitized grounds. Thus even Martin Noth, not a commentator noted for his lightness of touch, offers a final word worth pondering: "There is no indication of any punishment for the man who,

---

24. A great deal could be said, but I have explored this text at length elsewhere (cf. Briggs 2009b), and it would take us too far afield to try to do justice to all the details here.

in the case of the woman's being innocent, has entertained, out of 'jealousy,' an unjustified suspicion (v. 14b); perhaps he simply went free" (1968. 52).

However, I have argued elsewhere that the problem foregrounded in this text, which is self-described as a law "of jealousy" (v. 29), is at least in part the issue of what happens when suspicion is allowed to flourish without the usual recourse to corroborative testimony, witnesses, or discussion of the situation before it is brought to trial. In short, it is a mistake to read this text as restricting a privilege of suspicion to men. Rather, it is the according to men of a disastrous prerogative. The hermeneutical point, reading in terms of the implied "virtue" of suspicion, is that we are to be suspicious of the narrative events described in this text, since overall it poses for us the question of how to evaluate untrammeled suspicion. Could one suggest that the narrator of 2 Kings 18 knows that, left to its own devices, suspicion will self-destruct, imploding upon itself into despair (cf. Jacobs 2001: 88–90)?

The example of Numbers 5 offers a particularly clear test case of whether one could settle the question about the wise reader always agreeing with the text by simply parading a "problem" text, since it is a prime candidate for being a text more or less "unusable" in terms of making a constructive contribution to the believer's understanding of how God is at work in the world. And yet even here, the question is not whether one should adopt some such ritual as is described in the case of Numbers 5—clearly one should not—but larger matters concerning how the reader is drawn in to make judgments about matters such as trust and suspicion by the way in which the narrative is presented and framed in the book of Numbers (see Briggs 2009b for discussion of this point in some detail). A reader's response to a freestanding text is not the way to assess the question about wise dissent broached at the beginning of this chapter: every case ramifies out into a broader network of commitments and interpretive judgments, and—at least arguably—any text found in the canon has its role to play in developing those commitments and judgments.[25] All this brings

25. See further the balanced discussion of Robin Parry (2004: 219–42, esp. 242), where he talks of the interaction of "suspicion" and "faith" in similar terms.

us back to how the implied reader of these canonical texts might be characterized in terms of the interpretive virtue of trust.

The Interpretive Virtue of Trust

We began with the question, loosely phrased but understood as appropriately focused, does the wise reader always agree with the text? The virtue we have had in view has not been "agreement" as such, but trust. And we have seen that the implied reader of 2 Kings 18 is one who trusts God in the face of considerable evidence (and even logic) to the contrary. To bring this out, the text was required to provoke trust by the articulation of a counter-possibility. Three points suggest themselves by way of a conclusion concerning the interpretive virtue of trust.

First, in the midst of testimony and countertestimony, such as we find in the Old Testament in general (so, programmatically, Brueggemann 1997) and in this passage in particular, it is apparent that to trust one voice will perhaps inevitably involve extending suspicion to another. Trust and suspicion as modes of engagement require as careful balancing with texts as they do in any of the existential aspects of human relationships. In a study of their role in literary interpretation, Gabriel Josipovici writes: "The problem is how to keep suspicion from turning into cynicism and trust from turning into facileness. Trust without suspicion is the recipe for a false and meretricious art; but suspicion without trust is the recipe for a shallow and empty art" (1999: 3). In the conclusion to his account, Josipovici makes the striking observation that Wittgenstein's *On Certainty* could just as well have been called *On Trust* (Josipovici 1999: 271), since it insists that we trust not so much in the truth of some proposition or other but "in the responsiveness of the world to our agency" (1999: 271). With regard to the reading of texts, Josipovici concludes that "suspicion has to follow trust, not precede it; it is only by opening ourselves up to the literature of the past and the present that we can begin to see what works and authors are meaningful to us. . . . To begin with suspicion is to condemn ourselves to solipsism" (1999: 274; cf. also Steiner 1989: 89). Earlier in the book he has explored what this means in practice with readings of texts ranging from 1 Samuel and Genesis to Samuel Beckett and Kafka, in the process tracing a literary version of the "fall" of literary interpretation not too dissimilar to the theological one discussed by Frei.[26]

Second, an interesting question arises in transferring our focus from Hezekiah and his envoys in besieged Jerusalem to the reader of 2 Kings 18 hearing their tale told. Is the virtue of trust to be circumscribed closely as "trust in Yhwh," or can it be understood as trust in the word of Yhwh, especially in light of the discussion above, dealing with the theme of words and power (with reference to 18:20)? The difference this makes may be clear: is the interpreter of Scripture hereby enjoined to trust in the text, or in the God of the text? The various words of the prophet, which in the end lead to the overthrow of Sennacherib, suggest that this contrast could be overdrawn: perhaps an interpreter manifests trust in the God of the text by way of trusting the text itself. But this is probably to be understood as a mode of trust in the text that trusts it only insofar as it is received as the word of the God who remains a free agent over and above the text. In other words, if the communicative force of the canonical text requires assent from the wise reader, this is because it is attributed to the God who authorizes the canon.

We live at an odd time when most of the scholars who might want to make such a (theological) claim do not work with the text overmuch, and many who work with the text would prefer not to make such a claim. A very clear point at which our own text would bring this claim down from the stratosphere of theological abstraction and locate it in the midst of exegetical detail would be the verse we looked at earlier, 2 Kings 19:35. In this verse the angel of Yhwh strikes 185,000 Assyrians overnight. Can this text be trusted? Such a discussion, at least since Herodotus, has devolved on to the much less hermeneutically significant claim of whether or not it is historically accurate, as we have shown at various points in this chapter. The question of trust here is not in the record of history, however, but in the ascription of

---

26. A fascinating account of a catholic approach to literature in general by Nicholas Boyle (2004: 58–62) also draws upon Frei on its way to a discussion of the many modes of reading sacred and secular texts. Without using the vocabulary of trust and suspicion, it has several points of contact with Josipovici's (1999) work.

agency to Yhwh, who chooses in this case to resolve the matter that
has wrought the devastation on Israel to which such passages as Isaiah 1 and 10 seem to attest. Although there are moments in the Old
Testament when the death of the enemy is the occasion of rejoicing
(Exod. 15, with the Song of the Sea, springs to mind as one obvious
example), it is striking that the resolution of this conflict is presented
in Kings in bare detail, leading immediately to the story of Hezekiah's sickness unto death (20:1). In Isaiah, this complex of stories
leads directly to the exile. For every moment of apparent closure or
completion in the narrative, the onward rush of both the story and
of history reopens all judgments, reframes them with a hermeneutic
alert to provisionality, and offers the option either of grinding to a
halt, unable to ascribe anything to Yhwh, or of taking the wager and
moving ahead in trust.

All this leads us on in turn to a final point. Trust, as implied in
this narrative, is not primarily dependent on evidence or logic; rather,
it is the framework within which evidence and logic can play their
part. Such considerations may perhaps be familiar in philosophically
oriented discussions in the tradition of thinkers like Wittgenstein and
Polanyi[27] and are also found in the thought-provoking study of the
"ethics of belief" by Wolterstorff (1996).[28] But interestingly, what we
notice here in the Old Testament is already a recognition that the
question of trust in Yhwh can be put most forcefully at precisely the
moment when a good deal of the evidence seems to favor the Rabshakeh. In global terms, one may or may not have particular reasons
with respect to why trust in Yhwh is appropriate, but the delicate
balancing act wherein all the real work is done is in discerning how
to balance such global trust with local examples where trust appears

27. For theological reflection on the nature of trust in their work, see on the former
especially R. Williams 1988: esp. 37–41; and on the latter, note inter alia Louth 1983: 59–66,
as well as 73–95 on "tradition and the tacit."

28. Wolterstorff 1996 begins his analysis of Locke with a note about how he "became
perplexed over the challenge so widely issued to religious people that they must have evidence for their religious beliefs—evidence consisting of other beliefs. It was insisted that
at bottom a person might not *reason from* his or her religious beliefs but had to *reason to*
them from other beliefs. Why was this?" (1996: x). As Wolterstorff notes, in his reading
of Locke's approach to this issue, he found himself "present at the making of the modern
mind" (1996: xii).

to be a foolhardy wager on the impossible. This question of balance between the general and the specific will reappear in a different guise in our next chapter.

It is often noted that the Isaiah version of our story is deliberately constructed as an alternative vision of how the king trusts the prophetic word after meeting the enemy on the highway to the fuller's field—over against the story of Ahaz at the same location in Isaiah 7 (and noted, indeed, that Isa. 7:14 more than likely reads as a prophecy of Hezekiah as the one who will succeed where Ahaz fails). This is not the moment to enter into an analysis of this theme in Isaiah, but one cannot resist observing the way in which the promise of Isaiah 7:9b ("If you do not stand firm in faith, you shall not stand at all," in the Hebrew) has become, in the LXX, the profound claim that "if you do not believe, neither shall you understand."[29] And in the theological tradition that springs from this formulation, so central to Augustine's thought in the first instance, it is notable that profound questioning is characteristic of the kind of inquiry that springs from such belief. The interpretive virtue of trust may be understood to function similarly: if you do not trust, neither shall you interpret. Rather than foreclosing on questions of suspicion, this actually gives them their proper framework and allows them their place.

The wise reader knows that in matters of interpretation the commitment to trust is the commitment to stand firm in the midst of the hermeneutical siege. In due course this will lead on to a deepened awareness of what is at stake in the text in the process of wrestling with suspicion, exploring alternative ways ahead, and coming to a deeper grasp of how God may be at work "in, with, and under" the text before us.

---

29. This is the translation offered in NETS. On the ways in which this translational transmutation occurred, see Wong 1996; Menzies 1998.

5

LOVE IN THE TIME
OF MONOTHEISM

The Blessing of Interpretive Charity

I n the preceding chapters we have been building up a picture of
the implied virtues of the reader of the Old Testament that has
included humility, wisdom, and trust. It is time to turn to the topic
around which Augustine's own treatment of interpretive virtue is
focused: love. It is striking how little is often said about love in treatments of Christian ethics as they relate to the Old Testament. Rodd
offers only, "Terms like . . . 'love' are empty cells which have to be
filled with concrete ethical actions" (2001: 306). No one is going to
deny the centrality of love to any vision of the Christian life, but as
is well known, the problems start when specifics are envisaged.

The Desirability of Love in Biblical Interpretation

In the lead article of the three volumes of the SBL's "Character Ethics and Biblical Interpretation" group (discussed above, in chap. 1),
Lisa Sowle Cahill offers a perceptive analysis of how the Christian

135

ethicist looks askance at the biblical interpreter forever hiding behind conceptual complexity and the plurality of canonical perspectives. As she puts it, "From the standpoint of an ethicist, the simple celebration of diversity is quite an anemic response" to such matters as genocide, child exploitation, and so forth (2002: 11). In particular, though she is addressing New Testament ethics in the main, she writes, "I find it essential to Christian character ethics to define at least a few desirable *characteristics*. It is astounding to me that so many biblical interpreters today are so highly reluctant to acknowledge that a profile of such characteristics is clearly projected by the 'single, fairly coherent story' of Jesus as the Christ" (2002: 13).[1] When she comes to clarify what this kind of desirable character is, Cahill follows Wolfgang Schrage in seeing Christian ethics as removing all limits on the notion of love, redefining the most unlikely candidates into the category of "neighbour" (Cahill 2002: 13–14). In other words, love cannot be ceded to the biblical scholar's penchant for observing that this or that text is not interested in love; nor can the canonical witness be allowed to overturn any moral vision that does not leave love central in some way. Her article indicates that if Cahill finds New Testament scholars' celebration of diversity frustrating in this regard, she has even less time for Old Testament scholarship that is unable to locate any sort of thematic center to its canonical collection (2002: 10).

The questions concerning love in Old Testament discourse, to which we shall be turning our attention in due course, may be further illuminated, however, by staying a moment longer with the concerns of the New Testament's moral vision. In this regard, it is striking that Richard Hays's thorough analysis of just this topic locates the three "focal images" of the New Testament's moral vision as being community, cross, and new creation (1996: 193–200). But Hays is too aware of the richly multilayered nature of his task not to see the obvious comeback to this proposal: "It is widely supposed that love is the basic message of the New Testament. Indeed . . . [for Paul and John] love is fundamental to the moral life" (1996: 200). Nevertheless, he says that this does not warrant making love a central image, for reasons that he

---

1. The phrase "single, fairly coherent story" she attributes parenthetically to Carol Newsom with respect to her discussion of Bakhtin's "dialogism" (Newsom 1996), though in fact that article neither uses those words nor urges such an idea.

goes on to articulate. First, love is not present either significantly or at all in major parts of the New Testament canon (Acts being an obvious case); second, it is clear that the New Testament thinks love can only be grasped in terms of the cross (as, e.g., in 1 John 3:16), which is therefore the key image to be used instead; and third, "the term love has become debased in popular discourse," reduced to vapid generalities and a cover for a form of ostensibly easygoing relativism, a point he takes from the work of Stanley Hauerwas in particular (Hays 1996: 200–202; citing also Hauerwas 1981: 124). Again, how much more might such a critique apply to Old Testament ethical reflection.

However, we may take some cue from Hays's judicious analysis and make the following observations. With regard to the first point, the fact that love is not omnipresent across the canonical (and indeed New Testament) witnesses need not mean that we cannot see its centrality in the moral life of Israel. The Old Testament foregrounds the matter in the Shema, and Jesus takes this up as a summary of the law and the prophets. As we shall see, such a consideration is actually central to Augustine's own conception of the hermeneutical task. Since our own project does not aspire to the kind of comprehensive canonical purview that Hays has in mind, for better or for worse, we are spared the concern of having to explain how love can have such value while not being everywhere articulated. The second point raises an interesting question about the New Testament–specific aims of Hays's book that cannot detain us here.[2] The third point, in my judgment, is exceedingly powerful and perhaps gets to the heart of why he does not use love as a focal image for New Testament ethics. Here he is taking a different path from Lisa Sowle Cahill, who requires us to find love as something like a key characteristic of the one whose life is morally informed by Scripture. The way to negotiate this difference of opinion seems to depend on how much one predetermines what content will fill what we might call the pretheoretic notion of "love." Although his own purpose in making this point is different, Rodd sees this clearly with his striking example: "If incorrigible heresy results in eternal torment in hell, it is a loving action to torture the unfortunate heretic to save him or her from that fate" (2001: 306).

2. See, though, the brief discussion of Wenham 2000: 146–49, 153n4.

This reflection brings us to precisely our project in this book: to let the Old Testament determine the moral content we ascribe to the various categories of virtue ethics that go to portray the implied reader of its narratives. Given that love remains a predominant theological conception of what Christianity is all about and is the standard by which Christianity is often judged in the wider world (and often, of course, found wanting), it is particularly appropriate not to give up too quickly the label "love" when it comes to the Old Testament. Indeed, in its most simplified form, a common complaint against the Old Testament may be put in these terms: the Old Testament represents the morality of a former age, predicated upon a violent and/or jealous God, and largely to be set aside in our theological work in exchange for the kindnesses of Jesus (or of God newly revealed in Jesus).

In recent decades sensitivity to the voices and experiences of Jewish believers has perhaps mitigated this to some extent (though only to some extent), but nevertheless anyone who has ever taught or preached from the Old Testament will surely have encountered some form or other of this complaint. In the light of it, one might well say that, yes, it is uplifting indeed to consider such virtues as trust or humility, but this is to ignore the very real central problem for contemporary use of the Old Testament, that it is not at its heart talking in the language of love that can make sense to us today. This objection does, of course, merit careful reflection as to whether the problem is with the language or the subject matter, and often what is at stake in a particular text is the question of how various words and actions might be appropriately construed as loving. Indeed, one of the obvious traps awaiting the unwary who would study "love" in the Old Testament is the complexity of locating the appropriate passages where the relevant virtue is in view regardless of the vocabulary being used. We shall have to lay out quite carefully the way to focus on particular passages in this chapter.

The path we shall want to take is to let the Old Testament have some say in defining what constitutes love as a virtue. We may be helped here by Carter Lindberg's fine survey of the various manifestations and mutations of love as it has wended its way through the history of Western Christianity (2008). After his initial sober disclaimer, "It is possible under the rubric of love to include anything and everything" (2008: xi), Lindberg proceeds to offer a wide array of conceptualizations of love through the (Western Christian) ages. He starts with Anders Nygren's much-noted study *Agape and Eros* (English translation 1953), with its broad (if deeply problematic) distinction between the Christian concept of *agapē* as characterized by God's love reaching down to humanity in contrast to the Greek notion of *eros*, characterized by humanity's striving "upward" toward God. Lindberg then explores a range of critiques of this view, noting those who have urged that for Plato, *eros* was to be understood in fundamentally positive terms.[3] This more positive view is then the one adopted by Augustine, who sought a "synthesis of biblical agape and Hellenistic eros" under the governing rubric of *caritas*: grace, favor, love, benevolence (2008: 50–65, esp. 58–59).[4] In later models, Lindberg looks at Heloise's threefold characterization of love as passion, love as choice to love another, and love as friendship (Lindberg 2008: 76); love as the faculty of knowledge in Bernard of Clairvaux (2008: 79); Aquinas on love as charity, the emphasis very much captured in the KJV translation of *agapē* (most famously in 1 Cor. 13); and on to later emphases such as Luther's love as faith in action, love understood as service in many pietistic traditions, and the Romantic emphasis on love as feeling or yearning. In the face of such a rich historical survey, our current study will be modest indeed.

It is arguable that if "love" is expanded to serve as a catchall term for everything that counts in human living (at one point Lindberg cites a medieval scholar who wrote of love as "the virtue of virtues"; 2008: 10), then it makes no sense to offer a chapter on the topic in a study of specific virtues, since in one way or another every other chapter could be co-opted into the present one. There seem to be two reasons for persevering, however. First, the New Testament models a process whereby a pretheoretic notion of love is explicitly redefined. In 1 John, for example, we have "We know love by this, that he laid down his life

3. Additional critique is offered from a linguistic point of view by Barr 1987: 3–4 and throughout. Jeffrey's more tightly focused account, "Charity and Cupidity in Biblical Tradition" (2003: 55–74), completely ignores Nygren.

4. Some of the continuities between Augustine's view and that of Aquinas in the articulation of charity as a virtue allied to knowledge are drawn out in the detailed study of Sherwin 2005: esp. 63–118. Thus "Aquinas can join Augustine in describing prudence as 'love discerning well,' because 'love moves reason to discern'" (2005: 110).

for us" (3:16). This is Hays's point, noted above, that the cross redefines love. Though there is no comparable overall defining image for love in the Old Testament, images such as Yhwh's parenthood regarding Israel in Hosea 11 (e.g., 11:3–4) offer a rich vein of reflection. However, for reasons to do with our own ultimate concerns of interpretation, it will suit our project to pursue virtues modeled in the text by humans rather than by God. The New Testament's engagement with the topic provides one spur to persevere with seeking to let the Old Testament define love. A second reason is that Augustine's own understanding of interpretation is specifically framed around an analysis of love, of God and of neighbor, in his classic treatment of biblical interpretation, *On Christian Doctrine* (or *Teaching*). In our own pursuit of interpretive virtue, it will be important to ask how the Old Testament might contribute to the kind of approach found in Augustine, especially if one takes the time to note that "love of God" and "love of neighbor" are both, in the first instance, Old Testament texts.

In what follows, then, we shall begin with Augustine and an exploration of his "hermeneutics of love," from which two somewhat contrasting emphases will emerge. Each of these will provide the spur to consider a particular Old Testament passage: first is the book of Ruth and in particular its opening chapter's portrait of Ruth's declaration of faithfulness to Naomi; second is the story of Naaman in 2 Kings 5, which offers a rather different angle of approach to the issues raised by Ruth. In the light of these two passages, we shall then be in a position in the final section of the chapter to offer some conclusions regarding the interpretive virtue of "love," more commonly articulated as the virtue of interpretive charity.

Augustine and the Hermeneutics of Love

For Augustine, the goal and framing context for all Christian interpretation of Scripture is the love of God and the love of neighbor. The key text in which he lays out this hermeneutical approach is *De doctrina christiana*, or *On Christian Teaching*.[5] This work was written

---

5. Reference is made here to the translation of R. Green 1997, which is based on his critical edition (R. Green 1995), whose choice of title translation I have followed. Arnold

to set forth ways of rightly handling Scripture in the work of "sound doctrine" (or "teaching"). Most of its first three books were written around AD 395–397 and focused on the task of understanding what is in Scripture. The work was completed some thirty years later with a fourth book focusing on matters of presentation, in particular relating the eloquence of Scripture to the canons of classical rhetoric (cf. R. Green 1997: vii–xxiii; Jeffrey 2003: 39–53). The main passages relating to the link between interpretation and love occur at the end of book 1. They remain one of the most striking statements ever made about Christian interpretation of Scripture, in a work described overall by Stephen Fowl as "perhaps the clearest statement of the relationship between scriptural interpretation and the formation of virtue" (2005: 838).

The context of Augustine's discussion of scriptural interpretation in 1.40–44 is his discussion of the varieties of love and how to order them appropriately. After discussing the distinction between the use of something and the enjoyment of it, he claims that "the person who lives a just and holy life is one . . . who has ordered his love, so that he does not love what it is wrong to love, or fail to love what should be loved, or love too much what should be loved less" (1.28). O'Donovan argues that this way of relating enjoyment and use in rightly ordering love is only briefly characteristic of Augustine during this time in the mid-390s, but the conclusion remains significant for our purposes: "The use-enjoyment pair corresponded to the twofold command of love to God and neighbor" (O'Donovan 1980: 25; cf. 24–32 for his full discussion). Or as Augustine puts it when he arrives at the conclusion of this analysis:

> So anyone who thinks that he has understood the divine scriptures or any part of them, but cannot by his understanding build up this double love of God and neighbour, has not yet succeeded in understanding them. Anyone who derives from them an idea which is useful for supporting this love but fails to say what the writer demonstrably meant

---

and Bright 1995 is a useful resource for further exploring this work, although few of its essays actually touch on our own concerns.

in the passage has not made a fatal error, and is certainly not a liar. (*Doct. chr.* 1.41)[6]

These two sentences set out a positive and a "negative" vision. On the one hand, the positive vision is that all understanding of Scripture must contribute to the double love of God and neighbor. On the other, perhaps more remarkably, one can get by with misunderstanding the writer's purpose in the passage as long as one has found a way of building up this love. In the ensuing paragraphs, Augustine clarifies that in the long run failing to take a passage on its own terms will run into problems, since it may end up conflicting with other passages, but in the short term, love trumps exegesis, if one may put it in such bald and anachronistic terms.

Jacobs's probing study of "the hermeneutics of love" finds its anchor here amid the sea of competing readings upon which he sets sail with regard to the general reading of any literature by Christians concerned that their reading should be an act of discipleship (2001: 9–17).[7] He suggests that "an account of the hermeneutics of love is one of the great unwritten chapters in the history of Christian theology" (2001: 11), and it is worth quoting at length his own sketch (a "general or schematic" summary, as he calls it) of how it might play out, and indeed how he begins to articulate it himself in his own book-length analysis, entitled *A Theology of Reading*:

> But what makes the difference between a reading that is manipulative and selfish and one that is charitable? . . . Fundamentally, it is the reader's will that determines the moral form the reading takes: If the will is directed toward God and neighbor, it will in Augustinian terms exemplify *caritas*; if the will is directed toward the self, it will exemplify *cupiditas*. This terminology is of course Augustine's version of the Pauline distinction between living spiritually and living carnally. That one can read charitably only if one's will is guided by charity is

6. Jacobs (2001: 154n2) suggests that *non perniciose fallitur* ("has not made a fatal error") is better translated here as "has not been deceived," the point relating to making progress forward rather than being right or wrong as such.

7. Jacobs notes in particular Augustine's "astonishing statement" (2001: 11) and his part/whole approach to whether the love-building interpretation happens to be in accord with the writer's purposes (2001: 16).

a pretty obvious point, yet it is neglected in hermeneutical theory even more than the charitable imperative itself. (Jacobs 2001: 31)

In a nice twist, Jacobs is seeking to broaden out Augustine's concerns for reading Scripture to a generalized Christian theological account of reading (2001: 11), while I am wanting to bring Jacobs's analysis back to the very task that Augustine had in view in the first place: how to read Scripture according to the virtue of love, or as Jacobs has put it here, *caritas*. Writing of "study as love," Philip Cary observes, "'Charity' (*caritas*) in Augustine means rightly-ordered love and all its works, not simply alms-giving. Thus charity is the name for any act by which we willingly obey the twofold command of love for God and neighbor" (2000: 69). It is precisely the virtues of purity, humility, and charity, Cary suggests, that can offer us an "Augustinian vision" of education under the rubric "study as love" (2000: 63).[8]

In the context of this chapter, then, a terminological decision confronts us: whether to talk of love, beholden as the term is to all the vagueness noted by Richard Hays and Stanley Hauerwas, or whether to signal our determination to fill the concept with some particular value by adopting the English term "charity." This is a heuristic decision only and is not intended to foreclose on a whole range of other interesting questions one can ask about varieties of love, either in the abstract, in history, or in biblical texts. As is usually the case with questions of terminology, the issues in biblical interpretation can still be addressed (with care) to some extent independent of one's preferred vocabulary, and it is my judgment that the two phrases "interpretive charity" and "hermeneutics of love" are more or less functionally equivalent. More generally, "love" and "charity" work differently in the English language, so while the "virtue of love" might perhaps be more traditionally understood in terms of "the virtue of charity," I will attempt to use "love" for the sake of consistency through this chapter, but on the level of interpretive virtue I shall use the two terms interchangeably.

8. In a New Testament context, N. T. Wright has also suggested that the key to reading the New Testament rightly is "a hermeneutic of *love*," though his brief description of a way of reading that respects both self and "other" (text, author . . .) in a conversational model is, as he himself notes, in need of exploration "on another occasion" (1992: 64). Cf. also briefly, Thiselton 1992: 609, 612–13.

Augustine goes on from the discussion we have been following to draw an intriguing contrast that is not often considered in biblical hermeneutics today, in the age of print and mass literacy. Namely, he thinks there is a difference between the two cases of how, on the one hand, a believer understands rightly the nature of the holy life that is to be lived and how, on the other, one charged with the *teaching* of the Christian faith is to understand their indebtedness to the scriptural text: "A person strengthened by faith, hope, and love, and who steadfastly holds on to them, has no need of the scriptures except to instruct others. That is why many people, relying on these three things, actually live in solitude without any texts of the scriptures" (*Doct. chr.* 1.41). So one may live a holy life without explicit debt to Scripture, but one could not teach the way of a holy life without Scripture. It is arguable that this distinction could with profit be deployed in some discussions of biblical interpretation today. It is not that every individual needs to be able to account for how their conception of the Christian life is indebted to (or at least informed by) Scripture, but it is the case that this is a feature of the role of Scripture in the church's life. Equally, love of God and love of neighbor may be built up by all manner of readings of Scripture, but this needs to be anchored somewhere in the church by a reading that corresponds to the point of the text at hand. And such "anchoring" may need something of a critical edge at times—as Fowl puts it in his discussion of Augustine as an exemplar of the very virtue we are discussing: "Interpretive charity is not the same as being nice" (1998: 92).[9]

How then does one determine what a hermeneutic of love does and does not entail with respect to reading a particular text? One of the features of Jacobs's account is his exploration of a whole variety of modes of interpretive engagement that look a little like love in one way or another. A particularly acute example he gives is Derrida's zealous

9. In this context, Fowl (1998: 91–95) chooses Augustine as an example of "interpretive charity" and deliberately selects one of his polemical writings to exemplify it. Fowl offers a strong account of the virtue of charity, though his concluding thought that interpretive vigilance is directed not at Scripture but at "individuals and communities interpreting scripture" (1998: 96) takes a different path from the one we shall follow below and in the next chapter. Jeffrey (2003: 39–53) offers a concise account of some of the practical ecclesiastical and contextual factors that shaped *On Christian Teaching* in dialogue with those who were in disagreement with Augustine.

over-attention to texts, a "fanaticism" bordering on "immodesty itself" (Jacobs 2001: 54; citing Geoffrey Bennington from Bennington and Derrida 1993: 6–7). This oftentimes leads to a form of willful exploitation of possibilities in the text that deliberately steer away from the ways in which the author would have had us construct the meaning (a point that leads, of course, to the epithet "deconstruction").

Thus it is not enough to declare that one will love and then read as one pleases. But the striking possibility opened up by Augustine's and Jacobs's accounts of the hermeneutics of love is that in some cases, the interpretive virtue of love can consist of misreading for the sake of a greater good: not for those who teach, not for all texts at all times, and not (arguably) as a general theory of literature, but with respect to promoting the love of God and love of neighbor.[10]

We are then left with two models to pursue in the remainder of this chapter, two models that do not straightforwardly go together. In the first, we shall be interested in the question of love as a form of long-term commitment to the agenda of another, corresponding to Augustine's notion of love as the solid foundation for understanding the biblical text as a coherent whole. This will lead us to the book of Ruth. In the second, we shall take up Augustine's "astonishing statement" (Jacobs 2001: 11) that love in the short term can permit deviation from the longer-term path. There is an Old Testament text that models this issue and, as one might imagine, has created no little consternation down through the ages for its somewhat radical implications. It is the little detail of Naaman in the house of Rimmon in 2 Kings 5, and we shall turn to that narrative after looking at Ruth.

Defining Love: Can Ruth's Virtue Be Our Virtue?

The initial question confronting us is this: can we locate love in the Old Testament on anything other than our own terms? The story of Ruth offers a straightforward example of this issue: Ruth's striking

10. See here also the excellent collection of essays in D. Smith, Shortt, and Sullivan 2007—including Jacobs (2007) himself, Rine (2007), and especially Netland (2007)—for a discussion of how far one can push the limits of interpretive charity in the reading of literature from other cultures.

declaration to her bereaved mother-in-law, Naomi, who is about to set out and return to Bethlehem after many years in Ruth's native Moab:

> "Where you go, I will go;
> where you lodge, I will lodge;
> your people shall be my people,
> and your God my God.
> Where you die, I will die—
> there will I be buried.
> May Yhwh do thus and so to me,
> and more as well,
> if even death parts me from you!" (Ruth 1:16–17)

The elliptical Hebrew here could equally be rendered, for example, "Your people become my people, Your God is now my God,"[11] but this does not affect the discussion that follows.

What values (or virtues) are to be discerned in this text? A straightforward argument that here we see Ruth loving Naomi may in the end turn out to be right, but it is important to note that this is not to be affirmed on the basis of saying that Ruth's action strikes *us*, the twenty-first-century readers, as loving. Indeed, a considerable body of tradition sees the issue in Ruth 1 as relating not to love but to Gentile conversion. One of the problems for much traditional Jewish interpretation is that chapter 1 has opened with an account of a series of events that can barely if at all be construed positively. First, Elimelech has abandoned the land in a time of famine and has gone to Moab, of all places. Though it is hard to know how such an action might have been evaluated in the original context of the story of Ruth, it is striking to read it in a canonical context, which includes such texts as Deuteronomy 23:3–4 ("No Ammonite or Moabite shall be admitted to the assembly of Yhwh. Even to the tenth generation, none of their descendants shall be admitted") and the story told in Ezra 9–10. There Ezra rules on the need for the people of Judah to divorce their foreign wives, speaking of those who have married "peoples of the lands," peoples who are named (anachronistically) in 9:1 and include

---

11. Cf., e.g., Exum 1996: 135, citing also others.

the Moabites (cf. also Neh. 13:1). As a result, one can at least see why later readers sensed a question mark hanging over the actions of Elimelech's sons, who in Ruth 1:4 take Moabite wives. On the other hand, an alternative scenario is that Orpah and Ruth have converted in some sense to the faith of Israel, but then in that case it was felt that 1:12 reads rather harshly, with Naomi trying to send them back to Moab. Some have argued that what we have in verses 8, 11, and 12 ("Turn back!" and variations) are Naomi's requisite three attempts to dissuade Ruth, the would-be convert, from following her to Bethlehem, and that the result of the attempt is to discern that Orpah never had really converted, but had only made a pretense of following the God of her husband. Ruth, on the other hand, declares her commitment in verses 16–17, as already implied in Naomi's description of Ruth's "dealing kindly" (doing *hesed*) in verse 8. Several different rabbinic sources then read verses 16–17 as one side of a dialogue where questions are inserted into the text in order to draw out its logic, a device characteristic of much haggadic exegesis (such as the not dissimilar imagined conversation between Yhwh and Abraham in Genesis 22 over the four-step instruction to take his son, his only son, whom he loved, Isaac). Thus in this case it is suggested that Ruth's affirmations in verses 16–17 respond to questions concerning her various forms of self-identification put to her by Naomi. One by one, Ruth articulates ways in which she now belongs to Yhwh: she will *go* only where Torah permits, she will *lodge* only where Torah permits, she will identify herself with the people of the Torah, forsake idolatry, and submit even unto death to the way of Israel.[12]

Having said all this, it is important to note Ruth 4:15, where "the women" describe Ruth to Naomi as the "daughter-in-law who loves

12. Rashi's version of the paraphrase of Ruth 1:16–17, explicit down to details of categories of judicial death and subsequent locations of burial to which Ruth is now assenting, may be found in Beattie 1977: 104. Beattie (1977: 173–75) offers a comparison of five different but comparable ways in which this text is handled in haggadic exegesis. In addition to Beattie's detailed analysis, in this paragraph I am indebted to the survey of Bronner 1993 as well as the anthology of Jewish texts compiled by Zlotowitz 1976, though one might be uneasy with his enthusiasm for such observations as the numerical value of Ruth's name: he notes that *r-w-t* adds up to 606, indicating the number of Torah commandments (613) minus the seven Noachide commandments to which all peoples are subject (1976: 67); thus he suggests that Ruth functions as an exemplar of conversion.

you, who is more to you than seven sons." From this it seems fair to deduce, on the narrative's own terms, that Ruth does indeed love Naomi and that therefore 1:16–17 can be read as exemplifying in some sense the virtue of love.

If nothing else, the discussion above has demonstrated that we move too quickly if we describe the book of Ruth as a love story. This is especially pertinent in the light of Richard Hays's warning about the vague nature of "love" in most contemporary uses of the word. Ruth is often described as something of a pastoral idyll set "in the days when the judges ruled" (1:1), as in the work of Whybray, who suggests that it "stands out as a happy book. . . . The story has some resemblance to a fairy tale, . . . an idyllic tale portraying the good life as lived in a small community in faithfulness to Yahweh" (2002: 68–69). It is perhaps too easy to offer such a view as something of a pale projection of interpretive categories onto a text with harsher edges.

On the other hand, it is also possible so to emphasize the complexities of reading the text that one loses sight of something that is actually there. In more recent years, two notable readings of Ruth that play up the indeterminacy of the text and argue against seeing it in love-story terms are the studies of Danna Nolan Fewell and David Gunn in their *Compromising Redemption* (1990), and the commentary on Ruth by Tod Linafelt (1999). For all the insight these studies offer into the tropes of irony and suspicion, and for all that they are right to say that the reader has a vital role to play in a Hebrew narrative characteristically reticent with regard to character motivation where nevertheless "the plot is driven precisely by character motivation, . . . [which is] not unimportant, but rather unstated" (Linafelt 1999: 17), my own judgment is that the traditional view of the text as being persistently concerned with the practice of *ḥesed* has been overthrown a little too eagerly. Ideally, such a judgment needs a full engagement with such readings, but I suggest that the case is parallel to the one we faced (at length!) with regard to 1 Kings 3 in an earlier chapter. There the readings of the text that dissent from its presenting framework—on the grounds of the plausibility for today's readers of more suspicious approaches—in the end tend to tell us more about today's readers than about the text. This is not to deny the insights of the works in question, but it at least suggests that they are operating with different interpretive ends in view.[13]

In the interest of at least indicating some ways of evaluating such readings, however, let me offer some brief examples. Fewell and Gunn read Ruth 1:18, where Naomi understands Ruth's determination to follow her, as demonstrating a pointed silence on the part of Naomi (as against, perhaps, an unreported response). They characterize this silence as indicating "resentment, irritation, frustration, unease," for "Ruth the Moabite is to her an inconvenience, a menace even" (1990: 104). But this seems to be as likely an overreading of the text as any more familiar interpretive predilection might be that reads the book of Ruth as exemplifying divine providence in a text notably reluctant to attribute anything to Yhwh (e.g., Hubbard 1988: 69; such views are well critiqued by Linafelt 1999: xiv). Linafelt's work is better at emphasizing the sheer unknowability of much that interests us when reading Ruth, though in the end his work is driven by quite a strong thesis about the appropriate and original canonical location of Ruth between Judges and Samuel (1999: xvii–xxv), which he at best demonstrates only to be not impossible. Even then, Linafelt's reading does follow quite closely the contours of Fewell and Gunn's suspicion, as he himself acknowledges (Linafelt 1999: xiv).

Perhaps one may venture the suggestion that suspicious readings are sometimes (methodologically) simply mirror images of unduly credulous readings, and that each may be equally implicated in the practice of factoring in elusive details in the text to fit the overall reading being built up. A final and perhaps more overt example occurs in an essay on Ruth from a postcolonial perspective, where Laura Donaldson argues that there is something fundamentally troubling about Ruth's assimilating to Israel and abandoning her Moabite culture. Donaldson takes Orpah instead as the paradigm of postcolonial resistance, "a courageous act of self and communal affirmation" no less (Donaldson 1999: 144). Where then is the virtue of love as exhibited

---

13. With respect to Ruth, note the similar evaluation of Sakenfeld 1999: 13. Mills (2001: 114) characterizes this "suspicious" trend rightly by saying "more recently, the shadow side of this tale has been examined." Cf. her own slightly ambiguous reading (Mills 2001: 97 116) and the literature cited there, in particular Exum 1996: 129–74 exploring the representation of Ruth's story in various popular media.

by Ruth? It is transformed into a negative, and for Donaldson (more or less explicitly, though not in dialogue with Augustine), reading to build up love of God and love of neighbor requires a conscious reading against the values of the text. Such a move raises large questions concerning the status of the text, such as why one would persevere with this text at all when it so clearly fails to meet the predetermined criteria for that which can inspire one to love.[14] More problematically, in its own way Donaldson's reading essentializes the virtue of staying with one's own people and effectively inverts the evaluative hierarchy, so that now, apparently, it becomes impossible to demonstrate love through conversion, a judgment that seems no less "oppressive" on its own terms than the one to which Donaldson's reading first objected.[15] Perhaps trying to discern love in the Old Testament text without reference to the God of Israel is a project doomed to the task of staring down the well of interpretive possibilities and seeing only the reflection of one's own preferences.

How then shall we balance all these considerations? For our purposes it is not necessary to show what the purpose of the book of Ruth was, either in its original or canonical settings. Rather, we must demonstrate that the text concerns itself with the practice of *ḥesed*, though this has actually been one of the more prominent conjectures regarding the purpose of the book.[16] So in conclusion, one can find one's way through the interpretive maze to discern practices of love in the text, but these need to be defined in some sense by the text or context rather than being supplied by the reader who already "knows" what constitutes love.

14. Contrast, for example, Bauckham 1997, who makes a strong argument for a feminist reading that respects the book of Ruth's minority voice in the canon and uses this as leverage against the omission of the female voice elsewhere. (Bauckham's analysis of the book's "voice" is taken up more rigorously by Lim 2007, with cautiously positive results.)

15. A similar point was made in a response to Donaldson's paper on its original airing at the 1997 SBL conference, where a not unsympathetic Roland Boer (1999: 167) nevertheless asked, "But when such alternative histories, the histories of the forgotten and repressed, are written, an ethical question starts to come to the surface. By what criteria are such stories and histories to be valued? . . . [Given that it is] imperative to end oppression and suffering, . . . the question that arises is whether replacing official histories and stories with other stories merely replicates the existing patterns of dominance and suppression."

16. Cf. Bush 1996: 53–55. Larkin (1996: 56) cites the rabbinic dictum that the purpose of the book of Ruth is "to teach how great is the reward of those who do deeds of kindness" (*Ruth Rab.* 2.13).

One route suggested in the preceding analysis is by way of vocabulary markers for love, whether they be the covenantal kindness of *ḥesed*
as found in various places in the book or the broader term *'āhēb*, which
serves as the verb of loving in Ruth 4:15 (and which, indeed, we have
met earlier, in Solomon's love for foreign wives, as well as in the Shema
itself; Deut. 6:5). Yet word studies require caution on all manner of
conceptual levels and have perhaps never recovered from James Barr's
withering critique of how easy it is to reify concepts around word
occurrences and to suppose that one can track the singular notion
of a concept such as love across vast tracts of time and canon (Barr
1961: esp. 215–19; cf. also Barr 1987). In the case of *ḥesed*, one can
follow the development of linguistic sensitivity through the three major
published dissertations on this one word: Nelson Glueck studies how
the word is distributed across biblical usages pertaining to people,
people before God, or God toward people, emphasizing the notions
of relationship and reciprocity for understanding *ḥesed* (1967: esp.
70–102; original 1927). Katharine Doob Sakenfeld analyzes how the
word develops chronologically through the Old Testament, offering
a wide range of meanings for the term but often focused around the
notion of a freely chosen act of generosity and kindness toward someone in an inferior situation (or at least a situation of need), carried
out with an awareness of moral obligation to meet a need rather than
any formal or legal requirement (1978: 233–39). Gordon Clark offers
a full-fledged linguistics-oriented analysis of how the word functions
in contrast to or in support of a range of related terms (1993).[17] Clark
concludes his study by saying, "*Ḥesed* is a supreme human virtue,
standing as the pinnacle of moral values" (1993: 267), while earlier
noting on the same page: "it cannot be adequately translated in many
languages, including English." In his summary of findings he suggests
that it includes, but is more than, grace and mercy (*ḥnn*), compassion
(*raḥamîm*) and faithfulness or reliability (*'ĕmûnâ*), but is rather more
distantly related to *'āhēb*, though it does include notions of love.

In a later study, Sakenfeld has sought to disseminate the results
of her research more widely in a monograph entitled *Faithfulness*

17. Both Sakenfeld (1978: 1–13) and Clark (1993: 15–24) in turn offer full discussions
of other works on the term. Cf. also Routledge 1995, who seeks to defend and explore
Glueck's (1967) view.

in Action: Loyalty in Biblical Perspective (1985: esp. 39–42). In her commentary on Ruth, she brings this understanding to bear by calling attention to the book's emphasis on "examples of loyal living," with a focus on characters who choose "to act in ways that promote the well-being of others" (1999: 11–14).

Ḥesed is found in the text of Ruth at 1:8; 2:20; and 3:10, but in the light of the work of Sakenfeld and others, it is more significant that the narrative of Ruth consistently offers exemplars of the practice of *ḥesed*. As noted by Leila Leah Bronner in her study of rabbinic insights into Ruth, "What is remarkable in the narrative and the [rabbinic] commentary is that a foreigner/convert is allowed to take the lead as the epitome of *ḥesed*" (1993: 157). Ruth's actions and speech in 1:16–17 mark out a form of love that is so focused on offering loyalty to another (in this case to Naomi) that this even overcomes her natural allegiance to her own god (presumably Chemosh, the god of Moab, though the background is complex; cf. Müller 1999). The prime concern becomes to ally herself to another, come what may, wherever such loyalty might end, whether in life or death. (A comparable narrative is David's attempt to dissuade Ittai the Gittite from following him, answered by Ittai with "Wherever my lord the king may be, whether for death or life, there also your servant will be"; 2 Sam. 15:19–22.) The vocabulary of *ḥesed*, while not present in Ruth 1:16–17, does anchor our attention through the book as a whole to the broader concept of love and ensures that we do not overwrite it by using concepts drawn from our own prejudgment concerning what constitutes love. In this sense, Ruth's virtue can indeed be our virtue: we can let the text of Ruth fill out our own notion of what love is.

The kind of love exemplified by Ruth (and especially in 1:16–17) locates loyalty to another within the framework of willingness to belong to the people of Yhwh, the God of Israel. The following narrative does not play this out in any flat or moralizing way, as for instance in the considerable consternation caused to commentators by Naomi's instructions to Ruth to prepare herself to meet Boaz on the threshing floor at midnight (for a rare balanced appraisal of which, see van Wolde 1997: 84–86). Here one could easily imagine that not all Yahwists would have thought this to represent a prudent way forward, but then equally neither does the Old Testament's notion of walking with Yhwh fit hand in glove with modern conceptualizations of the moral life, as we have seen repeatedly. The reduction of the Old Testament's complex vision of the moral life to moralism (whether it is then affirmed or contested) is one of the great disappointments of much of the (perhaps relatively recent) interpretive tradition.

If we may draw a conclusion here about the virtue of love, it is that love is not an independent virtue exercised in interpersonal relationships such that it could be separated from the broader ways in which life requires allegiance to one god or another. The dynamics of this evaluation are then modeled in many and various ways in different Old Testament narratives, ranging from the submissive (Abraham willing to sacrifice Isaac in obedience to Yhwh in Gen. 22; Moses relaying God's condemnation on the revolt in Num. 16) through to the confrontational (Abraham arguing over the destruction of Sodom for the sake of his nephew Lot in Gen. 18; Moses standing against God's anger over the golden calf in Exod. 32), often in the life of one person. Even if love is the "virtue of virtues," this does not elevate it (at least in the Old Testament) to sit in judgment over the divine-human relationship.

Here Ruth's words may easily be appropriated for the task of conceptualizing interpretive virtue in particular. As Ruth pledges loyalty to Naomi, so the interpreter might pledge loyalty to the text: to go where it goes in the sense of following it on its own terms, even as far as trusting it in matters of life and death. While this overall framework does seem to describe what the Old Testament would take to be an interpretive virtue, it does not on its own paint the full picture. Indeed, it is easy to see how those who think that it is the full picture can transpose this vision of God into practicing a form of "love" that is harsh in the extreme, in the interests of what is perceived to be the greater good for those in their care. History is full of examples of just such endeavor, and it is the kind of approach alluded to by Rodd in the quote offered earlier: "If incorrigible heresy results in eternal torment in hell, it is a loving action to torture the unfortunate heretic to save him or her from that fate" (2001: 306). But in line with Augustine's distinction noted earlier, this kind of hard-line loyalty is not the only mode of love modeled in the Old Testament. Before we try to draw too many conclusions from the story of Ruth, we must turn to a very different kind of charity: that exercised by Elisha toward Naaman in 2 Kings 5.

Obedience and Charity in the House of Rimmon

Second Kings 5 tells the story of Naaman, the commander of the army of the king of Aram, to whom (military) victory has been given by Yhwh but who also has leprosy (v. 1). A captive Israelite girl (for whose story, see Kim 2005; Brueggemann 2001) informs him of an Israelite prophet who can cure leprosy. So Naaman sets off with a tribute from the king of Aram and presents himself before the king of Israel for healing, to the latter's evident dismay. The Aramean view portrayed here, that if healing can be found in Israel then it must be at the disposal of Israel's king, is clearly one of the points being critiqued in the narrative: it is Elisha, gifted by the spirit of God, who may heal, and not the king merely by virtue of his office. Verse 8 more or less has Elisha set his king straight on this very point.

So Naaman brings his retinue to Elisha's house, where he is told by the prophet (who does not even come out to give him this message in person) that he is to go and wash seven times in the Jordan, and then he will be clean. Naaman is unimpressed,[18] but his servants prevail upon him to submit to the prophet's command, and in due course he bathes and is made clean. Returning to Elisha (identified in v. 15 only as "the man of God"), Naaman urges him to accept some sort of gift, but Elisha refuses. Naaman's subsequent speech brings us to the point of interest in the story for our purposes:

> Then Naaman said, "If not, please let two mule-loads of earth be given to your servant; for your servant will no longer offer burnt offering or sacrifice to any god except Yhwh. But may Yhwh pardon [*yislaḥ*] your servant on one count: when my master goes into the house of Rimmon to worship there, leaning on my arm, and I bow down in the house of Rimmon, when I do bow down in the house of Rimmon, may Yhwh pardon your servant on this one count."
>
> He [Elisha] said to him, "Go in peace [*lēk lĕšālôm*]." (2 Kings 5:17–19)

The story continues with Elisha's servant Gehazi deciding to exact some sort of payment from Naaman after all. It ends with striking

---

18. In the article cited above on p. 33n17, Thomasset (2005: 86–88) uses this point in the story to explore a character ethic of anger and its resolution.

contrasts between Elisha's gracious treatment of Naaman, Naaman's gracious (if bemused) acquiescence to Gehazi's request, and Gehazi's own fall into punishment as a result of his manifest lack of either grace or generosity, as well as his lying to cover his tracks.

In the text quoted above, two points are clearly at issue. First, Naaman wants to take with him some physical token of his experience of Yhwh to indicate (and perhaps to remind him of) his decision no longer to sacrifice to any other god. This point is often portrayed unduly unsympathetically by suggesting that he perhaps operates with a territorial notion of Yhwh worship: if he can return with soil from the land of Israel, then he may be able to worship Yhwh alone even in Aram, as his heart (now) desires. But on the face of it, this request may symbolize nothing more (or less) than his enthusiastic new devotion. Second, however, he appears to succeed in obtaining permission to make an exception with regard to the worship of a "foreign" (i.e., non-Israelite) god. Elisha's "Go in peace" is surely, on any account, one of the most striking concessions to be found anywhere in the Old Testament, at least anywhere after the so-called "ecumenical bonhomie" of the patriarchal age, where one might build an altar to mark a theophany and travel on one's blessed way.[19] And while the vocabulary of love or charity is absent here, the issue is perhaps the paradigm case of charity with respect to the bending of a presupposed regulation, especially since Elisha's reply looks like a full-blown blessing rather than a grudging acceptance of a somewhat undesired scenario.

Commentators have not in general been slow to spot the issue, even if it is startlingly easy to find major commentaries having nothing at all to say on the matter (e.g., Hobbs 1985: 55–69). When Elisha's blessing is noted, it is often with a kind of bewildered gratitude rather than exploring it for its theological significance.[20]

19. Application of the phrase "ecumenical bonhomie" to the patriarchal period appears to have originated with Wenham (1980: 184).

20. This at least is my reading of the brevity of many commentaries' treatments. An example of puzzlement is Seow (1999: 198), who describes Naaman's views as "simplistic" and "inadequate," likely to provoke the reader's frustration; yet in a final comment, he adds, "There was much room for grace in Elisha's theology."

A quarter of a century before Mark Twain was pondering Solomon's dealings with the two women of 1 Kings 3 by way of projecting the text into the world of his novel, we find this passage in 2 Kings being given similar probing treatment in a novel of a very different kind: *Tom Brown's Schooldays*, by Thomas Hughes (1996; original 1857). Hughes's narrative is the very epitome of Victorian children's literature, where morality will always pay and where to step away from the way of the Lord is to descend into rakish dissolution of various sorts.[21] One incident recounted in Tom's later days at school concerns how he trained fellow schoolboy Arthur into a knowledge and love of Scripture. The passage around which this discussion is organized is 2 Kings 5 (1996: 154–56). Apart from a degree of attention to the text quite remarkable nowadays for a novel, what we find here is Tom holding Naaman at fault for asking for his concession. Tom avers that the true way of spiritual devotion is found, by way of contrast, in the tale of Shadrach, Meshach, and Abednego, who submit to the fiery furnace in Daniel 3 and explicitly affirm that even if their God does not save them, they will not bow down to Nebuchadnezzar's idol (Dan. 3:17–18). In what could pass as an epigram for many a discussion of biblical hermeneutics, Tom's friends tell him that with regard to his estimation of Naaman, he must "drive a nail where it'll go." "'And how often have I told you,' rejoined Tom, 'that it'll always go where you want, if you only stick to it and hit hard enough.' Not for him 'half-measures and compromises.'" Hughes concludes the episode by saying that Tom's interlocutors "didn't forget, and thought long and often over the conversation."

Hughes's point is clear: Naaman's asking for a concession in 2 Kings 5 falls short of devotion to the Lord, and Elisha, by extension, lowers the appropriate standards in granting it. Though this is a coherent Victorian position, it is far from evident that it is the expected reading of 2 Kings 5, where Elisha is the reliable central figure, and his bless-

---

21. I am indebted for my reading of *Tom Brown's Schooldays* in context to Musgrave (1985: esp. 47–65). An incidental point of perhaps some interest to biblical scholars here is Musgrave's analysis of Hughes's text in conjunction with the following year's similar boarding-school tale, *Eric: or, Little by Little*, by none other than Dean F. W. Farrar, author of the 1885 Bampton Lectures on *History of Interpretation* (1886), whose view of moral decay so colored his history of interpretation that it reduced that history to little more than a series of human errors.

ing upon Naaman's request is presumably to be taken at face value. Indeed, the two requests Naaman makes of Elisha in verses 17–18 should probably stand or fall together in terms of whether Naaman's perspective on matters is to be praised or criticized. Admittedly, translations generally interpose a "but" between them: on the one hand, the request to carry earth back home, "but," on the other hand, forgiveness for some sort of premeditated sin. The Hebrew simply juxtaposes the two petitions: *yūttan-nā' lě'abdĕkā* (let your servant now be given) and *laddābār hazzeh yislaḥ yhwh* (may Yhwh forgive this thing).

In his theologically oriented reflection on this passage, von Rad suggests that both requests indicate Naaman's desire to mark himself out as belonging to Yhwh in an alien world. With regard to the first: "A new-found faith here expresses anxiety about remaining alive out in the heathen world and asks for Palestinian soil as a temporary expedient, an insulating layer, so to speak, from on-rushing heathendom" (1980: 52). And translating the passage without the interposed "but," von Rad moves on to the second question, suggesting that Elisha's response is significant in its leaving Naaman to work out his newfound faith in the public arena in ways not yet circumscribed by Israel's own law (1980: 53–54). As far as Kim is concerned, "In this way, the narrator expresses how deeply Naaman was converted" (2005: 56). Perhaps slightly less sympathetic to the nuances of the text, but nevertheless with a strong theological intuition about Naaman's perforce public engagement with the consequences of his allegiance to Yhwh, Jacques Ellul offers the following:

> Naaman still entertains the ideas of his age, but he bends and subjugates them in the presence of the true God. It is to serve this true God that he acts in a way that seems ridiculous to us. It is in order to love exclusively, to make a rigorous demarcation, to affirm his break publicly, that adopting the manners and ideas and customs of his day, he uses them to show that his God is not the same as that of others. (1972: 36)

Little is known about Rimmon.[22] As Brueggemann suggests, "Rimmon's importance here is only that this God is *not Yahweh*" (2000:

---

22. Cf. Greenfield 1976, who surveys what little data there is before remarking engagingly that the deity "joined other Syro-Palestinian gods in obscurity" (1976: 198).

336), and one does not proceed particularly far into this text by pondering Rimmon's relationship to any Syrian pantheon or how far his characteristics may be compared to those of Hadad, a Syrian storm god (e.g., Hobbs 1985: 66; Greenfield 1999, noting, e.g., Zech. 12:11). But that allegiance to Yhwh is in conscious interaction with the alternative possibilities of other allegiance is very much at the heart of this story, as (arguably) of the whole book of Kings (e.g., Bostock 2006: 159–65). And in this context we may find, with Ellul, the virtue of charity as it is extended from Elisha to Naaman in verse 19.

If, with von Rad, we construe both of Naaman's requests "positively" (i.e., that they reflect an appropriate ordering of priorities for a convert to Yahwism), then Elisha's "Go in peace" is in effect demonstrating the appropriate response to one who is seeking a way of honoring Yhwh in a world where the practice of obedience to another god is presupposed. Elisha's evaluation appears to operate on the understanding that, while the worship of other gods is unacceptable in Israel, the options for Naaman, who has worshiped other gods anyway and is now declaring allegiance to Yhwh alone, may (at least in the short term) be different.

Naaman knows this is not the obvious way to consider his situation; hence comes his request for forgiveness. The narrator too has signaled a somewhat more probing analysis of divine power as far back as verse 1 of the same passage. Here we are told that Naaman's victories are attributable to Yhwh, though presumably this is a view not shared by Naaman—at least not before the events recounted later in this chapter. It would be precarious to build too much on this single passing observation. As Brueggemann rightly observes, "Nothing is subsequently made of that claim" (2000: 331), except that it leaves the reader alert to questions of how rightly to attribute claims of divine action to one god rather than another. Naaman's "conversion" in this chapter sees him confessing, "Now I know that there is no God in all the earth [$'\bar{e}yn$ $'\check{e}l\bar{o}h\hat{\imath}m$ $b\check{e}kol$-$h\bar{a}$ $'\bar{a}re\d{s}$] except in Israel" (v. 15). Possessed by this conviction (and a right one in the eyes of the orthodox in Israel), he is free to enter the house of Rimmon, knowing that his master bows before no god. The forgiveness, presumably, is thus for the way it will look to other people. (Readers who have read 1 Cor. 8–10 will find this issue strikingly familiar from

Paul's New Testament context too.) Naaman might say (as indeed perhaps Elisha might say) that the point is that Yhwh can be worshiped even in the house of Rimmon, since he is in fact the only God. Put this way, Elisha's "concession" may be read less as a failure to hold the line and insist on the purity of worship required by monotheism, and more as an affirmation that even in a world (Syria) that looks as though it is dominated by the worship of other gods, Yhwh may still actually be worshiped. The course of Naaman's life is set in a new direction. He will eventually have many cases to consider where his old practices clash with his new confession, and this is the first. As von Rad notes, though, Elisha responds not with casuistry (1980: 54) but with blessing. There has been long-running discussion concerning the extent of Naaman's "conversion" and the vexed question of how far Elisha's blessing models a practice of allowing a "convert" to remain in their old context and form of devotional expression. This discussion ranges from variant manuscript traditions in the Targumim[23] through to the myriad contemporary questions raised on this score by Effa, who says, "Such questions of culture and faith have challenged mission practitioners for centuries" (2007: 311). In all probability, at least part of the difficulty here derives from the fact that "conversion" is not quite the right category to describe changing allegiances in the Old Testament. Non-Israelites can affirm the relative greatness of Yhwh without thereby becoming Yahwists (e.g., Jethro in Exod. 18:10–12). However, a full discussion of conversion lies outside our scope. In this chapter, I have used the word only loosely to signify issues of allegiance.

As we have observed, 2 Kings 5 does not use the vocabulary of love. But Elisha's word of peace to Naaman is an interpretive act of charity par excellence. Rather than assimilating Naaman's situation to his own and bringing to bear a framework that works in Israel, Elisha blesses him and commissions him to discover for himself, in a kind of embodied Syrian *phronēsis*, what the way of Yhwh will look like back in his master's house. In an article reflecting on the task of

---

23. *Targum Jonathan of the Former Prophets* includes, in one manuscript, an additional comment by Elisha clarifying that he is not giving Naaman permission "to sacrifice outside Israel" (Harrington and Saldarini 1987: 274). On the other hand, the text is used as it stands to set a precedent in *b. Sanh.* 74b–75a.

the evangelist in the light of this narrative, Brueggemann suggests that "coercion is deeply inappropriate to the gospel" and that, with regard to a convert, one rather "lets them be with whatever they can make of their transformed lives" (2007: 270). It is possible that the apparent desirability of this conclusion might foreground the point unduly in this reading of 2 Kings 5—noting, by way of contrast, that the healing itself leads Brueggemann to draw no comparable conclusions for contemporary practice; nevertheless, for our own analysis, the point is simply that Elisha was right to bless Naaman and that we may learn from what is at stake in such a blessing.

In the long run, then, Naaman may learn the practices required of obedience to the exclusive God of Israel, and that Yahwism will not encourage him to persist in bowing down in the house of Rimmon. Elisha's blessing, though, grasps the fundamental point that charity in the short term can be more significant (theologically as well as socially) than assimilating the specific case straightaway into a general (theological) understanding. The obvious question thus raised, in terms of the narrative world of 2 Kings 5, is how Elisha knew to bless, and in terms of our reading today, how we may rightly discern when to bless rather than hold to account. Indeed, David Ford suggests that precisely this is one of the defining hallmarks of Christian wisdom in his book of that name: "The cry of blessing is fundamental to wise discernment. Whom to bless, what to bless, and when, how and whether to bless are questions whose answers are rooted in core conceptions of God and God's purposes" (2007: 16). Ford goes on to define "blessedness" as "being in the state that God most desires [us] to be in" (2007: 18). In the light of this, one should perhaps read Elisha as commissioning Naaman to go forth into the house of Rimmon and be a follower of Yhwh in the only way possible. In addition, he is affirming that this should not be a cause of concern to Naaman, who does not need to spend his energy worrying about whether this is compromise. Thus blessed, he goes in peace, knowing that it will now not be compromise after all.

As in the case of Ruth, though to different effect, the practice of love (or charity) is focused especially around allegiance to one God over another. Monotheism, we might say, makes love complicated and problematizes a notion of love that draws upon lack of constraint as one of its key notions—a view of love (quite common in our day) holding that it essentially connotes freedom or the unrestrained exercise of the will in affection, passion, or choice of direction through life. Such views sit uneasily with the demands of a monotheistic faith tradition, as has been seen quite clearly in works such as Regina Schwartz's *The Curse of Cain* (1997), though her solution, broadly speaking, is to turn the argument around and use a prior view of love as leverage against the claims of monotheism, which she then allies with notions of violence and scarcity instead.[24] The direction of our argument is different: what happens when the biblical text is allowed to shape our conception of the virtue concerned? And in any case, there is still room for a great expanse of love within the conception of monotheism that the biblical text imagines, in the light of which it is perhaps interesting to note the response to the single occasion in the New Testament when this incident concerning Naaman is mentioned: Jesus's sermon at Nazareth, where he points out that there were many lepers in Israel at this time, but only Naaman the Syrian was cleansed (Luke 4:27). In the midst of uncovering a range of responses to his own mission to the poor, the captives, the blind, and the oppressed, Jesus's citation of Naaman the Syrian provokes rage among those in the synagogue (4:28). One wonders if it is any part of Luke's agenda to suggest that those who rail most strongly against the limits placed on love by Jewish (and Christian) monotheism might think themselves to have a surer grasp of what constitutes appropriate love but in fact do not exemplify it.

Having now considered both Ruth and 2 Kings 5, it is time to draw together some conclusions about how such thinking about love might be harnessed to the task of understanding love as an interpretive virtue.

Interpretive Charity: The Interpretive Virtue of Love

How should the interpreter understand the role of love in reading the biblical text? In the light of Augustine's distinction between long-

24. I am aware of the debates concerning the nature, extent, and desirability of monotheism in recent writing and have surveyed them in Briggs 2006b; cf. also Bauckham 2004. These debates, I think, do not affect the basic points being made here.

term loyalty to the text and short-term edification derived from the use of it in one way or another, we have suggested that there is a range of ways in which love is operative in the hermeneutical task. But fundamentally, the narratives of Ruth and of Naaman offer two "poles" around which such approaches might cluster: the model of the loving interpreter loyally pledging to follow the text come what may (to exercise interpretation as a matter of *ḥesed*, one might say), and the model of the loving interpreter blessing some interpretation of the text that may seem to sit at odds with many other ways of rightly handling the words of Scripture. What are the implications of sketching out such a range of possibilities?

First, the context of interpretation makes a great deal of difference. Blessing, for one thing, does not occur in the abstract: it always requires a blesser and one who is blessed, who will occupy particular social (and other) locations, with the result that how Scripture is used as blessing in one place may not be transferrable to another place without considerable reconceptualization of the interpretation being offered. Preachers have long known this: a sermon addressing one context may or may not be one that can be "extracted from the file" when the same text comes up for a sermon in another context. But Augustine's insight in this matter suggests that one must probe further here and actually say that this piece of preacher's wisdom applies just as much to the basic question of what counts as an appropriate interpretation (or perhaps better, a reading) of the passage. There is a time, perhaps, for dwelling with textual indeterminacy and a time for bold conjectures; a time for source criticism and a time for the reading of redacted wholes; a time (as Jeremiah might have put it had he been a literary critic) for construction and for deconstruction.

To take a slightly different perspective on the same point, any reading of Scripture within the life of the church would not necessarily need to be critiqued by concerned teachers/theologians worried about exegetical infelicity. Rather, the point is that at some level, love must serve as the criterion for evaluating the extent to which a reading should be considered appropriate for the life of the church (or indeed any who are hearing the interpretation), even if, one might say, one can see the shortcoming of the proposed interpretation on exegetical grounds. Augustine's caveat—that this needs to be balanced out by the recognition that sometimes the short-term gain is costly in terms of longer-term theological construction—raises complicated issues that probably need to be considered case by case rather than theoretically, and this is what we have tried to do in the two case studies of this chapter, as examples. In general and for a variety of reasons, it seems likely that there may be no theoretical resolution to the question of how to discern whether an interpretation has problematic longer-term consequences. On the one hand, the consequences will sometimes relate to questions of relatively little theological import, such as typical "biblical studies questions" regarding, say, source-critical analyses of a text or questions relating to the historical influence one way or another between intertexts. On the other and perhaps more interesting hand, it is clear that sometimes differing exegeses make relatively little substantive theological difference: in some cases a range of ways of reading a text can be right and all still build toward a common (and love-encouraging or edifying) overall proposal.[25]

With a topic as vast as the question of rightly grasping the nature of love in the Old Testament, this chapter invites any number of caveats, qualifications, and further explorations. Alan Jacobs's point, noted earlier, that "an account of the hermeneutics of love is one of the great unwritten chapters in the history of Christian theology" (2001: 11), seems to me to invite the rejoinder at this point that trying to write a chapter on it simply highlights that an entire book is needed. Nevertheless, it has seemed better not only to say something rather than nothing but also to say something rather than deferring an attempt to say everything. But by way of conclusion, let me offer some limited reflections on ways in which our notion of the interpretive virtue of love (or the operation of interpretive charity) may need further consideration.

First, it is evident that a great many ways of handling the Old Testament material on love could have been attempted, rather than the somewhat selective decision to approach the subject via the consideration of *ḥesed* in Ruth and the charitable blessing Elisha offered

---

25. For an intriguing set of case studies of this point, see the exchange of essays discussing Oliver O'Donovan's use of the Old Testament in his *The Desire of the Nations* (1996) in the volume of essays devoted to this work (Bartholomew et al. 2002), including especially the reflection of Meilaender (2002).

to Naaman. Nevertheless, I have urged that these two scenarios do allow us to access the way in which love is constrained (though still expansive) within the broadly monotheistic conception of the Old Testament. This will not go quite as far as Lisa Sowle Cahill was wanting with her appeal to Schrage and the ethics of defining neighbor as inclusively as possible. The Old Testament does not (at least predominantly) envisage all people being grasped in the warm embrace of Israel, despite several notable attempts to read the dominant thrust of the narrative that way.[26] But a balance to be struck here suggests that our pretheoretic notion of love can indeed be related to the kind of love found persistently (though not everywhere) in the Old Testament. It is a balance that can only profit from continuing to attend to the many and various ways in which Judaism finds its Scriptures and its God to be life-affirming and love-encouraging.

A second observation is that there are many other different models of love that could have been considered too. Where we have thought through some of the implications of love as loyalty or love as blessing, it is obvious that one predominant strand not considered here is love as passion. This might be taken to be one of the prominent aspects of the books of Samuel, particularly in their intricate telling of David's court history.[27] Love as passion is also in view in the Song of Songs' various narrative portraits of its two lovers, as well as occurring at certain (arguably key) points in the Genesis narratives. What would this chapter have looked like if we had taken these emphases as indicative of the virtue of love?

In point of fact, such a project has in many ways already been undertaken in Dow Edgerton's striking and somewhat neglected book *The Passion of Interpretation* (1992). Here, with reference to a range of texts such as the binding of Isaac (Gen. 22) and the road to Emmaus (Luke 24), as well as rabbinic, Greek, and contemporary fiction texts (including a fascinating insight into the nature and possible relevance

26. For example, C. Wright 2006 urges a "missiological" reading that sees God's calling of Israel in the Old Testament as fundamentally for the sake of the broader mission to all peoples. By way of contrast, note Kaminsky 2007.

27. On this, see van Seters 1987, who looks at the link between passion and death that is unique to this narrative in the Old Testament, and Bailey 1990. However, Bailey actually wants to argue that love (and lust) are not the key issues in the plot development of 2 Samuel. Rather, the story is one of power and its pursuit.

of Hermes to the tasks of hermeneutics), Edgerton effectively pursues a similar kind of "feedback-loop" approach to that of the present volume in asking how the texts in question portray a kind of passion that can then be understood as a key to interpretation: "We are concerned here with stories of interpretation and what understanding of interpretation might emerge through our encounters" (1992: 15). His conclusion is that "interpretation is a work of passion" in a range of senses, which he takes to include love, hate, desire, hunger, intensity, determination, power, vocation, calling, and even, in a christological sense, suffering (1992: 142–43). There would perhaps be quite a conversation to be had regarding how to understand these characteristics in terms of "interpretive virtues" (Edgerton's book, I think, seeks to make its mark in the area of poetic resonance rather than hermeneutical analysis per se), but at least one can see that his discussion offers further areas of investigation for our own discussion of a hermeneutic of love.

Other questions remain, such as the basic one of whether Augustine is in fact right about interpretation. This could be asked in two ways (at least). First, must interpretation build up love of God and love of neighbor? Second, is it really possible to do what he clearly wants to do, which is to hold together the desire to read charitably with the desire to do justice to the text? Or does one come at the expense of the other? Another way of asking the same question is to ask about texts that threaten to overturn love as the key category, texts that can easily be read as operating with an implied virtue of a darker kind. We have seen such suggestions implicitly in the various "suspicious" readings of Ruth noted earlier, as well as in earlier chapters relating to various "problem texts" as they are familiar to readers of the Old Testament. In our earlier discussion, we have suggested that there is no value-neutral way of assessing this question in terms of whether texts objectively merit suspicion or dissent. These questions obviously merit a thorough treatment of their own, but to some extent and at this point, we need only offer the pragmatic observation that there are many ways of handling texts that step outside the framework offered by Augustine. I have adopted this framework because it works well to elucidate the issues involved in understanding the virtue of love as it pertains to interpretation. In analyzing the hermeneutical principles deployed by Barth, Richard Burnett devotes a lengthy discussion to Barth's "hermeneutics of love and trust" (2001: 184–220), noting that Barth's account was deeply indebted to Augustine's foundational insight (2001: 208). This would perhaps have been yet another way to approach the subject matter of the present chapter.

Interpretive charity, on the account developed in this chapter, is the virtue that will enable interpreters of Scripture to navigate wisely the different ways in which it is possible to bless those to whom Scripture is read or interpreted. Like Ruth pledging herself to Naomi, it may be present in a willingness to call hearers to account before the text, no matter where it leads. Like Elisha blessing Naaman, it may understand the need for leeway. But overall it will seek to affirm the hearer or reader "in the state that God most desires them to be in" (Ford 2007: 18), and, as such, interpretive charity should be understood as a blessing designed to build up the love of God and the love of neighbor in the practices of interpreting Scripture.

6

SUMMONED

The Virtue of Receptivity

How does an analysis of the implied virtues of the Old Testament take account of the summoning presence of the God whose presence and activity is the subject matter of so much of the Old Testament's testimony? This chapter attempts to round out the foregoing explorations of interpretive virtues by looking at what sort of virtue might be appropriate to a mode of "response" or "being summoned"—a recognition that it is not by the interpreter's native wit and moral resource alone that one is able to fathom the mysteries of the Old Testament text. Such an exploration may begin by situating this concern in the wider field of theological interpretation, to which, by the end of the chapter, our study may be able to make some contribution.

Exegesis and Theological Interpretation Today

There is no shortage of voices in theological hermeneutics today arguing that what is needed is a recovery of a working conceptuality of divine action and initiative in all our thinking about Scripture. In some ways, such programmatic proposals actually constitute one of the most prominent strands of the kind of theological interpretation discussed above, in chapter 1.[1] Even allowing for considerable diversity among its practitioners, one can certainly detect common themes and emphases in some of these writings. This is not the place for a detailed review and interaction with all these various proposals.[2] However, a general observation may be made by way of introduction to the topic of this chapter.

Over recent decades the pendulum has swung one way and another regarding the perennial question of how to integrate the concerns of biblical exegesis with serious Christian (and in a different sphere, Jewish) theological thinking. Biblical scholars have been found across a wide range of such positions, and the contested nature of what role theological thinking can, could, or should play in biblical interpretation is clearly going to be with us for a while yet to come. But a particular trend in some of these recent writings is to urge a properly theological account of biblical interpretation almost as an alternative to careful engagement with the actual biblical text. Of course, the claim is not that one *should* not engage carefully with the biblical text. Rather, what happens is that a strong claim is made that only a certain type of theologically characterized engagement can be acceptable to the church over against various more historical and critically oriented modes of reading. Sometimes the claim is even pressed that the church's theological business is nothing but "exegesis" thus defined, but in practice no examples of acceptable engagement are offered, and no exegesis of any sort takes place.[3] This curious double-edged strategy, I think, deserves a double-edged response. One

1. Examples include Webster 2001; 2003; 2007; Rae 2005; Bowald 2007; Topping 2007; Levering 2008; several entries in Vanhoozer et al. 2005; and many volumes of the Scripture and Hermeneutics series edited by Bartholomew et al. 2000–2007. A lucid introduction to the whole area is Treier 2008.

2. I have offered reviews of most of these publications in various places, including Briggs 2007a, which also discusses the slightly different emphases of Work 2002 and N. T. Wright 2005. The work of Vanhoozer (1998; 2002; 2005a; 2005b), discussed a little in chapter 1 (above), has points of contact with these concerns and over time has shifted more explicitly toward concerns with divine action. Cf. also Spinks 2007.

3. Treier 2008 is an exception to this trend, with repeated reference to a case study of the image of God, though it might have been interesting to consider what would have been at stake in having a focal passage rather than a topic.

might appreciate, indeed even applaud, the constructive theological vision set forth, and yet at the same time one may rightly wonder if by its own lights the analyses offered are not in fact guilty of the same problems they so easily critique in others. The difference is only that the theorizing in question is now theorizing about theological interpretation rather than hermeneutics more generally.

John Webster's work offers some interesting examples of this double-edged strategy. In his book *Holy Scripture*, for example, he starts by saying that "the primary theological task" is "exegesis" (2003: 3; cf. also 2001: 110) and then offers a lengthy and appreciative quote from Zwingli to underline that "I saw the need to set aside [philosophy and theology] and to learn the doctrine of God direct from His own Word" (2003: 102). Readers of Webster's book, though, are offered little chance to follow in such footsteps, even though they are assured that "dogmatic theology operates best when it is a kind of gloss on Scripture" (2003: 130), and they may be a little surprised by the observation that such dogmatics needs to be "light-weight, low-level, and approximate, something therefore less likely to compete with or displace Scripture" (2003: 130). Throughout the book a striking polarization of options is offered: the church is to receive Scripture either by way of "normed compliance" or "arbitrary *poiēsis*" (2003: 62), or the clarity of Scripture "is given, not the product of unaided exegetical prowess or technique" (2003: 94). Might one wonder whether arbitrariness is found as often in calls for compliance as in the exercise of *poiēsis*, or whether a good deal of exegetical prowess is conceived of as aided (and indeed compliant) rather than unaided? How much of the argumentative work is helped on its way by such uses of heavily weighted adjectives on one side of the analysis? Several of the more recent works in theological hermeneutics (esp. Bowald 2007) have effectively followed Webster in arguing that "as instruments of divine action, texts are prevenient, determining the shape of our reading not only by passive resistance but also by active presentation of the speech of God" (2001: 76). It is difficult, to say the least, to reconcile such claims of "determining" with much of the actual history of the shape of the church's reading of Scripture.

To come now to the focus of the present study, Webster says in a more recent article that "theology should disabuse itself of the

assumption that clarity about the nature of biblical interpretation
demands nothing more of us than exquisite discussion of such matters as exegetical technique or readerly virtue" (2007: 143). Leaving
aside the rhetorically loaded adjective "exquisite," and the perplexing
question of whom Webster thinks he is arguing against here (since it is
hard to find any scholar at all making the claim of which he is seeking
to disabuse his readers), the substantive issue raised by this sentence
is the idea of "nothing more." Indeed, in the very next sentence, he
adds, "These matters are certainly proper matters for reflection and
self-correction; but their resolution depends in large part upon prior
beliefs about the natures and ends of texts, interpreters and acts of
interpretation" (2007: 143). Well, maybe—perhaps a great deal depends here on the extent of the "large part"—but why would it ever
be assumed that such "proper matters for reflection" should be *all*
that is required and "nothing more"? The claim of the present work
is in fact precisely that *in addition to* (and not instead of) all these
factors listed by Webster, the subject-matter of the biblical texts in
all their specificity and variety should also be contributing (perhaps
even in "large part") to these "proper matters for reflection."

It may be that the foregoing analysis suggests dissent from Webster's
proposals, but I actually find myself in agreement with a good deal
of his constructive agenda, and indeed I have learned much from it.
Thus—and how could this be better said?—"whatever the church does
with Holy Scripture, its acts of reading, construing, and interpreting
have value only insofar as they are modes of attention" (2007: 150). It is
true that Webster means by this attention to divine presence (in terms
of the risen Jesus), but perhaps one might say that in light of some of
his other points, this attention is at least *exegetically mediated.*

It will by now, I hope, be clear that the double-edged problem being
addressed here is one that is caught between setting a powerful agenda
for the practices of biblical interpretation while at the same time offering
an unnecessarily bleak picture of the various ways in which such practices could be played out in contemporary theological interpretation. I
have focused on Webster's specific presentation of these issues because
it is both influential and broadly representative of other works (some
of which, indeed, announce conscious indebtedness to his approach).
To offer a final note, it is striking that he does not in practice offer

discussion of those whose work consciously seeks to integrate "aided" exegetical technique with systematic theological reflection on Scripture.[4] Such dialogue might temper a little the polarization noted above.

To try to demonstrate that the concerns considered above need not dissuade us from the analysis of "readerly virtue," as Webster puts it, in this chapter I want to explore a very particular virtue, that of "receptivity." I suggest that this receptivity represents a responsiveness both to the text and to the subject matter of the text. It will be demonstrated best by looking at a text that brings to the fore the notion of divine summons. The text we shall explore is the famous narrative of Isaiah 6: Isaiah's vision in the temple, with its apparently forbidding call to the prophet to embark on a ministry intended to be strikingly unfruitful by design. How may the summoned reader learn from the summoned prophet in considering this text?[5]

Isaiah 6: The Summoning of the Prophet and the Reader

The famous narrative of Isaiah 6 brings with it a whole host of well-known questions debated down through the centuries, most of which, we may as well say straightaway, will not be answered here.[6] Wider questions of the canonical framing of individual incidents in Isaiah

4. Works such as, most notably, Thiselton 2000; Moberly 2000; Seitz 1998; Schneiders 1991; 1999 (2nd ed.). All these writers had also written many other similarly "integrated" works before Webster's (2001; 2003) comments. The work of Francis Watson (1994; 1997) does merit one brief appreciative paragraph (Webster 2001: 51–52), but not in such a way as to affect the tenor of the critique.

5. On another occasion it would be worth exploring the congruence between the argument of this chapter and the powerful account of the "summoned self" with which Paul Ricoeur concluded his Gifford lectures (Ricoeur 1992), the published version of which omits the two explicitly theological lectures: "The Self in the Mirror of the Scriptures" (1997) and "The Summoned Subject in the School of the Narratives of the Prophetic Vocation" (1995). My thinking in this chapter is deeply indebted to Ricoeur's notion of the "summoned self," refigured by engagement with the subject matter of the text, but the complexity of Ricoeur's conceptual scheme mitigates against including an account of it here. For a brief analysis, see Briggs 2006a: 63–69.

6. Technical critical questions are given admirable expression in the lengthy treatment of Wildberger 1991: 246–78, though his own view is that we have here a prophet adapting traditional elements of descriptions of God drawn from foreign origins (e.g., Wildberger 1991: esp. 276–77), which has little in common with the approach adopted here. Childs 2001: 49–60 offers a more theologically constructive overview of background questions.

find several points of resonance here: if this is a call narrative, why
is it only found now, after five chapters of oracles? In what sense, if
at all, is Isaiah 6 to be read in some form of reciprocal relationship
to Isaiah 40?[7] And then there are the questions of the content of the
narrative: Where is Isaiah for this vision—on earth looking up to
heaven or caught up into the heavenly realms? Who (or what) are
the seraphim? What is the meaning of their cry, "The whole earth is
full of his glory" (v. 3b)? How is the final verse of the chapter to be
translated? But finally, the kernel questions relate, perhaps as always,
to the subject matter of the text: the *Sache* (content) of the story it
tells. What is the holiness that this chapter envisions? And in what
sense are we to understand that Isaiah's preaching has divine hardening as not just its result but also its divine purpose?

The structure of the narrative may be laid out as follows:

6:1   *I saw . . . the Lord (*'ădōnāy*) sitting
      Seraphim in attendance
      + description of seraphim
      + call of the seraphim ("Holy, holy, holy")
      + Isaiah's response ("Woe is me! . . .")
6:5   . . . *for my eyes have seen the King*

6:6–7   Touching of the coal to Isaiah's lips

6:8   *I heard . . . the voice of the Lord (*'ădōnāy*) saying
6:9–10   The commission
        Mind   *dull!*
          Ears   *stop!*
            Eyes   *seal!*
            Eyes   *seeing*
          Ears   *hearing*
        Mind   *grasping*
6:11   *I asked . . . How long, my Lord (*'ădōnāy*)?
      —until . . .
      —but while

7. This is the particular suggestion of Rendtorff 1993; see below. Note also Wells's
(2000: 147–52) reading of Isa. 6 in conjunction with both Isa. 1 and 40.

This analysis is indebted to Williamson (2005), who notes the following key points: the use of *wāw*-consecutive verbs of perception (seeing and hearing, as well as asking) to mark the three fundamental units of thought of the passage and to move the narrative forward (vv. 1, 8, 11; marked above with an asterisk *), with the deliberate use of *ădōnāy* ("Lord") in each instance as a further structural marker (to be contrasted with the use of the divine name Y*hwh* elsewhere—vv. 3, 5, 12); and the resultant division of the chapter into a first half regarding what Isaiah saw (vv.1–7) and a second half regarding what Isaiah heard (vv. 8–13). (Williamson [2005: 126–27] notes also the *inclusio*, where v. 5 brings us back to the opening announcement with details of what Isaiah saw.)

Of the many points that could be made regarding the interpretation of this text, a few must suffice, and we shall restrict the discussion to points that shall, in due course, cast light on the question of the kind of reader implied by this passage. The underlying theological dynamic of the passage as a whole is well set out by Moberly: "The seraph with the glowing coal relates to Isaiah, as Isaiah with his message relates to the people. Isaiah's purification by the coal is parallel to, and is the means towards, the people's purification by the prophetic message" (2003: 132; cf. the comparable analysis of Conrad 1991: 111). The recognition of holiness in Isaiah's vision, not least in the emphatic threefold repetition of *qādôš* (holy) in the song of the seraphim in verse 3, provokes Isaiah's response of recognizing his "uncleanness" (*ṭāmē'*) rather than his "unholiness." "Clean" and "unclean" do not operate in a straightforward way as categories of holiness in Israel. Without entering into a full analysis of such terminology, we shall follow Philip Jenson's summarizing conclusion: "Holiness (and its opposite, the profane) represents the divine relation to the world, and the clean (with its opposite, the unclean) embraces the normal state of human existence in the earthly realm" (1992: 47). Given the vagueness that the language of "sacred and profane" can so easily import into discussion of the biblical text, it seems wise to opt for the technical translation of "common/unholy" instead of "profane," and with this small change, the resulting schema looks like this:[8]

8. Here I draw upon the comparable diagrams of both Jenson (1992: 42) and Milgrom (in many places, but conveniently set out in 2000: 29).

Holy	"Common" (or unholy)
qādôš	ḥōl
Pure (or clean)	Impure (or unclean)
ṭāhôr	ṭāmē'

One can see then how unholiness and purity can coexist in one person (or place, thing, or time). This general vocabulary is found in something like this schematized form in Leviticus 10:10, where God calls on Aaron (and by implication the priestly role in general) to be able to distinguish between these various categories, relayed in the two pairs we have been discussing.[9] Further specifics, including gradations of holiness or impurity, depend on the particular contexts of any given use of the terms (so Jenson 1992: 45).

The two "active" categories in this schema are "holy" and "impure," in the sense that they are "contagious" (i.e., "they seek to extend their influence and control over the other two categories"; Milgrom 2000: 29). In the case of Isaiah 6, the prophet recognizes himself as under the influence of the one (impurity) but is clearly being offered more than a vision of its opposite (purity). In some sense he is being offered a vision of holiness itself. This transcending of his own perspective is perhaps a key to the transformative nature of the passage as a whole. It represents a conversion of status and perspective to which Isaiah himself could not attain only by his own effort: it has to be in some sense the initiative of the God here envisioned as three-times holy. The moment of divine deliberation that follows almost seems to *invite* the co-opting of the prophet rather than enforcing it: "Whom shall I send, and who will go for us?" (The "I" refers to God himself, and the "us" doubtless to the divine council gathered in the celestial court as the setting for the vision.) Isaiah's response is as recipient, as a "summoned self," in Ricoeur's terminology (see note 5 above). Hence: "Here I am [*hinnî*]," the same one-word response of readiness found at such key moments as the call for Abraham to sacrifice his son (Gen. 22:1, 7, 11) or Moses's response to the vision of the burning bush (Exod. 3:4), and indeed Yhwh's announcing his readiness to act for a repentant Israel in Isaiah 58:9. And then: "Send me!" Isaiah's

---

9. Though it is worth noting, with Jenson (1992: 45n1), that *ḥōl* is relatively rare: in P it appears only at Lev. 10:10.

whole response to the God who has summoned him is self-involving
and transformative in every sense: he allows all his own contribution
and perspective to be taken up into the purposes and perspectives of
God, even while he remains the human "agent" Isaiah throughout.

Striking though this is, the text moves on immediately to God's
next words, where we come upon the theological crux of the passage.
It is tempting indeed to stay with the rousing call to self-identification
with the mission of God, tempting to such an extent that Isaiah 6:1–8
serves to this day as the Old Testament reading for the ordination
service for those entering ministry in the Church of England, for
instance. Verses 9–10 and the rest of the passage cast the whole into
a different perspective.

Although no translation is perfect, there is merit here in laying out
these verses as transparently as possible, with their straightforward
Qal imperatives[10] in verse 9 (hear/hear! see/see!) and the Hiphil (caus-
ative) imperatives of verse 10, and thus here I follow the translation
of Robinson (1998: 172):

6:9   And he said, "Go, and say to this people,
        'Hear and hear, but do not understand;
        See and see, but do not perceive.'
6:10   Make the heart of this people fat
            and their ears heavy
            and their eyes blind
        Lest they see with their eyes,
            and hear with their ears,
            and understand with their hearts
            and return [*wāšāb*] and be healed."[11]

The interpretation of these verses began as early as the LXX, with its
softening of verse 10's imperatives to indicatives, and the addition of
a "for" (*gar*) to connect verse 10 to verse 9, thus changing "make the
heart fat" to "for this heart has grown fat." As a result, "lest they see"

10. Followed in each case by the infinitive absolute, the "postpositive infinitive absolute,"
which indicates "perfection or intensity of action" (J-M §123, II).

11. This last line is difficult, but it does not on the whole affect our reading. See Wildberger 1991: 250.

became "so that they might not see"—a result of their own hearts growing fat—and thus the blame for the hard-heartedness is left with the people of Israel rather than with God. The saying then occurs at various key moments in the New Testament, notably on the occasion of Jesus's discussing why he spoke in parables. In this context it is only clearly quoted in Matthew 13:14–15, but there are related allusions in the parallel passages, Mark 4:12 and Luke 8:10. It appears also in relation to John's claim that Jesus's signs (rather than his parables) had not brought about belief (John 12:40), in a reference to fulfilling the words of the prophet Isaiah, a reference to which we shall return. Isaiah 6:9–10 is also found at the end of Acts (28:25–27; perhaps programmatically for Luke's two-volume account, so Koet 2005: 95–96) as well as in Paul's reflection on Israel's hardness of heart in Romans 11:8 (though here drawing on Isaiah 29:10 as the point of reference).[12]

---

12. The continuing history of interpretation of Isaiah 6 is another area of considerable interest. Evans 1989 offers a thorough analysis of all the above references and more, and the New Testament use of the text is also well covered in Moyise and Menken 2005, as well as the various entries in Beale and Carson 2007 (note also Evans 1997). Evans reads the point of Isa. 6:9–10 in the canon in a manner similar to the approach of his sometime collaborator J. A. Sanders's (1984) notion of the canonical process, whereby it serves as a means of "monotheizing" the Israelite conception of the world as the theater of one God alone. Thus "I am interested in the text of Isaiah 6.9–10 because in a certain sense it epitomizes the struggle to monotheize. I believe that Isaiah 6.9–10 is perhaps one of the most important prophetic witnesses to the monotheistic hermeneutic, the hermeneutic that lies at the very heart of the canon" (Evans 1989: 16). Sanders's view is most clearly set out in Sanders 1984: 73, where he advises us to read the Bible as "paradigms of the struggles of our ancestors in the faith to monotheize, that is, to pursue the Integrity of Reality, in and over against their various polytheistic contexts." (For their joint work, see Evans and Sanders 1993.) Ultimately, if only Yhwh's action is determinative of all things, then Israel's "fat hearts" and "heavy ears" must also be the result of divine decree.

However, for Evans, the LXX and later uses of the text are unable to accept Isaiah's monotheizing and seek to get around it by turning the *announcement* of judgment into "an *explanation* of a pre-existing condition that necessitated, or unavoidably resulted in, judgment" (1989: 164). Evans goes on to trace the reception of the text among the church fathers (1989: 147–62), noting in particular that the focal point of the discussion becomes predestination and that, crucially, the text is understood to be speaking about others rather than about the community doing the interpreting. We shall return later to the significance of reading Isa. 6 as addressing the reader and the reader's community rather than "other people," although one must observe the hints of such a transition already occurring in the book of Isaiah itself when similar language is applied to idolaters in 44:18.

As a result of the change of the text (in translation), then, the history of interpretation offers a window to a set of interpretive debates that are different from the ones raised by the Hebrew text. For clear examples of how the theological debates set by Isa. 6 subsequently

The Hebrew text of Isaiah 6 certainly seems to hold out a bleak prospect for the prophet summoned to speak the prophetic word not only *to* a people who will not listen (which is clearly presupposed in some sense) but *in order that* people will not listen. Commentators have come up against a mystery here that seems to defeat all attempts to make sense of it, which is perhaps in itself more significant than is sometimes granted. We shall offer some brief considerations of some of the more common paths offered at this point, since it is the sense in which this text "summons" the reader that will be our concern.

On the one hand, some might simply throw their hands up in horror and reject completely the point apparently made by the passage. But even ignoring the view that such a verse is simply self-underminingly pointless, there are interpretive approaches that do seem to exhibit a kind of failure of theological nerve when confronted with this passage. Consider the view that the text records something like a failure on the part of Isaiah. It is sometimes urged that the prophet missed the opportunity, at a crucial moment, to argue the prophetic case against Yhwh's judgment, in comparison to the manner in which both Abraham (Gen. 18:22–33), Moses (Exod. 33:12–16), and others argued against the threat of divine retribution. Thus Marvin Sweeney, for example, suggests that "perhaps Isa 6 shows the reader the consequences of failing to challenge evil, even when it comes from the highest authority" (2005: 59–60). Evidently such a reading is not an impossible construal of the text,[13] but it is hard to see how the passage can in any sense have been designed to function as an illustration of prophetic failure or on what reading of the whole book it would serve any purpose to show off the character carrying the book's central human voice as fundamentally unable to rise to the prophetic calling.

---

develop into other sorts of (systematic) questions, see the fine studies of Wawrykow (2005: esp. 59–67) on Aquinas, and Steinmetz (1987) on Calvin. In what follows, references to "Isa. 6" (and vv. 9–10 in particular) refer to the substance of the Hebrew text, not to the LXX.

13. Though note that Savran 2003, offering a helpful form-critical analysis of "type-scenes," thinks that while there may be room in commissioning type scenes for expressions of prophetic reluctance to go, there is no real possibility within the form for prophetic objections to the divinely announced mission. Childs (2001: 52–53) helpfully deflates the significance sometimes attached to form-critical approaches here.

Less unlikely, but surely similarly misleading, is the "psychological" approach.[14] This view argues that the text serves in part as a later, retrospective reflection on what happened: Israel did not repent and avert judgment, and thus it turns out that the result of the prophetic preaching in this case was to cause people to turn *away* from God rather than *to* God. This is the cussedness of the human psyche, says this approach: offer God's good news, and people turn away. Although on this account the verse serves something of an encouraging function for Isaiah, who is hereby liberated from responsibility for any "failure" of his preaching (it is God's decree, not his own failing), it still is hard to see that the text is designed at this point to serve as encouragement for Isaiah. Neither is there any overall sense that Isaiah simply happens to have stumbled upon a general characteristic of the human race. This narrative is lifting Isaiah into a unique position, not making him into a model preacher. Nevertheless, variations on this approach remain popular, perhaps because they all at some point bring the text down to something a little more theologically manageable, though arguably only a little.[15]

A more promising line of approach is one we might call "temporal," and Seitz's commentary offers a fine example of it (1993: 55–60). Its underlying rationale is "canonical" in Childs's sense of the term (this is clearer in Childs's own version of the reading; 2001: 56–60), deliberately eschewing redactional explanations as to why what looks like an inaugural call occurs as late as chapter 6. It suggests instead that the function of the narrative in the finished book of Isaiah must be related to its position between the darkening gloom of Isaiah 5 (with its list of woes and final account of the land of "darkness and

14. So-called by Seitz (1993: 56) in his insightful analysis. Cf. also Childs 2001: 53–54, who broadens out the category into what he calls "etiological" and "retrospective" readings.

15. Although his survey is strikingly unsympathetic, A. Davies (2000: 173–86) offers a fair "metacommentating" overview of the ways in which scholars try to navigate around this text. Davies's own analysis, however, does not resolve the tension created by, on the one hand, arguing that the text must be addressed without theological bias—such that "God" is simply one character in a literary narrative—and then, on the other hand, affirming rather suddenly his own conviction that this "God" is the Christian God. The problematic result is that theology emerges late as a category swung about at the mercy of a literary construal of the text, with no role to play in shaping the judgments or habits of reading used to get there.

distress"; v. 30) and the resultant content of chapters 7 and following, where Isaiah's prophetic oracles are gathered for their purposes
of judgment leading up, eventually and after agonizing delay, to the
words of comfort of Isaiah 40.[16] In favor of this reading, perhaps
most notably, is the fact that Isaiah's response to these extraordinary
words in chapter 6 is not "Why?" or "How?" but "How long?" (Seitz
1993: 57). In other words, says Seitz, chapter 6 sets up the next phase
of the message of the finished book and explores the "dark side of
Zion theology; . . . when Israel chooses to become like the nations,
and is finally indistinguishable from them, the fury of Yahweh that
was to protect Zion is turned against his own people" (1993: 58).
Until, that is, "she has served her term," and "her penalty is paid"
(40:2), and we arrive at the expression of divine reembrace in 54:7–8,
difficult though that text is for those pondering the nature of faithful
relationships.

Seitz's approach, and others like it, do indeed "hold their nerve"
before this text, finding a way into its mysteries by focusing on the
temporal limitation indicated by the "How long?" Seitz also distinguishes between the part of the text commissioned to Isaiah to relay to
the nation (v. 9) and the part that describes, as it were, Yhwh's private
description to Isaiah of his task (v. 10). At this point, several commentators have asked whether we have any record of Isaiah duly delivering
the message given to him in verse 9. Gerald Sheppard, working along
not dissimilar canonical lines to Seitz, puts it this way: "What is 'the
central message' of the prophet as it is presented within the book as
a whole? . . . The answer is found clearly spelled out, initially, in the
narratives that follow the call report" (1996: 270–71). Sheppard's
approach here broadly follows the study of Rolf Rendtorff (1993),
which traces links between chapters 6 and 40 and sees them as offering
a canonically shaped "dual commissioning" of the various aspects
(or stages) of the message of the book. As a result, the key point of
interpretation is the desire to trace the import and impact of Isaiah 6

---

16. The contours of Isa. 1–39 are certainly more complex than this, with their own
sections of praise (chap. 12) and renewal (amid chaps. 24–27), and indeed Second Isaiah
is not all uplifting (cf. 44:18, noted earlier), yet something of this general trajectory (from
judgment to comfort) may nevertheless be discerned.

in the texts that follow it, regardless of the complex questions about the formation of the text as we have it.[17]

In the finished book of Isaiah, then, the commission of chapter 6 announces the judgment of God upon Israel, judgment for its failure to trust in God alone. The stinging critiques of Isaiah 1 have already anticipated that this is the thrust of the opening section(s) of the book. In the light of this, the terms of Isaiah's commission in verse 9 are in a certain sense ironic, since God's longer-term purpose is clearly for Israel to turn to him, although in the short/medium term it is clear in verse 9 that Israel cannot understand how this is to work.[18] For reasons that perhaps can never be clear either to Isaiah or to us, the long-term salvation of God's people requires the short-term hardening of Israel.

Perhaps most demanding of all, the final verse of the chapter, though one of the most complex to read in terms of simply understanding the text before us, seems in some way to suggest that the destruction will go on, even to the ravaging of any remnant of the faithful, even to the felling of any tree left in the land.[19] There is hope here, though it comes late and does not seem designed to function to overturn the tone of the passage. As Moberly puts it, "The assumption appears to be that such burning is intrinsic to the holy nature of YHWH, . . . and so burning continues constantly, primarily to purify and restore but also to consume those who do not respond" (2003: 134, noting also Isa. 1:28–31 and 66:24).

In terms of who is acting and initiating in this narrative: on one level all the action comes from God's side, but Isaiah's response is

17. On which, note especially Williamson 1994: 30–56, who also, though differently, sees the text as intricately linked to its surrounding, final, textual context.

18. On irony here, see Goldingay 2001: 61; Moberly 2003: 133; and note that there is clear irony to come in the book with texts such as Isa. 29:9–13, where we read, "Stupefy yourselves and be in a stupor, blind yourselves and be blind!" (v. 9) as well as "He has closed your eyes, you prophets" (v. 10).

19. It would be beyond our present needs to explore how to read the text of verse 13, but note Emerton 1982, whose main conclusion is that the verse foretells the destruction of the tenth part of the people who have thus far remained and that the reference to trees illustrates this destruction, but the leaving of the stumps of the trees allows a (later) mention of the "holy seed" as a sign of survival and hope (1982: 115). Beale (1991: 261–67) offers further analysis, suggesting a link with a critique of idolatry in the imagery of this verse. Cf. also Williamson 1997: 119–22.

also one of acceptance and a readiness to do what he is asked. As is generally the case for Old Testament prophets, it is not that Isaiah is given this vision because he has attained to some virtuous state that qualifies him to be brought before the holy God. But a little caution is required here in knowing how best to articulate the ever-present tension between divine initiative and human response. In his careful analysis of this issue with respect to holiness in Isaiah, John Gammie approaches the topic from "the perspective of empowerment and divine enablement or hallowing of humankind for the attainment of the goals held out by the divine sovereign." His conclusion is helpful: "The biblical focus is never on abstract causality but rather on divine intentionality in response to and in the light of human deeds" (1989: 94). He reads Isaiah 5:16b ("The Holy God shows himself holy by righteousness") as indicating that God's holiness is made manifest in human acts of righteousness and justice, acts that reflect "human initiative and an ultimate divine empowerment" (1989: 95).[20] The point is that human initiative and divine action are woven together inseparably in these texts. All in all, this seems to be a better balance than any desire to overplay the lack of a human contribution to the scope and nature of divine action. Isaiah's summoning, then, represents divine action but also results in human action, and we would do well not to unpick too emphatically the link between these two, both here and in our later discussion of how readers might be summoned to attend to the text wherein this dynamic is described.

Who Can Learn to Read Isaiah?

We come now, in our pursuit of interpretive virtue, to ask how this understanding of the God who summons, and of Isaiah as the summoned self, can contribute to our picture of the implied virtues of the reader of the Old Testament. Perhaps our own concerns may be helpfully focused around the question of what kind of reader can rise to the challenge of reading Isaiah, and in particular chapter 6. Let us note Hugh Williamson's analysis, speaking of chapter 1 in connection with its various intertextual echoes throughout the book: "It [chap. 1] . . . serves as an

20. For this understanding of Isa. 5:16, see also Moberly 2001.

introduction to the book in the sense of an appeal to the reader to repent in the light and on the basis of all that is to follow; it prepares the
reader's frame of mind at the start of the book rather than anticipat-
ing what is to come" (2006: 10). Slightly more broadly, Williamson in
an earlier piece wrote that the purpose of chapter 1 was "to invite the
reader to adopt a responsive attitude to all that is to follow" (1997: 127),
thereby exhorting the reader to a changed way of life, newly alerted to
the "blessings of obedience" and the "perils of disobedience" (1997:
127). This hermeneutical dynamic—whereby the text is understood
as leading the reader through a series of responses considerably more
wide-ranging than simply the apprehension of the meaning of a text—is
perhaps characteristic of much recent study of Isaiah.[21]

How then is the reader shaped in the reading of Isaiah 6? At this
point one path that seems to invite consideration is that the reader is
summoned to an appreciation (if not an experience) of the holiness
of God. In the somewhat theorized language of van Wieringen, "the
vision with the expression of the Lord's holiness becomes so striking
for the implied reader that the content thereof will function as a . . .
paradigm" (1998: 47). But having said this much, how exactly does one
grasp the significance of a notion such as being summoned before the
holiness of God? Perhaps, after all, the reader is simply brought to an
impasse in Isaiah 6. We noted above that it might be more significant
than is sometimes granted that commentators do not know "how to
go on" when confronted with the vision of God and the concomitant
commission in this chapter. One has sympathy with the poetic tour
de force offered by Brueggemann: "But first the stump! The stump of
failure and termination rooted in numbness and hard-heartedness.
. . . It will not surprise us that our verses of narcotization leave us
deeply stumped" (1998: 63). Maybe we too have erred in confidently
proclaiming one approach as insightful and another as problematic?
Would we have been better advised to keep a respectful silence before
the searching presence of the numinous in this text?

21. Thus, e.g., Gitay 1997; several of the essays gathered in Melugin and Sweeney 1996;
and the lengthy study of "the implied reader in Isaiah 6–12" by van Wieringen 1998, although
this ends up with insights surprisingly similar to those of more traditional commentary but
simply in a different register, as in the quote that follows above. Changing trends in Isaiah
study over recent years are ably documented by Tate 1996 and Tull 2006.

In fact, I do not think this is the case. It is clearly tempting to argue that there is really no way of understanding the purposes of God in judgment and mercy other than to wait upon divine initiative, or to suggest that any attempt to "reduce" the text down to manageable size marks the point at which we as readers step in with a pretension to a knowledge of good and evil that we do not have. On this view, one could imagine wanting to argue that interpretive virtue is less a key to knowing what to do with the text, and more that such virtue consists in knowing that we do not know what to do. To (mis)appropriate some words of Nicholas Lash: "The holy, in its fulness, lies outside our control. In the presence of the holy, you take off your shoes and silence the clamour of self-interest" (2004: 38).

In this chapter, we have already managed to say a good deal about what can and cannot be said with regard to Isaiah 6 and its content and purposes; so on what grounds, one may ask, have we concluded that reverent silence was not the route to take? The answer to this lies in the wider context that gives Lash's quote above its currency, a context that has been implicit throughout the present book. In particular we must recall the notion of "tradition-constituted inquiry," which we looked at in chapter 1 in discussing the work of Alasdair MacIntyre. Lash himself has made much of this way of thinking in his penetrating critique of the various categories of "religious discourse" so common among us in the late twentieth and early twenty-first century. Dating a good deal of such terminology (including such terms as "monotheism" and "atheism," as well as modern usages of the word "God") to the seventeenth century, he suggests that the "mistake lay in the expectation that the human grasp of truth could ever be other than tradition-constituted" (1996: 19). In the context of writing about the ways in which Christian traditions and those native to India might be able to understand each other's categories, he makes the point that there are no neutral "religious" terms that can without distortion mediate the realities being discussed (1996: 3–25).[22] And this will apply, in due course, to any discussion of "the holy" or "the numinous." Thus his later point about the presence of the holy must be understood in the

---

22. In his striking article, "What Might Martyrdom Mean?" (1986), Lash offers an account of how such thinking relates directly to biblical interpretation.

context of asking how any particular notion of the holy is introduced into the conversation, and what sorts of experiences it is intended to evoke. Holiness, in Lash's analysis, marks out the presence of the God whom we must learn to approach rightly. But this must be done in a way that respects our nature as human beings. The broader point he wishes to make is that "to be human is to be able to speak, to say 'Yes' or 'No'; to be able to *respond* to places, times and people, and, perhaps, to God" (2004: 63). The crucial point is the kind of "noise" that the response is: is it the egotistical noise of self-expression or the "outgoing" sound of communication, relationship, and building up communion? His answer: "The silence that is *attentiveness*—to God and to each other" is sound, not noise (2004: 92). In other words, the response we find at the key moment in Isaiah 6 constitutes ongoing communication and relationship, and in a certain sense the option to come to a (silent) halt before the numinous can sometimes be the decision to break off such communication.

Isaiah the prophet is not actually silent before the vision of God in chapter 6. Nor, significantly, does the book of Isaiah draw to a sudden, undone "closure" in the face of holiness. Indeed, there are sixty chapters still to go. And if Lash is right, we must attend to the ways in which the holiness of chapter 6 is presented in its narrative (or canonical) setting. It would be wrong to conclude, then, that Isaiah 6 simply takes us to the limit of our understanding and leaves us with no response. Rather, Isaiah 6 introduces us to the holiness of God in a very particular way, which is taken up in Isaiah's response and subsequent ministry. Earlier we looked at two important features of this: that Isaiah's action and initiative should not be overcontrasted with divine action and initiative, and that the unfolding of the book as a whole indicates ways in which the vision is to be grasped. It is here that we may attend with profit to the ways in which more reader-oriented approaches to the book help us to see the narrative dynamics of Isaiah 6 in a proper context.

Van Wieringen offers a helpful way into the broader setting of chapter 6 when he notes the important point that Isaiah 6 poses a question about the temporal placement of the implied reader that it does not in itself answer: "Does he [the implied reader] read the narration looking back after the *until*, or does he still read the narration before the realization of the *until*?" (1998: 49). The "until" in question is that found in 6:11–12 (and by implication v. 13): "until cities lie waste . . . until Yhwh sends everyone far away . . . it will be burned again. . . ." In other words, has the reader already seen this destruction wrought and now looks back on the narrative promising that it would happen? Or is the reader left with the sense that this destruction is hereby announced but is still to come? Where is the reader to be located (temporally) with respect to the judgment in 6:11–13, and how does that in turn affect our reading of Isaiah?

A persuasive answer to this question is offered by Edgar Conrad's bold analysis in his *Reading Isaiah* (1991).[23] Conrad's approach has many points of contact with other literary and canonical readings, although he is equally willing to invest in historical-critical insights for the value of understanding the various aspects and structural features of the book. In particular he draws fresh insight from looking at well-known structural features of the book understood as a literary whole, an exercise that casts new light on such familiar features as the narrative section of chapters 36–39, which he sees as fundamentally offering an Assyrian denouement in anticipation of the Babylonian one in chapters 40–47. These two climactic sections are flagged in advance (though in reverse order) in chapters 13–14 (Conrad 1991: 52–82).

Our own concerns with Isaiah 6 are illuminated by Conrad's approach, in two ways. First, he suggests that chapter 6 serves to set out a portrait of Isaiah designed to resonate with the implied audience of the (overall) book. In chapters 59 and 63–64, this audience comes somewhat into focus as what he calls "survivors" of the Babylonian exile. On this view, in Isaiah 6 "Isaiah is presented as the first of the survivors, and his actions and words make the present meaningful for the book's implied audience" (1991: 111). As readers progress through the book, therefore, they consciously identify with Isaiah's experiences as in some sense paradigmatic for their own. Among the many similarities that Conrad identifies between Isaiah and the "survivors of exile," we may note the following: both recognize

23. See his own further account in Conrad 1996 as well as a somewhat differently oriented "new canonical" approach indebted to Umberto Eco in Conrad 2003: esp. 182–242.

their need for repentance in the midst of people who have strayed
from Yhwh (6:5–7; 59:12; 64:5), both are sent willingly (6:8; 66:5,
19), and both wrestle with hardness of heart (6:10; 63:17). Overall,
Conrad suggests, the "until" description of 6:11–13 would resonate
with the implied readers of the book, who have experienced the
reality of the desolation here described. Isaiah's words and actions
in chapters 6–8 are "paradigmatic for the community of survivors"
(1991: 113).

The second way in which Conrad's approach clarifies some of the
dynamics of chapter 6 is with regard to the repeated theme of the
reading of books in Isaiah 28–35. This theme occurs in 34:16 and
especially in 29:11–12, where the people cannot "read" God's word,
immediately before a description of their flawed worship in 29:13–14.
This description (they "draw near with their mouths, and honor me
with their lips, while their hearts are far from me"; v. 13) obviously
takes the reader back to 6:9–10. Furthermore, Isaiah anticipates and
symbolizes this future inability to grasp the word of God in 8:16,
where his testimony is bound up and sealed for a future age (Conrad
1991: 130–43). Now it is possible to take Conrad's basic observation
about failure to understand and the "binding up" of prophecy and
explore the historical trajectory of how this dynamic of sealing and
opening did actually play out in the reception of Isaiah.[24] But Conrad's own point, on a literary level, is that Isaiah 6–39 constituted an
earlier "vision of Isaiah" text that is "now" (i.e., in the time of the
survivors) related to the new experiences of the implied community
(the readers). As a result, the handling of this "book" theme within
Isaiah allows us to understand how the dynamics of grasping the
word of the Lord might be understood in terms of the overall book of
Isaiah (1991: 117–53). The inability to hear or see, as foretold in Isaiah
6:9–10, is explicitly rolled back in 29:18: "On that day the deaf shall
hear the words of a scroll, and out of their gloom and darkness the
eyes of the blind shall see." The day in question, says Conrad (1991:
137–40), finally arrives in chapter 40, where this word of the Lord is

_____

24. This is the project undertaken by Blenkinsopp 2006. Note also the sharp, if slightly
inconclusive, study of R. P. Carroll 1997.

to be "cried out" (or "read"; 40:3) in anticipation of the servant of the Lord, who will "open the eyes that are blind" (42:7).[25]

Who then can read Isaiah 6? Or more precisely, where does this leave readers of Isaiah 6 as they make their way through the whole book? The implied reader is not just someone summoned by God, or confronted by awe-inspiring holiness, in a single moment of divine encounter. Rather, it is someone introduced into a specific narrative that includes, but is not stalled at, Isaiah's vision in chapter 6—a narrative that goes on to characterize the reader as a member of the community that has survived (perhaps in ways never fully understood) the divine hardening involved. The reader has thus lived through the "until" of 6:11–13, has survived exile, and thus knows that judgment leads on to mercy. The mystery of chapter 6 explores a blindness and a deafness that can be characteristic of even the people of God. But out of this blindness and deafness, God will lead (or has led) his people in the new day foretold in the succeeding chapters of First Isaiah (or "Isaiah's vision," in Conrad's terms), a day that dawns (or has dawned) in Second Isaiah.

Conrad's two points above combine to give us the following: Isaiah is a model for the implied reader, confronted with the mystery of God's judgment but aware that this particular implementation of divine punishment lies in the past. The "implied reader" is to be part of the "implied community" of the book of Isaiah, summoned by the God to whom this text witnesses. One might even say that the point of deafness and blindness could be missed by those who presume to know how God's purposes will be worked out in a text like Isaiah 6:9–10. Rather, readers must allow themselves to be summoned by the specific strangeness of this text in its wider context, and then follow where it leads, even though this looks like the hardest and most uninviting of places. In short, only readers who hold their theological nerve before the terrible and entirely unnerving spectacle of Isaiah's vision will be able to see that they are invited to be transformed through the processes of judgment and restoration.

---

25. Elsewhere Conrad (1992) has further explored the notion that "books" in the Old Testament are effectively "texts" as likely to be oral as written.

Attending to the *Sache* of the Text: The Virtue of Receptivity

But what is at stake in this description of the reader's being summoned by a holy God? Here we return to our opening comments about theological interpretation in an attempt to delineate more clearly the relevant virtue, which we can perhaps call "receptivity" (a virtue listed first, indeed, by Gregory Jones in the quote with which we began our inquiry in chapter 1; 2002: 32).

The reader of scriptural texts, I am urging, is called to attend to the *Sache*, or content, of the text before them. The German word *Sache* here seems better suited to our task than any English equivalent: it is the reality, the subject matter, the "what it is about" of the text. I shall use it here as shorthand for this sense of "what is really there," and for the purposes of this discussion I shall not enter into an argument over the question of whether there is really anything there at all, an argument that has exhausted the brightest and best of the postmodern firmament in many other places.[26] This *Sache* includes perhaps the meaning of the text, or maybe the author's intended figuration of reality, or arguably the agents described in the text. In this case, the reader of Isaiah 6 is called to attend to the kinds of issues we have been considering in the foregoing analysis. We have characterized these as "holding one's nerve" before the text, but I want to draw out explicitly how this kind of inquiry factors into thinking about the practices of theological interpretation.

What we have to observe is the demanding and searching complexity of the basic categories of the text's *Sache*, which on any reading include notions of sin, holiness, blindness and deafness, and divine laying waste. A category such as sin, or uncleanness, can on one level be labeled and discussed as an abstract noun with whatever implications are thought to attach to it. But as we saw with the work of Nicholas Lash noted above, the point of engaging with the *Sache* of the text is

---

26. I note only the eloquent treatment of George Steiner (1989), offering a theopoetic affirmative answer to his subtitle *Is There Anything* in *What We Say?* even if the God he invokes is not self-evidently the one narrated in Christian Scripture (though such an identification seems to be at least implicitly at work in his strong critique of literary approaches to the Bible [Steiner 1988; cf. also Steiner 1996]).

that one must come (at some secondary, deeper level) to recognize that labeling is not a neutral exercise and that all sorts of self-involving judgments are involved in grasping the sense of what "sin" (or any of these categories) really means in the life-world imagined by the text. The grammar of all these terms, as we have seen in earlier chapters too, at some point ramifies into how the reader grasps the conceptuality of the God who is entirely implicated in the various value judgments and understandings of the text.

Obviously, there is some kind of limit to this analysis. One can hold the line at phenomenology and urge, "The text speaks of God this way, but I myself have no stake in believing what such language affirms." My point is that when one draws a line in the self-involving conceptuality of the text and steps instead to a place of detached judgment, that is the moment at which the "summoning" of the text is curtailed. It then becomes much harder to continue to think through the implications of this or that detail with regard to how it refigures the *Sache* of the text. It is a deep irony of some recent work in theological hermeneutics that this step outside of the grammar of the specific text, to a place where the text is subsumed into some judgment regarding "what it is about," can occur too soon in equal and opposite ways. Thus on the one side we might find critics announcing that the *Sache* of the text must be rejected (on the basis of some evaluative criteria, of course), but on the other side we might find others affirming the *Sache* of the text without having stayed long enough to see what it is.

At this point, it is important to reflect that our own manner of proceeding in this chapter (as indeed in every chapter) has been to approach the text with the aid of any and every interpretive tool available to us. It simply makes no sense to suppose that an interest in theological interpretation can allow one to bypass basic questions of how the words and illocutions of the text function, just as it makes no sense to claim that one can tackle the *Sache* of the text with the words alone (i.e., without the wider judgments about their conceptualities and significances in a world of human relationships and divine action). As an example: one question floated at the beginning of our reading of Isaiah 6 related to the meaning of "the whole earth is full of his glory." This worship by the seraphim in verse 3 is, if history is a reliable guide, easier to sing and affirm than it is to understand. Hugh Williamson's study of this verse reads it along lines similar to the claim made about the king of Assyria in 8:7 ("the king of Assyria and all his glory") and suggests that it should be rendered "the fullness of the earth is his glory [*kābôd*]," with *kābôd* understood as armies, or military might (1999: 186; also 2005: 133–36). The point is that Isaiah's vision reveals that the Lord of Israel has at his disposal more than just Israel: implicitly the song of the seraphim offers an alternative perspective to any self-assured belief on the part of Israel that they must be acceptable in God's eyes simply because they are God's. Such a reading leads quite naturally on to the shock and challenge of the later verses in the chapter, as well as offering real insight into what one might call Isaiah's political theology (cf. Lind 1997). This entire discussion has all manner of theological implications, which are not our concern here. Our point is formal rather than material: the discussion is actually accessible only to those who have stayed with the text long enough and neither prescinded from it too quickly nor affirmed it and marshaled it into their preexisting theological framework too quickly. But equally, this is not the same as saying that one "stays with" the text forever, never moving to a judgment about the *Sache*.

The conclusion about theological interpretation, as it is illuminated by the dynamics found in our text, may be put this way. Theological interpretation is interested in the *Sache* of the text, and as such it is more naturally compared with other such approaches (typically ideological or "advocacy" readings, which also engage with what the text is about). But it operates in detailed dialogue with any and every manner of approach to the text and so should not be seen as an alternative methodology or a separate discipline. What sets it apart, if anything, is its willingness to be summoned by the God of Christian (or in a different framework, Jewish) faith. But one may go further and suggest that one cannot section off the different aspects of interpretation from each other. Heuristically, it is the case that one may concentrate here on points of linguistic detail, and there on points of ideological or theological resonance, but all these aspects of interpretation are interrelated. So it follows that separating out the theological questions of interpretation from other aspects not only affects the theological interpretation but in due course also affects the other aspects. In the case of Isaiah 6, this is the issue raised above about the self-involving dynamics of most of the key terms and concepts at stake in the passage. To stop short of an analysis of what sin is, or uncleanness, or holiness, and to stop short on the grounds of not wishing to engage with the theological ramifications of these notions—such a maneuver will in the end curtail almost any manner of interpretation, even down to the ways in which the meanings and functions of individual words such as "sin," "uncleanness," or "holiness" (and their Hebrew/Greek equivalents) are grasped. It is not that disinterested lexical analysis has no place, but rather that much serious and pressing language in human existence requires engagement with the realities of which the text speaks before one can actually be in a position to carry out such disinterested analysis, by which time it is hardly disinterested any more.[27]

Once we say this, it seems to me that the *Sache* of the text in front of us (Isa. 6, in this case) cannot be separated off from its wider implications, its reception history, its reuse in other contexts, including, for example, the way that John 12:38–41 seems to suggest that Isaiah actually saw Jesus in this vision. Obviously this is John's conceptuality, not Isaiah's, but on the level of the *Sache* of the text, it is germane to the discussion (cf. C. Williams 2006).

If the discussion in this book has been anywhere near right, then the humble, wise, trusting, and loving interpreter will be well equipped to ponder Isaiah 6 with eyes as open as could be wished for, but the point of the present chapter has been to suggest that this is not in itself enough. In Isaiah's vision we discern another kind of virtue, another manner of bringing oneself to (or being brought to) the text, and this is the virtue of "receptivity." The kinds of judgments that must go into conceiving of oneself as being summoned by the text, willing to have one's perspectives transcended and taken up into mysterious divine

---

27. In Nicholas Lash's way of putting the point: "Is there not a sense in which it is a necessary condition for understanding, with any depth and sensitivity, what [scriptural texts] 'originally meant,' that we have some articulated grasp of those fundamental features of the human predicament to which those texts were constructed as elements of a response?" (1986: 80). This is a comment on the hermeneutics of what I have been calling "self-involvement."

purposes, are searching indeed but fundamentally rest upon the notion of God being the one who summons the interpreter. Isaiah 6 offers us a picture of receptivity to the words of God that we can transpose to the interpretive virtue of receptivity to the scriptural text.

This study comes after the others because I did not want to suggest that being summoned is somehow hermeneutically prior to engaging with the specifics of the text with all care and attention. The corollary is that in coming last, it might look as though it is offered as an add-on or supplement to our account of interpretive virtue. Rather, receptivity operates in, with, and under all our other human modes of interpreting, setting a context for them but also being shaped by them. As we saw to be the case within the book of Isaiah itself, human initiative is not separate from, but is also not obscured by, divine initiative. In the process, I have argued, we may understand some of the ways in which theological interpretation allows a place at the table to the God who summons, with all the implications this has for every subdiscipline of scriptural interpretation if any other subdiscipline is underrepresented or excluded.

7

THE VIRTUOUS READER
OF OLD TESTAMENT
NARRATIVE

From the Implied Reader to the Real Reader

J ust as the interpretations of texts are shaped, in whatever measure, by readers, so readers in turn are shaped by the texts they read. Any text that detains a reader long enough to provoke a response, whether of delight or disgust, will play its part in contributing to who that reader becomes as they turn to the next text or return again to the present one for a rereading. The dynamics of delight and disgust with respect to the biblical text are played out on public stages at conferences and in hundreds of new books and articles every year on almost every conceivable aspect of the text(s) of Scripture. Given how much time is spent engaged in the various activities of reading in such discussions, it is striking how little serious theological attention is paid to the disciplines involved in being a reader.

There are signs, however, that this is changing. In addition to volumes like the Scripture Project's *The Art of Reading Scripture*

(E. Davis and R. Hays 2003), which we have discussed earlier, there is evidence of new attention to the concerns of how to be a reader who reads well. As Nicholas Lash so memorably put it: "The fundamental form of the Christian interpretation of scripture is, in the concrete, the life, activity and organization of the Christian community" (1986: 90), the point taken up by Stephen Fowl and Gregory Jones in their emphasis on the reading of Scripture *in communion* (1991). Others have sought to recover reading "as a spiritual discipline" related to, but not identical with, other modes of reading[1] or have urged the recovery of a form of *lectio divina*.[2] Subtle treatments of reading in the theological economy typically dig deep into the tradition and look for insight from premodern modes of reading. Alan Jacobs's *A Theology of Reading* (2001), for example, seeks a theological account of the general activity of reading any literature, taking significant cues from Augustine. Peter Candler's fine study of reading texts that are designed to lead the reader to God (2006) draws on Aquinas and the medieval *Glossa ordinaria*. Candler explores "manuduction," a process of being led by the hand through the text to create a new learning experience, indeed a new "text" of sorts. Thus he develops the thesis that "the kind of 'texts' which we produce is altogether inseparable from the kind of people we are, or from the forms of life which might be said in some sense to constitute us" (2006: 9). Meanwhile, other treatments still focus on "how to read the Bible," as the titles of several books in any theological library will testify. Here the resources seem more easily traced back not to the giants of the theological tradition but to the practical words of wisdom of Mortimer Adler in his 1940 work *How to Read a Book* (rev. ed. 1972). Adler's goal (the highest level of reading to which he thought one should aspire) was the ability to read one text alongside others on the same subject and to compare

---

1. E.g., Griffiths 2002; cf. also his book-length treatment (Griffiths 1999), which distinguishes between "religious reading" and "consumerist reading."

2. See the introductory accounts of Magrassi 1998; Dumont 1999; Peterson 2006: 81–116; and Gargano 2007. Peterson (2006: 81) defines *lectio divina* as a practice designed "to discipline us, the readers of Scripture, into appropriate ways of understanding and receiving the text so that it is formative for the way we live our lives." Magrassi (1998: 68–69) offers the memorable image that "we cannot venture into the Bible as tourists, we must become inhabitants of the land. . . . Only after repeated listening do we detect the secret harmonies, discover the language, catch the dominant themes."

and contrast critically (what Adler called a "syntopical" reading, a fourth level after one had gone through elementary, inspectional, and analytical reading). A good many books and college courses on Bible reading seem to be more influenced by Adler than Augustine, with the strange result that the character of the reader can be factored out of consideration as a relevant aspect of the reading of Christian Scripture. The moral formation of the reader, on such accounts, is left as an optional extra to be considered, if at all, after the hard work of critical analysis has been done.

One of the burdens of the present work has been to urge that a concern with the moral formation of the reader must go hand in hand with the deployment of as wide a range as possible of interpretive insights from the various critical methodologies of biblical studies. To be a wise reader is more than attaining to a mastery of critical tools, but it is not less than that. In a book that seeks to model much this blend of the critical and the wise in New Testament studies, Markus Bockmuehl suggests that "the implied interpreter of the Christian Scripture is a *disciple*" (2006: 92). An earlier version of the chapter where he says this was entitled "Reason, Wisdom and the Implied Disciple of Scripture" (2003: cf. 63).[3] There seem to be many ways in which one could pursue the insight that who we are as readers is inextricably woven into all our practices of interpretation. I have chosen the path of seeking to build up a description of the ideal reader (Bockmuehl's "implied disciple") by way of looking at certain virtues that such a reader may be supposed to possess: a series of portraits, in other words, of the kinds of virtues implicit or implied in Old Testament narratives. Working with the assumption that the Old Testament has something to contribute to our thinking about the nature of the virtues most suited to reading it, we have pursued studies of the "interpretive virtues" of humility, wisdom, trust, love, and receptivity. The whole endeavor has been conceived as something of an attempt to take up the challenge implicit in the quote from Gregory Jones with which we began the discussion in chapter 1: "We need several interpretive virtues for wise and faithful reading of Scripture.

---

3. A comparable notion from a literary point of view is explored in Mark's Gospel by Rhoads, Dewey, and Michie (1999: 137–46).

Prominent among them are receptivity, humility, truthfulness, courage, charity, and imagination" (2002: 32). Immediately, one can see that other virtues could have been chosen, other passages explored for each virtue that was chosen, and other paths taken at almost every point along the way. For example, it would be intriguing to explore the virtues noted by David Lyle Jeffrey: "Through many years of reading and teaching literature I have come to believe that to read well one needs two apparently contradictory virtues—intellectual toughness and imaginative sympathy" (2003: 173). Such virtues are without a doubt called for in the reading of the Old Testament, but perhaps they do not arise so obviously from its own vision of the implied reader and thus have had to remain unexplored here.

This final chapter therefore has two (related) goals. First, I want to offer explicitly an acknowledgment, or a series of acknowledgments, concerning ways in which the present study is incomplete, whether conceptually or in practice. Some of these areas requiring further exploration probe potential limitations in the notion of the implied (or model) reader of the Old Testament with regard to various real readers. Second, therefore, I want to address directly the challenge left hanging in chapter 1, which related to this very question, and thus ask: What is at stake in making the transition from the implied reader to the actual reader? This will clearly move the discussion into a whole area of debate regarding how the Old Testament is being read and has been read in practice, and it will not be possible to do more than outline a general way of thinking about this issue. A third goal, which will become apparent and will be taken up in the discussion of the other two, is to highlight areas requiring further exploration.

The Virtuous Reader: A Modest Proposal

I have argued that the virtuous reader of Scripture is possessed of certain interpretive virtues. Chapter 1 explored why there could be no "canonical" list of such virtues, nor conceptual core to the kinds of characteristics that could be considered above and beyond the basic concern with *eudaimonia*. For a Christian project, it would certainly be important to conceptualize what constitutes the appropriately Christian frame of reference for the notion of *eudaimonia*. To some extent, I have supposed that the concerns of discipleship can be understood as the Christian version of such a way of thinking: that is, whatever contributes to the life of discipleship is a suitable candidate for a Christian sense of virtue. In theory, it would be interesting to pursue this conceptual question and ask exactly how the framework of virtue or character ethics can relate to the kingdom of God, and such considerations loom large in the fine discussion of Hauerwas and Pinches, who seek explicitly to find a way of negotiating between these different frameworks, especially in their brief section "On Being Happily a Christian" (1997: 14–16). I have instead chosen a piecemeal, case-study approach in the conviction that unless or until one can demonstrate any prospects at all for thinking about how the Old Testament shapes our notions of the categories of virtue, then the broader conceptual task is somewhat lacking in interest, at least to those engaged in the practices of actually reading the Old Testament.

Nevertheless, several questions could easily be posed at this point that clarify some of the built-in limitations of my proposal. I shall take five of them in no particular order.

Major Characters and Everyday Life

First, how significant is it that the characters we have studied are often major Old Testament figures? Can the virtues of Moses, Solomon, and Isaiah really be virtues to which all the people of God aspire? Clearly, not everyone is a Moses, but in the studies undertaken in this book, I have tried to pay attention to the question of the extent to which even a unique ascription of a characteristic to a major figure still operates within the narrative as some kind of commended characteristic for wider consideration.[4] Thus Moses is uniquely "humble" on the face of the earth, but Moses's work before God, as we saw when we looked at the canonical significance of Deuteronomy 34, is still to be carried on by others. Solomon's wisdom, too, is in some

---

4. New Testament readers will appreciate that the same question arises with regard to the figure of Jesus in the Gospels: an approach to the moral life that left no room for practicing the imitation of Christ after reading the New Testament would be strange indeed.

sense paradigmatic. And Isaiah's unique vision nevertheless invites us as readers to identify with his commitment to the word of God. Conceptually, at least, it should have made relatively little difference if the exemplars had all been rank-and-file Israelites. Perhaps the reason so many of the studies devolved onto major characters is no more profound than that they are allotted much greater narrative space, and this for the reason that they did indeed manage to exemplify characteristics worthy of consideration.

Male and Female Readers

Second, is it significant that the characters studied here have been mainly male? Is the implied reader constructed through these portraits, in other words, a somewhat male-oriented picture? I suspect that this question opens out into a whole different discussion, which we shall come to below, regarding the sense (if any) in which our portrait of the virtuous reader is intended normatively. With regard to the specific question of gender, it is of course true that certain constructions of certain virtues read differently for women and for men. We saw an example of this briefly in our study of humility. But suitably defined, as we have tried to do throughout these studies, it is at least not obvious that any of the virtues we have considered need to be differentiated with respect to gender, and the study of Ruth in chapter 5 did not seem to raise different types of questions regarding the role that the relevant virtue could play in the overall portrait of the virtuous reader.

Perhaps this is a good moment to note one of the earliest accounts of the "virtuous reader," found as one of the many prefaces to Aemilia Lanyer's celebrated poem "Salve Deus Rex Judaeorum" in 1611, a preface that she titled "To the Vertuous Reader" (Lanyer 1611a).[5] The poem as a whole is a reading of Christ's passion with particu-

---

5. For the text of Lanyer's poem, see the edition edited by Woods 1993 (Lanyer 1611b), presented along with its eleven prefaces, the last of which is "To the Vertuous Reader." There has been much speculation regarding Lanyer's possible identity in various Shakespearean sonnets (or indeed, theories that she was the real Shakespeare, which would muddy the gender waters still further!). Here I am indebted to Grossman 1998, as well as to helpful conversations with Hilary Elder, whose doctoral research at Durham has included a focus on Lanyer's reading of Scripture.

lar regard to the roles and perspectives of women in the tale. This preface, sometimes described by critics as "protofeminist," is a brief review of some of the scriptural reasons that women have to disavow strong claims made against them by some "evil disposed" men, claims that women are guilty of the rise of evil in the world. By contrast, Lanyer urges that it is men who "dishonoured Christ his Apostles and Prophets, putting them to shamefull deaths," and thus:

> Therefore we are not to regard any imputations, that they undeservedly lay upon us, no[t] otherwise than to make use of them to our own benefits, as spurs to virtue, making us fly all occasions that may colour their unjust speeches to pass current [i.e., appear true]. Especially considering that they have tempted even the patience of God himself, who gave power to wise and virtuous women, to bring down their pride and arrogance. (1993: 49)[6]

For Lanyer, then, the virtuous reader (of her poem, in the first instance) is a woman taking her stand against the schemes of evil *men*, although it is only fair to notice that this is presented as a constructive agenda *for women* rather than an attack as such on men. It is even clearer in her preface "To all vertuous Ladies in generall" (Woods 1993: 12–16) that her controlling metaphor is that she is forming her readers into brides of Christ, with the result that her "ideal reader" is in some sense only fully realizable as a woman. Arguably, one can hear her constructive agenda for women as written against the backdrop of an assumption that the world is full of *male* virtuous readers, so that one need not conclude from her account that virtuous reading is a feminine prerogative. Here all I wish to draw from this discussion is that the conceptuality of "the virtuous reader" is susceptible to being filled with content applicable to both male and female readers. Thus the question one would need to ask with respect to the present work is not whether the (biblical) texts in view are inherently either male oriented or female oriented but whether the specific virtues being discussed are apprehended in ways that allow them to be embodied by either men or women, or by both. This can only be settled case by case, and

---

6. I have modernized the spelling in this quotation and added bracketed material in two cases.

one need not doubt that various traditional construals of virtue have indeed maintained certain gender-specific ways of thinking, against which, perhaps, a work such as Lanyer's is especially aimed. But in the particular cases we have examined, where the Old Testament has been allowed to define the content of the relevant virtues rather than just working with "traditional" versions of them, virtuous male and female readers may well find themselves quite equal before the text.

More Problematic Texts

A third question to consider is whether some obvious candidates for implied virtue could have been considered that might have shed quite a significantly (indeed disastrously) different light upon the overall inquiry undertaken here. Is there not, for example, a virtue of aggression without mercy attested to in such texts as the famous *ḥerem* passages of Deuteronomy 7?[7] Or in the puzzling story of Saul's being condemned for sparing the best of the sheep and the cattle from the Amalekites as well as their king (1 Sam. 15)? Should we have included such a study and pondered the resultant virtue of commitment to wiping out one's enemy? And how would such a conclusion have in turn impacted any of the other considerations of love, humility, and so forth with which we have been occupied?

Short of engaging in a full and careful study of such passages as these, it is hard to say exactly what the outcome would be. At various points in the preceding chapters I have touched on the question of what sorts of issues are raised by "problem passages," with all their self-involving complexity (in particular with the discussion of suspicion in chapter 4 (above), where I tried to show why the strategy of parading a problematic text and saying "and that is unacceptable" raises too many questions). Further, one would at least need to handle a question such as that posed by the *ḥerem* passages with enough care to make sure that the right categories were used: *ḥerem* is neither a virtue nor a vice, but a practice (whether of "holy war," or "putting

---

7. The word *ḥerem* is variously translated as "utterly destroy" or "devote for destruction" (NRSV) and is found in texts such as Deut. 7:1–5 (specifically v. 2) and its various "fulfillments" or "enactments," such as Josh. 6:17. Stern 1991 offers a comprehensive review of relevant data.

under the ban," or however one would best translate the term), and the question must surely be about what kinds of virtues are implicit in the *ḥerem* narratives.

In the case of Saul in 1 Samuel 13 and 15, for instance, the relevant virtue that he is found to be lacking, according to the narrative, and to Samuel's "You have done foolishly" (13:13), is the virtue of obedience to the requirements of Yhwh. The problem we have as modern readers of this text is that we cannot grasp the grounds on which the particular forms of obedience were enjoined (though again, one should hesitate to make such a judgment short of careful engagement with the text). The virtues of the conquest narrative in Joshua include strength and courage (Josh. 1:9) and again obedient service (24:15). These too are not difficult to appreciate today, but the problem lies within the context in which these virtues were demonstrated: the violent arrival of the Israelites in the land of the Canaanites. That these accounts are not intended as history in the modern sense, and serve all manner of ideological and/or identity-forming purposes in being told in the subsequent generations in Israel—all this does not really remove the ethical edge with which they cut against the grain for the modern reader.[8]

Some brief comments by way of response must suffice, perhaps merely as an indication of further work that needs to be done on the sorts of virtues implicit in such "problem" texts, where it seems that the problems actually lie not so much in the virtue implicit in the narrative as in the narrative setting and assumptions within which the virtue is commended. Suppose, for the sake of simplifying the discussion at present, that "obedience" is indeed one of the virtues enjoined by the Joshua narratives. Then perhaps we could have explored obedience as an interpretive virtue, noting that the contexts in which it is modeled may in turn require us to do some serious thinking about discerning the right contexts today where reading should be translated into "obedience to what is read." Such hermeneutical considerations are always present to any who read the Bible carefully.

8. For a constructive account of how the book of Joshua might have been intended to function, see Douglas Earl (2010, forthcoming), who makes a strong case for reading such texts under the rubric of identity-formation, understanding the book as a narrative that, while taking conquest as its setting, is not essentially about conquest. Cf. also Earl 2009 on *ḥerem*.

In a useful study of "morally difficult passages in the Hebrew Bible," Harry Lesser surveys four different ways in which Jewish tradition has dealt with the problem: (1) judging an act to be wrong (even though faithfully recorded in the narrative), (2) arguing that at the time such an act was not wrong (usually with respect to the patriarchs and various issues surrounding marriage and sexual behavior), (3) contending that in cases of apparent divine punishment there was always a chance to repent or understand the divine justice involved, or (4) concluding that such "incidents are always seen as taking place under special circumstances, and not in any way to be imitated" (2000: 298).[9] In a helpful conclusion, Lesser observes:

> The [Jewish] tradition does not, like the truly fundamentalist tradition, simply bow before the wisdom and justice of God and take the text as defining what is just and sensible. It acknowledges that human commonsense and feelings of justice can be transcended, but takes it that they cannot be utterly wrong and that the justice of God cannot be utterly different from human justice. . . . The complexity of traditional Jewish interpretation arises partly because it accepts both [the rightness of Scripture and the concerns of justice and common sense] . . . , and when faced with scriptural passages that do not seem to meet normal moral requirements endeavours by close study to find an interpretation which will. (2000: 302)

For some, of course, this is merely a capitulation to the desire to safeguard the holy text at all costs against all reasonable inquiry. But setting aside the rhetoric that characterizes so much such discussion, it is at least worth noting that Jewish tradition does not look all that much like a self-protecting discourse interested simply in exonerating the text from harsh edges and pointed ethical challenge.

In a striking article, Diana Lipton has suggested that "the Hebrew Bible itself offers a model for addressing, if not solving, the problem of unpalatable sacred texts" (2003: 139). In one case study she argues that "the very text that seems to us unacceptable for its violent hostility towards outsiders may in fact have been intended to address

---

9. In his third approach, Lesser (2000: 297) includes some sample Jewish strategies for reading 1 Sam. 15.

precisely this form of violent hostility in an earlier text" (2003: 152). Critique of outsiders, in other words, is often fiercely aimed back at Israel itself: in the words of Amos, "You only have I known of all the families of the earth; therefore I will punish you for all your iniquities" (3:2).[10] Other (well-known) points could be made. Thus, clearly, every "problem" text has been variously interpreted down through the centuries, and perhaps it often is not wise to suppose that we have once and for all demonstrated that a biblical text is beyond acceptable limits.[11] Furthermore, most biblical texts speak for some persons and against others, and often the social/political/ecclesial location of the reader is one key to whether a text is experienced as having a life-giving role or as profoundly challenging and unsettling. From this it will follow that many judgments about biblical texts, at any one time, will be true for some readers and not for others.[12] Perhaps all I have succeeded in doing here is showing that more needs to be said on this issue, but I hope also to have shown that there are a good many paths available to the serious reader of a biblical text beyond a choice between "I accept it" and "I reject it."

The Role of Didactic Texts

A fourth point must be added to our list of areas requiring further reflection or exploration. Put simply, it is this: Why narrative? Why has our study of interpretive virtue chosen to work with implicit virtues in narratives, rather than addressing head-on the passages in Scripture that discuss what we might take as the Old Testament categories of virtue? This decision was partly taken for heuristic reasons: narratives

10. In Briggs 2007b: 179–80, I have offered further brief thoughts on the problematic issues raised here.

11. A striking case of thoughtful reinterpretation is found in C. Hays 2005, who looks at Ps. 137 as "an intellectual prank—a resistance technique employed by an oppressed population" (2005: 37). If Hays is right, most commentary on the psalm has missed the joke and taken the offense intended only for the Babylonian oppressors.

12. For example, I think one can never hear too often the words of Miroslav Volf, a theologian himself scarred by the warfare in his native Balkans: "It takes the quiet of a suburban home for the birth of the thesis that human nonviolence corresponds to God's refusal to judge. In a scorched land, soaked in the blood of the innocent, it will invariably die. And as one watches it die, one will do well to reflect about many other pleasant captivities of the liberal mind" (Volf 1996: 304).

actually do unearth quite profound configurations of values, as John
Barton has showed in his various studies on Old Testament ethics,
discussed above on pp. 32–34. Barton has not only explored particular
narratives, such as looking at how a story like Genesis 19 reveals a
network of value judgments about sexuality that are nowhere plainly
set out in the text (1998: 44–53). He has also given good accounts of
how something like the present approach works with Martha Nussbaum's treatments of Aristotle (Barton 2003: 55–64). There he notes
that "narrative prose can be the ideal vehicle for moral reflection. . . .
Literature is important for ethics because literature is as complicated
as life itself, and cannot be decoded or boiled down. Ethical insight
comes from reading it—first sequentially and then reflectively—*not*
from trying to extract a 'message' from it" (2003: 63). In essence, I
follow Barton's approach here because I think it works in practice,
although for reasons set out at length in chapter 6 (above), I have dif-
fered from him in thinking that carefully reading biblical literature
does not require the separating off of theological dimensions to all the
interpretive questions one might ask. Even so, John Barton's account
gives a good answer to the question "Why narrative?" But obviously a
Jewish scholar might point out that the Torah is supposed to set the
agenda. Perhaps, such an interlocutor would say, it is slightly odd to try
to approach the moral vision of the Old Testament by way of chipping
away at specific narratives rather than proceeding front and center
with the great demands of Deuteronomy or the lengthy disquisitions
of the wisdom narratives and poetry. In the end, I think one must try
to do both. At least in Jewish traditions, it is unlikely that in so doing
one would end up with two markedly different moral visions. In this
regard it is instructive to recall the title of Gordon Wenham's book
Story as Torah, which undertakes an analysis of various Old Testament narratives (particularly in Genesis and Judges) for their ethical
value (2000). Wenham's title, and the analysis it heralds, indicate that
one can overplay the significance of the distinction between narrative
and law code, and that, in terms of ethical conclusions, there need
be little problem here.

On one level, therefore, I want to affirm the desirability of starting
with the Torah or wisdom texts just as much as the approach taken in
this book, and I have indeed tried to take some account of the specifics

of didactic texts in each case study. So a further study of our topic in other genres would certainly be welcome, but I remain persuaded by John Barton's (and Gordon Wenham's) point that ethical reflection in narrative mode offers a nuanced picture, one that is actually well suited for the transposition to the task of describing a virtuous reader of the Old Testament. Although there are occasions where reading is the direct topic of discussion in the Old Testament itself (cf. Venema 2004; we shall consider one of them below), they are few and far between: I think that the tangential approach—building up to the notion of the implied reader by considering the virtues they are supposed to appreciate—offers a more fruitful line of approach for our specific task.

Revisiting the "Old Testament"

In the opening chapter we addressed the question of the "Old Testament" as a Christian construction and the difference that pursuing our topic with specific reference to the Old Testament might make to our conclusions. At that point I counseled a wait-and-see approach of assessing what profit might result from our various case studies. A brief word is therefore due in response, but it in fact turns out to be very brief. This is because, in practice, it does not seem that the limitation to Old Testament texts has skewed our project, in the sense either that New Testament perspectives are crying out to counterbalance our specific conclusions or that our reading of Old Testament texts has been misshapen by an agenda alien to these particular texts. This does not amount to a demonstration that there simply is no difference between the moral "visions" of the two Testaments, such that a continuity of emphasis in moral formation could be found across both. However, more modestly, it does indicate that in the relatively central and specific moral concerns that we have addressed (wisdom, humility, and so forth), the differences are not fundamental in nature. Broader questions about discontinuity (alongside continuity) between the two Testaments were broached in chapter 1 and need not be revisited here.

Finally, the various questions considered here do make it clear that the present proposal is modest in various ways. Much more could yet be done with the investigation of the virtues discussed in the preceding chapters, and even with the five cases examined, there would be other narratives to consider and further nuances to add regarding each virtue.[13]

What Is Normative about This Picture? Real Readers of the Old Testament

No blood flows in the veins of implied readers. They are literary-critical constructs, ideal (no pun intended) for getting at the kinds of interpretive judgments required of any reader of a given text. The implied reader of the Old Testament is not a straightforward category, however. For example, does the implied reader of the Old Testament also have a knowledge of the New Testament (presumably this would be a key difference from an implied reader of the Hebrew Bible)? Is such an implied reader addressed in community? Is such a reader supposed to be incapable of attaining to perfect reading—in other words, is the implied reader "sinful" in some sense and thus assumed to be equipped to read the text only by the various graces of the God who summons the reader to the text in the first place?

It is finally time to come to the question of how far all of our discussion relates to real readers of the Old Testament. For the sake of focusing this discussion, let us suppose that we have gotten everything right so far and have accurately constructed a portrait of the character of the implied reader of the Old Testament by way of delineating various key virtues that such a character possesses. What follows?

Another way to put some of the points considered in the first part of this concluding chapter would have been to argue that the real reader needs to judge the desirability of occupying the space of the implied reader: perhaps the real reader wishes to say, in practice, "I am not like Moses," or "The construct is too male," or "Too many problematic passages undermine my ability to trust the ones that seem

13. It would be interesting also to consider whether there would be profit in exploring "interpretive vices" as these are presented in the Old Testament, given that one way in which the Old Testament offers ethical discourse is by describing paths not to be taken. For example, would Psalm 1:1 indicate that a "scoffer" is unlikely to be a wise reader of texts?

to offer more life-giving possibilities." It is one of the ironies of much writing on biblical interpretation that real readers are often simply assumed to be able and willing to step up to the insights of theoretical analyses of biblical texts and embrace them somehow without regard to questions of their character, location, or other influencing factors.[14] Real readers can aspire to imitate the implied reader, but the two categories remain distinct.

On the other hand, real readers cannot be entirely divorced from implied readers either. Though no actual reader of a text is its perfect reader, or model reader, a certain interpretive empathy is required for the real reader even to understand what sorts of characteristics they may or may not be refusing to take on board. In one of the rare discussions of precisely this issue, Wayne Booth points out that one can only "feel" or "sense" the emotions of a text's narrative by entering into its world and grasping what is at stake for its characters (1988: 204–5). On one level, we can always remind ourselves that "it's only a movie," as he puts it, but to watch the entire movie while saying just that is really not to watch the movie at all. As Booth sees it, the conclusion, at least with regard to the specific point about how texts inculcate desires or longed-for rewards, is that "the distinction between what the implied reader does and what the flesh-and-blood reader does becomes blurred" (1988: 205). This blurring does not render the two categories identical, but it does suggest that a whole range of judgments will be in play with respect to the real reading of any particular text. Such a conclusion will not be a surprise if our earlier discussion of "problem texts" was on the right lines: real readers are operating along a whole spectrum of possibilities with regard to "interpretive empathy" with the text. Real readers are invited to ponder carefully a good many values and characteristics in the midst of whatever general tendencies lead them to prefer either "accepting" or "rejecting" a given narrative.

Real readers, then, still have a choice. They can say that while they understand the "offer" of the text (assuming that some exercise of interpretive empathy has allowed them to see it for what it is), they are not themselves interested in aspiring to be the kind of person such

---

14. The empirical study of real (i.e., nonprofessional) readers is still somewhat in its infancy, but for stimulating initial thoughts, see Pattison, M. Cooling, and T. Cooling (2007); Village (2007); and Powell 2001: 172–84, also 28–56 (expanded in Powell 2007).

an implied reader models. Real readers do this all the time with large numbers of texts, and a good number of real readers do it with the biblical text too. The reasons one might give for why a real reader should *not* take this path of unwillingness to be "summoned" by the biblical text relate, once again, to the various self-involving questions of one's stance and commitment with respect to the *Sache* of the text: the world described as God's creation, and God as the active participant in all human affairs as understood in the Jewish and Christian traditions. To real readers wanting to make such commitments, the portrait of the implied (or model) reader of the Old Testament constructed in this way will be of more than passing interest. It will indicate the kind of character that, it is supposed, will allow the reader best to understand and grasp the point(s) of the biblical texts in front of them.

This argument does not run all one way or the other. As we were careful to explore in the opening chapter, Scripture is not a closed book to those not yet virtuous enough to behold in it what is written. Such a critique is often aimed at virtue-oriented approaches to biblical interpretation. It is suggested that they seem to require the work of moral formation to take place in the interpreter as a self-contained project, now conceived of as a kind of entrance requirement to the task of reading the Bible in the first place. Clearly this is not right. But on the other hand, neither is it right to think that one starts blankly from the text, devoid of concerns about what manner of approach will best allow the reader to grasp the reality of what is going on in the text, as if virtues were to be pasted onto a tabula rasa of disinterested (disembodied?) inquiry. The loving reader is freshly caught by the notion of humility. The humble reader notices the challenge to trust. The trusting reader follows the summoning of the text. The summoned reader inspects the value judgments implicit in their attempts at offering wise discernment. From one virtue to another, in no necessary or particular order, the *virtuous reader* is led along a path of discipleship, toward a deeper and richer notion of what it means to live one's life for the God of Abraham, Isaac, and Jacob, the God of Jesus Christ, as well as toward a deeper and richer notion of what it means to practice reading as an act of discipleship.

In the real world, with real readers, such progress is by no means straightforward. Wise readers get texts wrong. Wise Christians fall into sin. There are no programs or safeguards by which virtue guarantees "results," whether in discipleship or hermeneutics. Neither can insights into texts (or any displays of virtue) come only from those advancing in the virtuous life. For example, in the case of nineteenth- and twentieth-century biblical scholarship, it is sad but true that many notable insights have come from scholars whose views, political and otherwise, could be fairly characterized as "anti-Semitic."[15] There is no point in trying to argue for some generalized maxim such as "only wise people make good readers" or vice versa, but equally this does not mean that the only alternative is that virtue is irrelevant. In chapter 1 we noted Stephen Fowl's striking summary statement: "Given that Christians are called to interpret Scripture as part of their ongoing journey into ever-deeper communion with God, it is not surprising that those who have grown and advanced in virtue will tend to be masterful interpreters of Scripture" (2005: 838). There we pointed out that "caveats and variables should not obscure the general point." In earlier chapters we have considered in effect the "objection of the academy" to this quote: that it appears to be perfectly possible to get on with biblical interpretation without having any interest in "ever-deeper communion with God," and we have suggested some of the self-involving ways in which the practices of interpretation work. But from the other end of the spectrum might come a quite different and typically Lutheran objection to this quote: that not only is there no way in practice to correlate the virtuous life and the good interpreting of texts but that to do so confuses moral categories where the only proper source of human insight must be the free and unmerited grace and gift of God. But the kinds of virtues we have explored in the present book have come back time and again to theocentric ways of conceiving of such notions as humility and wisdom, as well as the notion of receptivity to divine summons. This must at the very least problematize such a separation between human endeavor and divine initiative. As we saw with Isaiah, he remained Isaiah, the preacher and prophet, in and

---

15. On the anti-Semitism often identified in Wellhausen's writing, note Silberman 1983 and the cautious analysis of John Barton 1995: 327, who thinks the case can be overplayed but that it is nevertheless "not to be ignored." The celebrated case of Kittel's involvement in Nazism alongside his work as a New Testament lexicographer is charted with care in Meeks 2004. See also the sobering survey of Steinweis 2006: esp. 64–91 (66–76 on Kittel).

with and under the working out of the divine summons on his life
and work. The real reader who wishes to read Scripture will not find
it easy to correlate their progress along the path of the moral life with
their handling of the text; but in various and perhaps unpredictable
ways, the one who is engaging with God in the mysteries of holiness,
justice, forgiveness, and wisdom will find that their meditations on
texts witnessing to these realities are drawn deeper and further than
they would previously have had the capacity to see.

If this is a slightly individualistic way of putting the point, it is
perhaps worth adding that as readers progress toward new insights,
they will in general arrive at a point already occupied by others. Reading in community, or indeed *reading in communion*, will remain a
key to grasping the resonances and interconnections of many of the
ways in which the virtuous life is to be lived, and lived with others.
Real readers of the Old Testament will often read from within the
church or the synagogue, structures that serve in their own ways as
"plausibility structures" for encouraging ways of reading that foreground questions of moral formation and the appropriation of the
text for today.[16] The virtuous life is not lived by native (interpretive)
wit or individual effort alone.

Hermeneutics as a Virtuous Reader: "I Perceived in the Books . . ."

If the argument of this book has been anywhere near right, then the
concerns of virtue ethics are germane to the tasks of biblical interpretation, and in particular to theological understandings of those
tasks. The interpretation of biblical texts is not thereby simplified
down to some sort of "virtue method" that can now be "applied."
Rather, the promise is held out that the virtuous reader will bear
"hermeneutical fruit" in due season. This is the image of Psalm 1:
the reader who meditates on Torah day and night will be like a tree
planted by streams of water, yielding its fruit in season. The point is
not that this verse of Torah or that command can be suddenly seen

16. This notion is explored by, among others, Newbigin 1989: 222–33, in a chapter titled
"The Congregation as Hermeneutic for the Gospel."

to "apply" to a particular point at issue in the present day, but rather that the reader has been shaped, from the inside out, to be the kind of person who knows what to do in the present situation. The link between the text upon which they meditated, and the action they then performed, does not proceed via some "principle" or method of application of the text, but by way of the transformed character of the one doing the reading and meditating. Text and action are bound together, we might say, in the reader.

As noted above, the Old Testament does not often explicitly consider moments of reading the "biblical" (or "sacred") text.[17] There are obvious reasons for this. For one thing, the complex processes of canon collection and formation suggest that it would have been uncommon for there to be a prominent set of sacred texts available for characters within Old Testament narratives to read (i.e., without anachronism). Furthermore, for us as interpreters, these considerations make it hard to pinpoint any particular moment in any text when we could say for sure what sorts of texts might have been available to the writer (or characters in the narrative) to have before them. One exception to this vast sea of indeterminacy is the book of Daniel, without a doubt (one of) the latest canonical texts in the Old Testament. By the time the book of Daniel is written, some collection of sacred books clearly already existed, though for our purposes it is not important to know what collection exactly. All we need to assume is that some notion of authority would have attached to some nascent collection of texts, still in the process of compilation, as it would doubtless have been.

Thus in Daniel 9 we find a scene that is unusual for an Old Testament text: a man reading Scripture. On the one hand, it is true that the second-century BC book of Daniel portrays here a figure of Daniel who, in one sense, is not a "real reader," since he is himself a literary construct, a figure in the book's narrative. But the point is simply that the book of Daniel offers to its own readers this picture of reading Scripture. When we examine this scene, we find in miniature many of the concerns of the present book.

17. Though see Venema 2004. There is of course much of interest to say about the many and various ways in which particular Old Testament texts interact with other texts, in intertextual or "inner-biblical" resonance (cf. Fishbane 1985), but that is a different matter.

Daniel is reading the sacred texts and through them is seeing something about his present circumstances: "I, Daniel, perceived in the books the number of years that, according to the word of Yhwh to the prophet Jeremiah, must be fulfilled for the devastation of Jerusalem, namely, seventy years" (Dan. 9:2). The reference to seventy years clearly indicates that Daniel has been reading Jeremiah 25:11–12 (and perhaps 29:10), and the subsequent vision from Gabriel in 9:20–27 makes it clear that it is the recalculation of how such a figure relates to the end of exile and contemporary events that is the point at issue. A simple point may be made about this prototypical example of a man of God reading the holy books: we notice that Daniel is driven to prayer and confession by his "perceiving in the books" the way in which the word of Yhwh relates to his own situation.

Significantly, Daniel has been portrayed throughout the book as a wise man: humbling himself in prayer, trusting God in the face of overwhelming odds (in the lions' den, and equally as Israel is among the beasts in Dan. 7), and always obedient to the divine summons. Daniel's life is implicitly a model for any attentive reader.[18] Without stretching a point, one might suggest that here at the very (chronological) end of the Old Testament, Daniel comes in as a virtuous reader: the final acts of Israel's scriptural narrative played out in ways that already model the key point that the right sort of person will be able to "perceive in the books" what needs to be seen. The book of Daniel does not tell us about his "hermeneutic," but it tells a good deal about his character, and perhaps that is significant. To understand Scripture, we might say, consider the person of Daniel and what kinds of virtue he exemplified.

This is at best a hint, but it is a hint at the end of many long scriptural texts that have said very little at all about how to interpret the sacred texts, so perhaps we should not pass over it too lightly. The Scriptures of Israel invite humble, wise, trusting, and loving interpreters to be summoned to attend to their subject matter. Such virtuous readers may yet bear fruit in due season.

---

18. Humphreys (1973) called it "a life-style for diaspora" in his notable analysis of the setting and function of the court tales in Dan. 1–6, though he complicates this thesis by arguing that this lifestyle is undercut by linking these tales to the visions in the second half of the book.

BIBLIOGRAPHY

Adam, A. K. M., et al.
2006   *Reading Scripture with the Church: Toward a Hermeneutic for Theological Interpretation.* Grand Rapids: Baker Academic.

Adler, Mortimer J., and Charles van Doren
1972   *How to Read a Book: The Classic Guide to Intelligent Reading.* 1940. Rev. and updated ed. New York: Simon & Schuster.

Allen, Charles W.
1989   "The Primacy of *Phronēsis*: A Proposal for Avoiding Frustrating Tendencies in Our Conceptions of Rationality." *Journal of Religion* 69.3:359–74.

Arnold, Duane W. H., and Pamela Bright, eds.
1995   *De doctrina christiana: A Classic of Western Culture.* Notre Dame, IN: University of Notre Dame Press.

Baetzhold, Howard G., and Joseph B. McCullough, eds.
1995   *The Bible according to Mark Twain: Irreverent Writings on Eden, Heaven, and the Flood by America's Master Satirist.* New York: Touchstone.

Bailey, Randall C.
1990   *David in Love and War: The Pursuit of Power in 2 Samuel 10–12.* Journal for the Study of the Old Testament: Supplement Series 75. Sheffield: JSOT Press.

Barber, Bernard
  1983   *The Logic and Limits of Trust*. New Brunswick, NJ: Rutgers
          University Press.
Barclay, John M. G.
  1996   *Jews in the Mediterranean Diaspora: From Alexander to
          Trajan (323 BCE–117 CE)*. Edinburgh: T&T Clark.
Barr, James
  1961   *The Semantics of Biblical Language*. Oxford: Oxford
          University Press.
  1987   "Words for Love in Biblical Greek." Pages 3–18 in *The Glory
          of Christ in the New Testament: Studies in Christology in
          Memory of George Bradford Caird*. Edited by L. D. Hurst and
          N. T. Wright. Oxford: Clarendon.
Barth, Karl
  1936   *The Doctrine of the Word of God*. Translated by G. T.
          Thomson. Vol. 1.1 of *Church Dogmatics*. Edinburgh: T&T
          Clark.
  1963   *Evangelical Theology: An Introduction*. London: Weidenfeld
          & Nicolson.
Bartholomew, Craig G., et al., eds.
  2000   *Renewing Biblical Interpretation*. Scripture and
          Hermeneutics Series 1. Grand Rapids: Zondervan; Carlisle,
          UK: Paternoster.
  2000–   Scripture and Hermeneutics Series. 8 vols. Grand Rapids:
    2007 Zondervan; Carlisle and Milton Keynes, UK: Paternoster.
  2002   *A Royal Priesthood? The Use of the Bible Ethically and
          Politically; A Dialogue with Oliver O'Donovan*. Scripture and
          Hermeneutics Series 3. Grand Rapids: Zondervan; Carlisle,
          UK: Paternoster.
  2004   *Out of Egypt: Biblical Theology and Biblical Interpretation*.
          Scripture and Hermeneutics Series 5. Grand Rapids:
          Zondervan; Milton Keynes, UK: Paternoster.
Barton, John
  1986   *Oracles of God: Perceptions of Ancient Prophecy in Israel
          after the Exile*. London: Darton, Longman & Todd.
  1995   "Wellhausen's *Prolegomena to the History of Israel*:
          Influences and Effects." Pages 316–29 in *Text and Experience:
          Towards a Cultural Exegesis of the Bible*. Edited by Daniel
          Smith-Christopher. Biblical Seminar 35. Sheffield: Sheffield
          Academic Press.
  1998   *Ethics and the Old Testament*. London: SCM Press.

2003 *Understanding Old Testament Ethics: Approaches and Explanations*. Louisville: Westminster John Knox.

Bauckham, Richard
1997 "The Book of Ruth and the Possibility of a Feminist Canonical Hermeneutic." *Biblical Interpretation* 5.1:29–45.
2003 *Bible and Mission: Christian Witness in a Postmodern World*. Grand Rapids: Baker Academic; Milton Keynes, UK: Paternoster.
2004 "Biblical Theology and the Problems of Monotheism." Pages 188–232 in *Out of Egypt: Biblical Theology and Biblical Interpretation*. Edited by Craig Bartholomew et al. Scripture and Hermeneutics Series 5. Grand Rapids: Zondervan; Milton Keynes, UK: Paternoster.

Bauder, W., and H.-H. Esser
1976 "Humility." Pages 256–64 in vol. 2 of *New International Dictionary of New Testament Theology*. Edited by Colin Brown. Grand Rapids: Zondervan; Carlisle, UK: Paternoster.

BDB
A Hebrew and English Lexicon of the Old Testament. By Francis Brown, S. R. Driver, and Charles A. Briggs. Oxford: Clarendon, 1907.

Beale, G. K.
1991 "Isaiah VI 9–13: A Retributive Taunt against Idolatry." *Vetus Testamentum* 41.3:257–78.

Beale, G. K., and D. A. Carson, eds.
2007 *Commentary on the New Testament Use of the Old Testament*. Grand Rapids: Baker Academic; Nottingham, UK: Apollos.

Beattie, D. R. G.
1977 *Jewish Exegesis of the Book of Ruth*. Journal for the Study of the Old Testament: Supplement Series 2. Sheffield: JSOT Press.

Bechtel, Lynn
1993 "Rethinking the Interpretation of Genesis 2.4b–3.24." Pages 77–117 in *A Feminist Companion to Genesis*. Edited by Athalya Brenner. Feminist Companion to the Bible 2. Sheffield: Sheffield Academic Press.

Becking, Bob
2003 "Chronology: A Skeleton without Flesh? Sennacherib's Campaign as a Case-Study." Pages 46–72 in *"Like a Bird in a Cage": The Invasion of Sennacherib in 701 BCE*. Edited by

Lester L. Grabbe. Journal for the Study of the Old Testament: Supplement Series 363. European Seminar in Historical Methodology 4. London: Sheffield Academic Press.

Ben Zvi, Ehud
1990   "Who Wrote the Speech of Rabshakeh and When?" *Journal of Biblical Literature* 109.1:79–92.

Bennington, Geoffrey, and Jacques Derrida
1993   *Jacques Derrida.* Translated by Geoffrey Bennington. Chicago: University of Chicago Press.

Beuken, W. A. M.
1989   "No Wise King without a Wise Woman (I Kings III 16–28)." Pages 1–10 in *New Avenues in the Study of the Old Testament: A Collection of Old Testament Studies Published on the Occasion of the Fiftieth Anniversary of the Oudtestamentisch Werkgezelschap and the Retirement of Prof. Dr. M. J. Mulder.* Edited by A. S. van der Woude. Oudtestamentische Studiën 25. Leiden: Brill.

Bird, Phyllis A.
1997   "The Harlot as Heroine: Narrative Art and Social Presupposition in Three Old Testament Texts." Pages 197–218 in *Missing Persons and Mistaken Identity: Women and Gender in Ancient Israel.* By Phyllis A. Bird. Overtures to Biblical Theology. Minneapolis: Fortress. Originally published in *Semeia* 46:119–39.

Black, C. Clifton
2002   "Exegesis as Prayer." *Princeton Seminary Bulletin* 23.2:131–45.

Blenkinsopp, Joseph
2006   *Opening the Sealed Book: Interpretations of the Book of Isaiah in Late Antiquity.* Grand Rapids: Eerdmans.

Bockmuehl, Markus
2003   "Reason, Wisdom and the Implied Disciple of Scripture." Pages 53–68 in *Reading Texts, Seeking Wisdom: Scripture and Theology.* Edited by David F. Ford and Graham Stanton. London: SCM Press.
2006   *Seeing the Word: Refocusing New Testament Study.* Studies in Theological Interpretation. Grand Rapids: Baker Academic.

Boer, Roland
1999   "Culture, Ethics and Identity in Reading Ruth: A Response to Donaldson, Dube, McKinlay and Brenner." Pages 163–70 in

Ruth and Esther: A Feminist Companion to the Bible. Edited by Athalya Brenner. Feminist Companion to the Bible, 2nd ser., 3. Sheffield: Sheffield Academic Press.

Booth, Wayne C.
1961   *The Rhetoric of Fiction*. Chicago: University of Chicago Press.
1983   *The Rhetoric of Fiction*. 2nd ed. London: Penguin Books.
1988   *The Company We Keep: An Ethics of Fiction*. Berkeley: University of California Press.

Bostock, David
2006   *A Portrayal of Trust: The Theme of Faith in the Hezekiah Narratives*. Paternoster Biblical Monographs. Milton Keynes, UK: Paternoster.

Boswell, James
1979   *The Life of Johnson*. 1791. Repr. London: Penguin.

Botha, P. J.
2000   "'No King Like Him . . .': Royal Etiquette according to the Deuteronomistic Historian." Pages 36–49 in *Past, Present, Future: The Deuteronomistic History and the Prophets*. Edited by Johannes C. de Moor and Harry F. van Rooy. Oudtestamentische Studiën 44. Leiden: Brill.

Bowald, Mark Alan
2007   *Rendering the Word in Theological Hermeneutics: Mapping Divine and Human Agency*. Aldershot: Ashgate.

Boyle, John F.
1995   "St. Thomas Aquinas and Sacred Scripture." *Pro ecclesia* 4.1:92–104.

Boyle, Nicholas
2004   *Sacred and Secular Scriptures: A Catholic Approach to Literature*. London: Darton, Longman & Todd.

Brawley, Robert L., ed.
2007   *Character Ethics and the New Testament: Moral Dimensions of Scripture*. Louisville: Westminster John Knox.

Brenner, Athalya, ed.
1994   *A Feminist Companion to Exodus to Deuteronomy*. Feminist Companion to the Bible 6. Sheffield: Sheffield Academic Press.
1999   *Ruth and Esther: A Feminist Companion to the Bible*. Feminist Companion to the Bible, 2nd ser., 3. Sheffield: Sheffield Academic Press.
2000   *Exodus to Deuteronomy: A Feminist Companion to the Bible*. Feminist Companion to the Bible, 2nd ser., 5. Sheffield: Sheffield Academic Press.

Brichto, Herbert Chanan
  1992   *Toward a Grammar of Biblical Poetics: Tales of the Prophets.*
          New York: Oxford University Press.

Briggs, Richard S.
  2001   *Words in Action: Speech Act Theory and Biblical
          Interpretation.* Edinburgh: T&T Clark.
  2003   *Reading the Bible Wisely.* London: SPCK; Grand Rapids:
          Baker Academic.
  2006a   "What Does Hermeneutics Have to Do with Biblical
          Interpretation?" *Heythrop Journal* 47.1:55–74.
  2006b   *One God among Many?* Grove Biblical Series B42.
          Cambridge: Grove Books.
  2007a   "Perspectives on Scripture: Its Status and Purpose; A Review
          Article." *Heythrop Journal* 48.2:267–74.
  2007b   "The Role of the Bible in Formation and Transformation: A
          Hermeneutical and Theological Analysis." *Anvil* 24.3:167–82.
  2008   "Speech-Act Theory." Pages 75–110 in *Words and the Word:
          Explorations in Biblical Interpretation and Literary Theory.*
          Edited by David G. Firth and Jamie A. Grant. Nottingham,
          UK: Apollos.
  2009a   "Juniper Trees and Pistachio Nuts: Trust, Suspicion and
          Biblical Interpretation." *Theology* 112:353–63.
  2009b   "Reading the *Soṭah* Text (Numbers 5:11–31): Holiness and
          a Hermeneutic Fit for Suspicion." *Biblical Interpretation*
          17:288–319.

Bright, John
  1960   *A History of Israel.* London: SCM Press.

Bronner, Leila Leah
  1993   "A Thematic Approach to Ruth in Rabbinic Literature." Pages
          146–69 in *A Feminist Companion to Ruth.* Edited by Athalya
          Brenner. Feminist Companion to the Bible 3. Sheffield:
          Sheffield Academic Press.

Brown, Francis. *See* BDB

Brown, Jeannine K.
  2007   *Scripture as Communication: Introducing Biblical
          Hermeneutics.* Grand Rapids: Baker Academic.

Brown, William P.
  1996   *Character in Crisis: A Fresh Approach to the Wisdom
          Literature of the Old Testament.* Grand Rapids: Eerdmans.

Brown, William P., ed.
  2002   *Character and Scripture: Moral Formation, Community, and
          Biblical Interpretation.* Grand Rapids: Eerdmans.

Brueggemann, Walter

1980   "Psalms and the Life of Faith: A Suggested Typology of
        Function." *Journal for the Study of the Old Testament*
        17:3–32.

1997   *Theology of the Old Testament: Testimony, Dispute,
        Advocacy.* Minneapolis: Fortress.

1998   *Isaiah 1–39.* Westminster Bible Companion. Louisville:
        Westminster John Knox.

2000   *1 and 2 Kings.* Smyth & Helwys Bible Commentary 8.
        Macon, GA: Smyth & Helwys.

2001   "A Brief Moment for a One-Person Remnant (2 Kings 5:2–3)."
        Biblical Theology Bulletin 31:53–59.

2002   "Miriam." Pages 132–33 in *Reverberations of Faith: A
        Theological Handbook of the Old Testament.* By Walter
        Brueggemann. Louisville: Westminster John Knox.

2005   *Solomon: Israel's Ironic Icon of Human Achievement.*
        Columbia: University of South Carolina Press.

2007   "2 Kings 5: Two Evangelists and a Saved Subject." *Missiology*
        35.3:263–72.

Burnett, Richard E.

2001   *Karl Barth's Theological Exegesis: The Hermeneutical
        Principles of the "Römerbrief" Period.* Tübingen: Mohr
        Siebeck.

Bush, Frederic

1996   *Ruth and Esther.* Word Biblical Commentary 9. Nashville:
        Nelson.

Byron, Lord (George Gordon)

1812   "The Destruction of Sennacherib." Online: http://
        englishhistory.net/byron/poems/destruct.html.

Cahill, Lisa Sowle

2002   "Christian Character, Biblical Community, and Human
        Values." Pages 3–17 in *Character and Scripture: Moral
        Formation, Community, and Biblical Interpretation.* Edited
        by William P. Brown. Grand Rapids: Eerdmans.

Calvin, John

1855   *Commentary on the Four Last Books of Moses Arranged in
        a Harmony.* Translated by Charles William Bingham. Vol. 4.
        Edinburgh: Calvin Translation Society. Originally published
        in 1563.

Camp, Claudia V.

2000   *Wise, Strange and Holy: The Strange Woman and the Making
        of the Bible.* Gender, Culture, Theory 9. Journal for the Study

of the Old Testament: Supplement Series 320. Sheffield: Sheffield Academic Press.

Candler, Peter M., Jr.
2006   *Theology, Rhetoric, Manuduction, or Reading Scripture Together on the Path to God.* Radical Traditions. Grand Rapids: Eerdmans.

Carr, David McLain
1991   *From D to Q: A Study of Early Jewish Interpretations of Solomon's Dream at Gibeon.* Society of Biblical Literature Monograph Series 44. Atlanta: Scholars Press.

Carroll R. [Rodas], M. Daniel
2001   "Seeking the Virtues among the Prophets: The Book of Amos as a Test Case." *Ex auditu* 17:77–96.
2007   "'He Has Told You What Is Good': Moral Formation in Micah." Pages 103–18 in *Character Ethics and the Old Testament: Moral Dimensions of Scripture.* Edited by M. Daniel Carroll R. and Jacqueline E. Lapsley. Louisville: Westminster John Knox.

Carroll R. [Rodas], M. Daniel, and Jacqueline E. Lapsley, eds.
2007   *Character Ethics and the Old Testament: Moral Dimensions of Scripture.* Louisville: Westminster John Knox.

Carroll, Robert P.
1997   "Blindsight and the Vision Thing: Blindness and Insight in the Book of Isaiah." Pages 79–93 in *Writing and Reading the Scroll of Isaiah: Studies of an Interpretative Tradition.* Edited by Craig C. Broyles and Craig A. Evans. Supplements to Vetus Testamentum 70. Formation and Interpretation of Old Testament Literature 1. Leiden: Brill.

Cary, Phillip
2000   "Study as Love: Augustinian Vision and Catholic Education." Pages 55–80 in *Augustine and Liberal Education.* Edited by Kim Paffenroth and Kevin L. Hughes. Aldershot: Ashgate.

Chapman, Stephen B.
2000   *The Law and the Prophets.* Forschungen zum Alten Testament 27. Tübingen: Mohr Siebeck.

Charles, J. Daryl
1997   *Virtue amidst Vice: The Catalog of Virtues in 2 Peter 1.* Journal for the Study of the New Testament: Supplement Series 150. Sheffield: Sheffield Academic Press.
2002   "The Function of Moral Typology in 2 Peter." Pages 331–43 in *Character and Scripture: Moral Formation, Community,*

and *Biblical Interpretation*. Edited by William P. Brown. Grand Rapids: Eerdmans.

Chatman, Seymour
1978   *Story and Discourse: Narrative Structure in Fiction and Film.* Ithaca, NY: Cornell University Press.

Childs, Brevard S.
1967   *Isaiah and the Assyrian Crisis.* Studies in Biblical Theology 2.3. London: SCM Press.
2001   *Isaiah.* Old Testament Library. Louisville: Westminster John Knox.

Clark, Gordon R.
1993   *The Word "Ḥesed" in the Hebrew Bible.* Journal for the Study of the Old Testament: Supplement Series 157. Sheffield: JSOT Press.

Clark, Kenneth
1969   *Civilisation: A Personal View.* London: BBC and John Murray.

Clines, David J. A.
1990   *What Does Eve Do to Help? And Other Readerly Questions to the Old Testament.* Journal for the Study of the Old Testament: Supplement Series 94. Sheffield: JSOT Press.

Clines, David J. A., David M. Gunn, and Alan J. Hauser, eds.
1982   *Art and Meaning: Rhetoric in Biblical Literature.* Journal for the Study of the Old Testament: Supplement Series 19. Sheffield: JSOT Press.

Coats, George W.
1988   *Moses: Heroic Man, Man of God.* Journal for the Study of the Old Testament: Supplement Series 57. Sheffield: JSOT Press.
1993   "Humility and Honor: A Moses Legend in Numbers 12." Pages 88–98 in *The Moses Tradition.* Journal for the Study of the Old Testament: Supplement Series 161. Sheffield: JSOT Press. Originally pages 97–107 in *Art and Meaning: Rhetoric in Biblical Literature.* Edited by David J. A. Clines, David M. Gunn, and Alan J. Hauser. Journal for the Study of the Old Testament: Supplement Series 19. Sheffield: JSOT Press, 1982.

Cochran, Elizabeth Agnew
2008   "Jesus Christ and the Cardinal Virtues: A Response to Monika Hellwig." *Theology Today* 65:81–94.

Cogan, Mordechai
2000   "Sennacherib's Siege of Jerusalem." Pages 302–3 in *Monumental Inscriptions from the Biblical World.* Edited and

translated by W. W. Hallo and K. L. Younger. Vol. 2 of *The Context of Scripture*. Leiden: Brill.

Cogan, Mordechai, and Hayim Tadmor
1988   *II Kings: A New Translation with Introduction and Commentary*. Anchor Bible 11. New York: Doubleday.

Conrad, Edgar W.
1991   *Reading Isaiah*. Overtures to Biblical Theology. Minneapolis: Fortress.
1992   "Heard but Not Seen: The Representation of 'Books' in the Old Testament." *Journal for the Study of the Old Testament* 54:45–59.
1996   "Prophet, Redactor and Audience: Reforming the Notion of Isaiah's Formation." Pages 306–26 in *New Visions of Isaiah*. Edited by Roy F. Melugin and Marvin A. Sweeney. Journal for the Study of the Old Testament: Supplement Series 214. Sheffield: Sheffield Academic Press.
2003   *Reading the Latter Prophets: Towards a New Canonical Criticism*. Journal for the Study of the Old Testament: Supplement Series 376. London: T&T Clark.

Cosgrove, Charles H.
2004   "Toward a Postmodern *Hermeneutica Sacra*: Guiding Considerations in Choosing between Competing Plausible Interpretations of Scripture." Pages 39–61 in *The Meanings We Choose: Hermeneutical Ethics, Indeterminacy and the Conflict of Interpretations*. Edited by Charles H. Cosgrove. Journal for the Study of the Old Testament: Supplement Series 411. London: T&T Clark.

Cross, Frank Moore
1973   *Canaanite Myth and Hebrew Epic: Essays in the History of the Religion of Israel*. Cambridge, MA: Harvard University Press.

Davies, Andrew
2000   *Double Standards in Isaiah: Re-evaluating Prophetic Ethics and Divine Justice*. Biblical Interpretation Series 46. Leiden: Brill.

Davies, Eryl W.
1995   *Numbers*. New Century Bible. Grand Rapids: Eerdmans.

Davis, Ellen
2000   *Proverbs, Ecclesiastes, and the Song of Songs*. Westminster Bible Companion. Louisville: Westminster John Knox.
2001   *Getting Involved with God: Rediscovering the Old Testament*. Cambridge, MA: Cowley.

2002   "Preserving Virtues: Renewing the Tradition of the Sages."
        Pages 183–201 in *Character and Scripture: Moral Formation,
        Community, and Biblical Interpretation.* Edited by William P.
        Brown. Grand Rapids: Eerdmans.

Davis, Ellen F., and Richard B. Hays, eds.
2003   *The Art of Reading Scripture.* Grand Rapids: Eerdmans.

Davis, Mac
1980   "It's Hard to Be Humble." From *It's Hard to Be Humble.* By
        Mac Davis. Casablanca Records.

Dawes, Stephen B.
1988   "Walking Humbly: Micah 6.8 Revisited." *Scottish Journal of
        Theology* 41:331–39.
1990   "Numbers 12.3: What Was Special about Moses?" *Bible
        Translator* 41.3:336–40.
1991a   "'Ănāwâ in Translation and Tradition." *Vetus Testamentum*
        41.1:38–48.
1991b   "Humility: Whence This Strange Notion?" *Expository Times*
        103.3:72–75.

D'Costa, Gavin
2001   "Other Faiths and Christian Ethics." Pages 154–67 in *The
        Cambridge Companion to Christian Ethics.* Edited by Robin
        Gill. Cambridge: Cambridge University Press.

DeSilva, David A.
1998   *4 Maccabees.* Guides to Apocrypha and Pseudepigrapha.
        Sheffield: Sheffield Academic Press.

De Vries, Simon J.
1985   *1 Kings.* Word Biblical Commentary 12. Waco: Word.

Dickens, Charles
1966   *David Copperfield.* 1849–50. Repr. London: Penguin.

Dickson, John P., and Brian S. Rosner
2004   "Humility as a Social Virtue in the Hebrew Bible?" *Vetus
        Testamentum* 54.4:459–79.

Donaldson, Laura E.
1999   "The Sign of Orpah: Reading Ruth through Native Eyes."
        Pages 130–44 in *Ruth and Esther: A Feminist Companion to
        the Bible.* Edited by Athalya Brenner. Feminist Companion to
        the Bible, 2nd ser., 3. Sheffield: Sheffield Academic Press.

DQVirtGen
        "On the Virtues in General: Thirteen Articles." In *Disputed
        Questions on the Virtues.* By Thomas Aquinas. Edited by
        E. M. Atkins and T. Williams. Translated by E. M. Atkins.

Cambridge Texts in the History of Philosophy. Cambridge: Cambridge University Press, 2005.

Dumont, Charles
1999   *Praying the Word of God: The Use of "Lectio Divina."* Oxford: SLG Press.

Eagleton, Terry
1986   *Against the Grain: Essays 1975–1985.* London: Verso.
2003   *After Theory.* London: Penguin.

Earl, Douglas S.
2009   "The Christian Significance of Deuteronomy 7." *Journal of Theological Interpretation* 3.1:41–62.
2010   *Reading Joshua as Christian Scripture.* Journal of Theological Interpretation: Supplement Series. Winona Lake, IN: Eisenbrauns.

Eco, Umberto
1992   *Interpretation and Overinterpretation.* Edited by Stefan Collini. Cambridge: Cambridge University Press.

Edgerton, W. Dow
1992   *The Passion of Interpretation.* Literary Currents in Biblical Interpretation. Louisville: Westminster John Knox.

Effa, Allan L.
2007   "Prophet, Kings, Servants, and Lepers: A Missiological Reading of an Ancient Drama." *Missiology* 35.3:305–13.

Ellul, Jacques
1972   *The Politics of God and the Politics of Man.* Translated by Geoffrey W. Bromiley. Grand Rapids: Eerdmans.

Emerton, J. A.
1982   "The Translation and Interpretation of Isaiah vi.13." Pages 85–118 in *Interpreting the Hebrew Bible: Essays in Honour of E. I. J. Rosenthal.* Edited by J. A. Emerton and Stefan C. Reif. Cambridge: Cambridge University Press.

Eslinger, Lyle
1989   *Into the Hands of the Living God.* Journal for the Study of the Old Testament: Supplement Series 84. Bible and Literature 24. Sheffield: Almond.

Evans, Craig A.
1989   *To See and Not Perceive: Isaiah 6.9–10 in Early Jewish and Christian Interpretation.* Journal for the Study of the Old Testament: Supplement Series 64. Sheffield: JSOT Press.
1997   "From Gospel to Gospel. The Function of Isaiah in the New Testament." Pages 651–91 in *Writing and Reading the Scroll*

of Isaiah: Studies of an Interpretative Tradition. Edited by Craig C. Broyles and Craig A. Evans. Supplements to Vetus Testamentum 70. Formation and Interpretation of Old Testament Literature 1. Leiden: Brill.

Evans, Craig A., and James A. Sanders
1993   Luke and Scripture: The Function of Sacred Tradition in Luke-Acts. Minneapolis: Fortress.

Exum, J. Cheryl
1996   Plotted, Shot and Painted: Cultural Representations of Biblical Women. Journal for the Study of the Old Testament: Supplement Series 215. Gender, Culture, Theory 3. Sheffield: Sheffield Academic Press.

Fairweather, Abrol, and Linda Zagzebski, eds.
2001   Virtue Epistemology: Essays on Epistemic Virtue and Responsibility. Oxford: Oxford University Press.

Farrar, Frederic W.
1886   History of Interpretation. London: MacMillan.

Felder, Cain Hope
1991   "Race, Racism, and the Biblical Narratives." Pages 127–45 in Stony the Road We Trod: African American Biblical Interpretation. Edited by Cain Hope Felder. Minneapolis: Fortress.

Fewell, Danna Nolan
1986   "Sennacherib's Defeat: Words at War in 2 Kings 18.13–19.37." Journal for the Study of the Old Testament 34:79–90.

Fewell, Danna Nolan, and David Gunn
1990   Compromising Redemption: Relating Characters in the Book of Ruth. Literary Currents in Biblical Interpretation. Louisville: Westminster John Knox.

Fidler, Ruth
1994   "Problems of Propaganda: On King Solomon's Visit to Gibeon." Pages *31–*38 in Proceedings of the Eleventh World Congress of Jewish Studies, Div. A, The Bible and Its World. Jerusalem: World Union of Jewish Studies.
2005   "Halomot ha-shav yedaberu"? . . . ["Dreams Speak Falsely?" Dream Theophanies in the Bible; Their Place in Ancient Israelite Faith and Traditions.] Jerusalem: Hebrew University Magnes Press [in Hebrew].

Fischer, Irmtraud
2000   "The Authority of Miriam: A Feminist Rereading of Numbers 12 Prompted by Jewish Interpretation." Pages

159–73 in *Exodus to Deuteronomy: A Feminist Companion to the Bible*. Edited by Athalya Brenner. Feminist Companion to the Bible, 2nd ser., 5. Sheffield: Sheffield Academic Press.

Fishbane, Michael
1985   *Biblical Interpretation in Ancient Israel*. Oxford: Clarendon.

Fitzgerald, John T.
1992   "Virtue/Vice Lists." Pages 857–59 in vol. 6 of *The Anchor Bible Dictionary*. Edited by David Noel Freedman. New York: Doubleday.

Flanagan, J. W.
1972   "Court History or Succession Document? A Study of 2 Samuel 9–20 and 1 Kings 1–2." *Journal of Biblical Literature* 91:172–81.

Fletcher-Louis, Crispin H. T.
1996   "4Q374: A Discourse on the Sinai Tradition; The Deification of Moses and Early Christology." *Dead Sea Discoveries* 3:236–52.
2002   *All the Glory of Adam: Liturgical Anthropology in the Dead Sea Scrolls*. Studies on the Texts of the Desert of Judah 42. Leiden: Brill.

Ford, David F.
1992   *A Long Rumour of Wisdom: Redescribing Theology*. Cambridge: Cambridge University Press.
1999   *Theology: A Very Short Introduction*. Oxford: Oxford University Press.
2007   *Christian Wisdom: Desiring God and Learning in Love*. Cambridge Studies in Christian Doctrine. Cambridge: Cambridge University Press.

Ford, David F., and Graham Stanton, eds.
2003   *Reading Texts, Seeking Wisdom: Scripture and Theology*. London: SCM Press.

Fowl, Stephen E.
1990   "The Ethics of Interpretation, or What's Left Over after the Elimination of Meaning." Pages 379–98 in *The Bible in Three Dimensions*. Edited by David J. A. Clines, Stephen E. Fowl, and Stanley E. Porter. Journal for the Study of the Old Testament: Supplement Series 87. Sheffield: JSOT Press.
1991   "Could Horace Talk with the Hebrews? Translatability and Moral Disagreement in MacIntyre and Stout." *Journal of Religious Ethics* 19:1–20.

1995   "The New Testament, Theology, and Ethics." Pages 394–410
        in *Hearing the New Testament: Strategies for Interpretation.*
        Edited by Joel B. Green. Grand Rapids: Eerdmans.
1998   *Engaging Scripture.* Oxford: Blackwell.
2000   "The Role of Authorial Intention in the Theological
        Interpretation of Scripture." Pages 71–87 in *Between Two
        Horizons: Spanning New Testament Studies and Systematic
        Theology.* Edited by J. B. Green and M. Turner. Grand
        Rapids: Eerdmans.
2005   "Virtue." Pages 837–39 in *Dictionary for Theological
        Interpretation of the Bible.* Edited by Kevin J. Vanhoozer.
        Grand Rapids: Baker Academic; London: SPCK.

Fowl, Stephen E., and L. Gregory Jones
1991   *Reading in Communion: Scripture and Ethics in Christian
        Life.* Biblical Foundations in Theology. London: SPCK.

Fowler, Robert M.
1991   *Let the Reader Understand: Reader-Response Criticism and
        the Gospel of Mark.* Minneapolis: Fortress.

Fox, Everett
1995   *The Five Books of Moses: A New Translation with
        Introductions, Commentary, and Notes.* Schocken Bible 1.
        Dallas: Word.

Frankel, Ellen
1997   *The Five Books of Miriam: A Women's Commentary on the
        Torah.* San Francisco: HarperOne.

Frei, Hans W.
1974   *The Eclipse of Biblical Narrative: A Study in Eighteenth
        and Nineteenth Century Hermeneutics.* New Haven: Yale
        University Press.
1975   *The Identity of Jesus Christ: The Hermeneutical Bases of
        Dogmatic Theology.* Philadelphia: Fortress.
1986   "The 'Literal Reading' of Biblical Narrative in the Christian
        Tradition: Does It Stretch or Will It Break?" Pages 36–77
        in *The Bible and the Narrative Tradition.* Edited by Frank
        McConnell. New York: Oxford University Press. Repr. as
        pages 117–52 in *Theology and Narrative: Selected Essays.* By
        Hans W. Frei. Edited by George Hunsinger and William C.
        Placher. New York: Oxford University Press, 1993.
1993   *Theology and Narrative: Selected Essays.* Edited by George
        Hunsinger and William C. Placher. New York: Oxford
        University Press.

Fretheim, Terence E.

1999   *First and Second Kings*. Westminster Bible Companion. Louisville: Westminster John Knox.

Gallagher, William R.

1999   *Sennacherib's Campaign to Judah: New Studies*. Studies in the History and Culture of the Ancient Near East 18. Leiden: Brill.

Gammie, John G.

1989   *Holiness in Israel*. Overtures to Biblical Theology. Minneapolis: Fortress.

Gargano, Innocenzo, OSB

2007   *Holy Reading: An Introduction to Lectio Divina*. Translated by Walter Vitale. Norwich, UK: Canterbury.

Garsiel, Moshe

2002   "Revealing and Concealing as a Narrative Strategy in Solomon's Judgment (1 Kings 3:16–28)." *Catholic Biblical Quarterly* 64.2:229–47.

Geyer, John B.

1971   "II Kings XVIII 14–16 and the Annals of Sennacherib." *Vetus Testamentum* 21:604–66.

Gitay, Yehoshua

1997   "Back to Historical Isaiah. Reflections on the Act of Reading." Pages 63–72 in *Studies in the Book of Isaiah: Festschrift Willem A. M. Beuken*. Edited by J. van Ruiten and M. Vervenne. Bibliotheca ephemeridum theologicarum lovaniensum 132. Leuven: Leuven University Press.

Glueck, Nelson

1967   *"Hesed" in the Bible*. Translated by Alfred Gottschalk. Cincinnati: Hebrew Union College Press. Originally published in 1927.

Goldingay, John

2001   *Isaiah*. New International Biblical Commentary on the Old Testament 13. Carlisle, UK: Paternoster.

Grabbe, Lester L.

2003a   "Introduction." Pages 2–43 in *"Like a Bird in a Cage": The Invasion of Sennacherib in 701 BCE*. Edited by Lester L. Grabbe. Journal for the Study of the Old Testament: Supplement Series 363. European Seminar in Historical Methodology 4. London: Sheffield Academic Press.

2003b   "Of Mice and Dead Men: Herodotus 2.141 and Sennacherib's Campaign in 701 BCE." Pages 119–40 in *"Like a Bird in a Cage": The Invasion of Sennacherib in 701 BCE*. Edited by

Lester L. Grabbe. Journal for the Study of the Old Testament: Supplement Series 363. European Seminar in Historical Methodology 4. London: Sheffield Academic Press.

Gray, George Buchanan
1903   *Numbers*. International Critical Commentary. Edinburgh: T&T Clark.

Gray, John
1963   *I and II Kings*. Old Testament Library. London: SCM Press.

Green, Garrett
2000   *Theology, Hermeneutics, and Imagination: The Crisis of Interpretation at the End of Modernity*. Cambridge: Cambridge University Press.

Green, Garrett, ed.
1987   *Scriptural Authority and Narrative Interpretation*. Philadelphia: Fortress.

Green, Joel B.
2007   *Seized by Truth: Reading the Bible as Scripture*. Nashville: Abingdon.

Green, R. P. H., trans.
1995   *Augustine: De Doctrina Christiana*. Oxford Early Christian Texts. Oxford: Oxford University Press.
1997   *Saint Augustine: On Christian Teaching*. Oxford World's Classics. Oxford: Oxford University Press.

Greenfield, Jonas C.
1976   "The Aramean God Rammān/Rimmōn." *Israel Exploration Journal* 26.4:195–98.
1999   "Hadad." Pages 377–82 in *Dictionary of Deities and Demons in the Bible*. Edited by Karel van der Toorn, Bob Becking, and Pieter W. van der Horst. 2nd ed. Grand Rapids: Eerdmans.

Grenberg, Jeanine
2005   *Kant and the Ethics of Humility: A Story of Dependence, Corruption, and Virtue*. Cambridge: Cambridge University Press.

Gressman, Hugo
1907   "Das salomonische Urteil." *Deutsche Rundschau* 130:212–28.

Griffiths, Paul J.
1999   *Religious Reading: The Place of Reading in the Practice of Religion*. New York: Oxford University Press.
2002   "Reading as a Spiritual Discipline." Pages 32–47 in *The Scope of Our Art: The Vocation of the Theological Teacher*. Edited

by L. Gregory Jones and Stephanie Paulsell. Grand Rapids: Eerdmans.

Grossman, Marshall, ed.
1998   *Aemilia Lanyer: Gender, Genre, and the Canon.* Lexington: University Press of Kentucky.

Groves, Joseph W.
1987   *Actualization and Interpretation in the Old Testament.* Society of Biblical Literature Dissertation Series 86. Atlanta: Scholars Press.

Gunn, David M., and Danna Nolan Fewell
1993   *Narrative in the Hebrew Bible.* Oxford Bible Series. Oxford: Oxford University Press.

Hahn, Scott
2003   *Scripture Matters: Essays on Reading Scripture from the Heart of the Church.* Steubenville, OH: Emmaus Road.

Handy, Lowell K., ed.
1997   *The Age of Solomon: Scholarship at the Turn of the Millennium.* Studies in the History and Culture of the Ancient Near East 11. Leiden: Brill.

HaQoton, Chaim
2007   "Moses' Black Wife." Online: http://rchaimqoton.blogspot.com/2007/07/moses-black-wife.html.

Harrington, Daniel J., SJ, and James F. Keenan, SJ
2002   *Jesus and Virtue Ethics: Building Bridges between New Testament Studies and Moral Theology.* Lanham, MD: Rowman & Littlefield.

Harrington, Daniel J., SJ, and Anthony J. Saldarini
1987   *Targum Jonathan of the Former Prophets: Introduction, Translation and Notes.* Aramaic Bible 10. Edinburgh: T&T Clark.

Hauerwas, Stanley
1981   *Vision and Virtue: Essays in Christian Ethical Reflection.* Notre Dame, IN: University of Notre Dame Press.

Hauerwas, Stanley, and Charles Pinches
1997   *Christians among the Virtues: Theological Conversations with Ancient and Modern Ethics.* Notre Dame, IN: University of Notre Dame Press.

Hays, Christopher B.
2005   "How Shall We Sing? Psalm 137 in Historical and Canonical Context." *Horizons in Biblical Theology* 27.2:35–55.

Hays, Richard B.
1996   *The Moral Vision of the New Testament: A Contemporary Introduction to New Testament Ethics.* Edinburgh: T&T Clark.
1999   "Wisdom according to Paul." Pages 111–23 in *Where Shall Wisdom Be Found? Wisdom in the Bible, the Church and the Contemporary World.* Edited by Stephen C. Barton. Edinburgh: T&T Clark.
2005   "A Hermeneutic of Trust." Pages 190–201 in *The Conversion of the Imagination: Paul as Interpreter of Israel's Scripture.* Grand Rapids: Eerdmans.

Hens-Piazza, Gina
2003   *Nameless, Blameless, and without Shame: Two Cannibal Mothers before a King.* Interfaces. Collegeville, MN: Liturgical Press.
2006   *1–2 Kings.* Abingdon Old Testament Commentaries. Nashville: Abingdon.

Higton, Mike
2004   *Christ, Providence and History: Hans W. Frei's Public Theology.* London: T&T Clark.

Hobbs, T. R.
1985   *2 Kings.* Word Biblical Commentary 13. Waco: Word.

Hollis, Martin
1998   *Trust within Reason.* Cambridge: Cambridge University Press.

Hooft, Stan van
2006   *Understanding Virtue Ethics.* Chesham, UK: Acumen.

Horner, David A.
1998   "What It Takes to Be Great: Aristotle and Aquinas on Magnanimity." *Faith and Philosophy* 15.4:415–44.

Hubbard, Robert L.
1988   *The Book of Ruth.* New International Commentary on the Old Testament. Grand Rapids: Eerdmans.

Hughes, Thomas
1996   *Tom Brown's Schooldays.* 1857. Repr. London: Parragon.

Humphreys, W. Lee
1973   "A Life-Style for Diaspora: A Study of the Tales of Esther and Daniel." *Journal of Biblical Literature* 92:211–23.

Hunsinger, George
1993   "Afterword: Hans Frei as Theologian." Pages 235–70 in *Theology and Narrative: Selected Essays.* By Hans W. Frei.

Edited by George Hunsinger and William C. Placher. New
York: Oxford University Press.

Husser, Jean-Marie
1999   *Dreams and Dream Narratives in the Biblical World.* Biblical
        Seminar 63. Sheffield: Sheffield Academic Press.

Ipsen, Avaren E.
2007   "Solomon and the Two Prostitutes." *The Bible and Critical
        Theory* 3.1:2.1–2.12.

Iser, Wolfgang
1974   *The Implied Reader: Patterns of Communication in Prose
        Fiction from Bunyan to Beckett.* Baltimore: Johns Hopkins
        University Press.
1978   *The Act of Reading: A Theory of Aesthetic Response.*
        Baltimore: Johns Hopkins University Press.

Jacobs, Alan
2001   *A Theology of Reading: The Hermeneutics of Love.* Boulder,
        CO: Westview.
2007   "On Charitable Teaching." Pages 13–24 in *Teaching
        Spiritually Engaged Reading.* Edited by David I. Smith, John
        Shortt, and John Sullivan. A special issue of the *Journal of
        Education and Christian Belief* 11.2.

Jeffrey, David Lyle
2003   *Houses of the Interpreter: Reading Scripture, Reading
        Culture.* Waco: Baylor University Press.

Jenson, Philip Peter
1992   *Graded Holiness: A Key to the Priestly Conception of
        the World.* Journal for the Study of the Old Testament:
        Supplement Series 106. Sheffield: Sheffield Academic Press.
2008   *Obadiah, Jonah, Micah: A Theological Commentary.* Library of
        Hebrew Bible. Old Testament Studies 496. London: T&T Clark.

Jepsen, Alfred
1974   "ʾĀman." Pages 292–323 in vol. 1 of *Theological Dictionary
        of the Old Testament.* Edited by G. J. Botterweck, H.
        Ringgren, and H.-J. Fabry. Grand Rapids: Eerdmans.
1975   "Bāṭach." Pages 88–94 in vol. 2 of *Theological Dictionary of
        the Old Testament.* Edited by G. J. Botterweck, H. Ringgren,
        and H.-J. Fabry. Grand Rapids: Eerdmans.

J-M
        A Grammar of Biblical Hebrew. By Paul Joüon, SJ.
        Translated and revised by T. Muraoka. Subsidia biblica 14.
        Rome: Pontifical Biblical Institute, 1991.

Jobling, David
  1991   "'Forced Labour': Solomon's Golden Age and the Question of
          Literary Representation." *Semeia* 54:57–76.

Jones, G. H.
  1984   *1 and 2 Kings*. Vol. 1. New Century Bible. Grand Rapids:
          Eerdmans; London: Marshall, Morgan & Scott.

Jones, L. Gregory
  1990   *Transformed Judgment: Toward a Trinitarian Account of
          the Moral Life*. Notre Dame, IN: University of Notre Dame
          Press.
  2002   "Formed and Transformed by Scripture: Character,
          Community, and Authority in Biblical Interpretation."
          Pages 18–33 in *Character and Scripture: Moral Formation,
          Community, and Biblical Interpretation*. Edited by William P.
          Brown. Grand Rapids: Eerdmans.
  2003   "Embodying Scripture in the Community of Faith." Pages
          143–59 in *The Art of Reading Scripture*. Edited by Ellen F.
          Davis and Richard B. Hays. Grand Rapids: Eerdmans.

Josipovici, Gabriel
  1999   *On Trust: Art and the Temptations of Suspicion*. New Haven:
          Yale University Press.

Joüon, Paul, SJ. *See* J-M

Kaminsky, Joel S.
  2007   *Yet I Loved Jacob: Reclaiming the Biblical Concept of
          Election*. Nashville: Abingdon.

Keil, C. F.
  1980   *The Pentateuch*. Vol. 3 of *Commentary on the Old Testament
          in Ten Volumes*. By C. F. Keil and F. Delitzsch. 1865. Repr.
          Grand Rapids: Eerdmans.

Kenik, Helen A.
  1983   *Design for Kingship: The Deuteronomistic Narrative
          Technique in 1 Kings 3:4–15*. Society of Biblical Literature
          Dissertation Series 69. Chico, CA: Scholars Press.

Keulen, Percy S. F. van
  2005   *Two Versions of the Solomon Narrative: An Inquiry into the
          Relationship between MT 1 Kgs. 2–11 and LXX 3 Reg. 2–11*.
          Supplements to Vetus Testamentum 104. Leiden: Brill.

Kim, Jean Kyoung
  2005   "Reading and Retelling Naaman's Story (2 Kings 5)." *Journal
          for the Study of the Old Testament* 30.1:49–61.

Kitchen, K. A.
  2003   *On the Reliability of the Old Testament.* Grand Rapids:
          Eerdmans.
Knauf, Ernst Axel
  2003   "701: Sennacherib at the Berezina." Pages 141–49 in *"Like
          a Bird in a Cage": The Invasion of Sennacherib in 701 BCE.*
          Edited by Lester L. Grabbe. Journal for the Study of the Old
          Testament: Supplement Series 363. European Seminar in
          Historical Methodology 4. London: Sheffield Academic Press.
Koet, Bart J.
  2005   "Isaiah in Luke-Acts." Pages 79–100 in *Isaiah in the New
          Testament.* Edited by Steve Moyise and Maarten J. J. Menken.
          London: T&T Clark.
Lanyer, Aemilia
  1611a   "Preface: To the Vertuous Reader." Repr. as pages 48–50 in
          The Poems of Aemilia Lanyer: Salve Deus Rex Judaeorum.
          Edited by Susanne Woods. Women Writers in English 1350–
          1850. Oxford: Oxford University Press, 1993.
  1611b   "Salve Deus Rex Judaeorum." Repr. as pages 51–129 in *The
          Poems of Aemilia Lanyer: Salve Deus Rex Judaeorum.* Edited
          by Susanne Woods. Women Writers in English 1350–1850.
          Oxford: Oxford University Press, 1993.
Larkin, Katrina J. A.
  1996   *Ruth and Esther.* Old Testament Guides. Sheffield: Sheffield
          Academic Press.
Lash, Nicholas
  1986   "What Might Martyrdom Mean?" Pages 75–92 in *Theology on
          the Way to Emmaus.* By Nicholas Lash. London: SCM Press.
  1996   *The Beginning and the End of "Religion."* Cambridge:
          Cambridge University Press.
  2004   *Holiness, Speech and Silence: Reflections on the Question of
          God.* Aldershot: Ashgate.
Lasine, Stuart
  1987   "Solomon, Daniel, and the Detective Story: The Social
          Functions of a Literary Genre." *Hebrew Annual Review*
          11:247–66.
  1989   "The Riddle of Solomon's Judgment and the Riddle of
          Human Nature in the Hebrew Bible." *Journal for the Study of
          the Old Testament* 45:61–86.
  1991   "Jehoram and the Cannibal Mothers (2 Kings 6.24–33):
          Solomon's Judgment in an Inverted World." *Journal for the
          Study of the Old Testament* 50:27–53.

1993   "The Ups and Downs of Monarchical Justice: Solomon and Jehoram in an Intertextual World." *Journal for the Study of the Old Testament* 59:37–53.

1995   "The King of Desire: Indeterminacy, Audience, and the Solomon Narrative." *Semeia* 71:85–118.

2001   *Knowing Kings: Knowledge, Power, and Narcissism in the Hebrew Bible.* Semeia Studies 40. Atlanta: Society of Biblical Literature.

Leclerc, Thomas L.
2001   *Yahweh Is Exalted in Justice: Solidarity and Conflict in Isaiah.* Minneapolis: Fortress.

Lee, David
1999   *Luke's Stories of Jesus: Theological Reading of Gospel Narrative and the Legacy of Hans Frei.* Journal for the Study of the New Testament: Supplement Series 185. Sheffield: Sheffield Academic Press.

Leithart, Peter
2006   *1 and 2 Kings.* SCM Theological Commentary on the Bible. London: SCM Press.

Lesser, Harry
2000   "'It's Difficult to Understand': Dealing with Morally Difficult Passages in the Hebrew Bible." Pages 292–302 in *Jewish Ways of Reading the Bible.* Edited by George J. Brooke. Journal of Semitic Studies Supplement Series 11. Oxford: Oxford University Press.

Levering, Matthew
2008   *Participatory Biblical Exegesis: A Theology of Biblical Interpretation.* Notre Dame, IN: University of Notre Dame Press.

Levin, S.
1983   "The Judgment of Solomon: Legal and Medical." *Judaism* 32:463–65.

Levine, Baruch A.
1993   *Numbers 1–20.* Anchor Bible 4A. New York: Doubleday.

Lewis, C. S.
1961   *An Experiment in Criticism.* Cambridge: Cambridge University Press.

Lienhard, Joseph T., ed.
2001   *Exodus, Leviticus, Numbers, Deuteronomy.* Vol. 3 of *Ancient Christian Commentary on Scripture.* Downers Grove, IL: InterVarsity.

Lierman, John
 2004 *The New Testament Moses.* Wissenschaftliche
    Untersuchungen zum Neuen Testament 2.173. Tübingen:
    Mohr Siebeck.

Lim, Timothy H.
 2007 "The Book of Ruth and Its Literary Voice." Pages 261–82 in
    *Reflection and Refraction: Studies in Biblical Historiography
    in Honour of A. Graeme Auld.* Edited by Robert Rezetko,
    Timothy H. Lim, and W. Brian Aucker. Supplements to Vetus
    Testamentum 113. Leiden: Brill.

Linafelt, Tod
 1999 "Ruth." Pages vi–90 in *Ruth and Esther.* By Tod Linafelt and
    Timothy K. Beal. Berit Olam. Collegeville, MN: Liturgical
    Press.

Lind, Millard C.
 1997 "Political Implications of Isaiah 6." Pages 317–38 in *Writing
    and Reading the Scroll of Isaiah: Studies of an Interpretative
    Tradition.* Edited by Craig C. Broyles and Craig A. Evans.
    Supplements to Vetus Testamentum 70. Formation and
    Interpretation of Old Testament Literature 1. Leiden: Brill.

Lindberg, Carter
 2008 *Love: A Brief History through Western Christianity.* Oxford:
    Blackwell.

Lipton, Diana
 2003 "Remembering Amalek: A Positive Biblical Model for Dealing
    with Negative Scriptural Types." Pages 139–53 in *Reading
    Texts, Seeking Wisdom: Scripture and Theology.* Edited by
    David F. Ford and Graham Stanton. London: SCM Press.

Long, Burke O.
 1984 *1 Kings, with an Introduction to Historical Literature.* Forms
    of Old Testament Literature 9. Grand Rapids: Eerdmans.

Louth, Andrew
 1983 *Discerning the Mystery: An Essay on the Nature of Theology.*
    Oxford: Clarendon.

MacIntyre, Alasdair
 1981 *After Virtue: A Study in Moral Theory.* Notre Dame, IN:
    University of Notre Dame Press.
 1984 *After Virtue: A Study in Moral Theory.* 2nd ed. Notre Dame,
    IN: University of Notre Dame Press.
 1988 *Whose Justice? Which Rationality?* Notre Dame, IN:
    University of Notre Dame Press.

1990   *Three Rival Versions of Moral Enquiry.* Notre Dame, IN:
        University of Notre Dame Press.

Magrassi, Mariano
1998   *Praying the Bible: An Introduction to "Lectio Divina."*
        Collegeville, MN: Liturgical Press.

Maier, Gerhard
1977   *The End of the Historical-Critical Method.* Translated by
        Edwin W. Leverenz and Rudolf F. Norde. St. Louis: Concordia.

Makiello, Phoebe
2007   "Was Moses Considered to Be an Angel by Those at
        Qumran?" Pages 115–27 in *Moses in Biblical and Extra-
        Biblical Traditions.* Edited by Axel Graupner and Michael
        Wolter. Beihefte zur Zeitschrift für die alttestamentliche
        Wissenschaft 372. Berlin: de Gruyter.

Mayer, Walter
2003   "Sennacherib's Campaign of 701 BCE: The Assyrian View."
        Pages 168–200 in *"Like a Bird in a Cage": The Invasion of
        Sennacherib in 701 BCE.* Edited by Lester L. Grabbe. Journal
        for the Study of the Old Testament: Supplement Series 363.
        European Seminar in Historical Methodology 4. London:
        Sheffield Academic Press.

Meeks, Wayne A.
2004   "A Nazi New Testament Professor Reads His Bible: The
        Strange Case of Gerhard Kittel." Pages 513–44 in *The Idea of
        Biblical Interpretation: Essays in Honor of James L. Kugel.*
        Edited by Hindy Najman and Judith H. Newman. Journal for
        the Study of Judaism: Supplement Series 83. Leiden: Brill.

Meilaender, Gilbert
2002   "Ethics and Exegesis: A Great Gulf?" Pages 259–64 in *A Royal
        Priesthood? The Use of the Bible Ethically and Politically;
        A Dialogue with Oliver O'Donovan.* Edited by Craig G.
        Bartholomew et al. Scripture and Hermeneutics Series 3.
        Grand Rapids: Zondervan; Carlisle, UK: Paternoster.

Melina, Livio
2001   *Sharing in Christ's Virtues: For a Renewal of Moral Theology
        in Light of "Veritatis Splendor."* Translated by William E.
        May. Washington, DC: Catholic University of America Press.

Melugin, Roy F., and Marvin A. Sweeney, eds.
1996   *New Visions of Isaiah.* Journal for the Study of the Old
        Testament: Supplement Series 214. Sheffield: Sheffield
        Academic Press.

Menzies, Glen W.
1998   "To What Does Faith Lead? The Two-Stranded Textual
          Tradition of Isaiah 7.9b." *Journal for the Study of the Old
          Testament* 80:111–28.

Milgrom, Jacob
1990   *Numbers*. JPS Torah Commentary. Philadelphia: Jewish
          Publication Society.
2000   "The Dynamics of Purity in the Priestly System." Pages 29–32
          in *Purity and Holiness: The Heritage of Leviticus*. Edited by
          M. J. H. M. Poorthuis and J. Schwartz. Jewish and Christian
          Perspectives Series 2. Leiden: Brill.

Mills, Mary E.
2001   *Biblical Morality: Moral Perspectives in Old Testament
          Narratives*. Aldershot: Ashgate.

Moberly, R. W. L.
1997a   " *'mn*." Pages 427–33 in vol. 1 of *New International
          Dictionary of Old Testament Theology and Exegesis*. Edited
          by Willem A. van Gemeren. 5 vols. Grand Rapids: Zondervan;
          Carlisle, UK: Paternoster.
1997b   "*Bṭḥ*." Pages 644–49 in vol. 1 of *New International Dictionary
          of Old Testament Theology and Exegesis*. Edited by Willem
          A. van Gemeren. 5 vols. Grand Rapids: Zondervan; Carlisle,
          UK: Paternoster.
1999   "Solomon and Job: Divine Wisdom in Human Life." Pages
          3–17 in *Where Shall Wisdom Be Found? Wisdom in the Bible,
          the Church and the Contemporary World*. Edited by Stephen
          C. Barton. Edinburgh: T&T Clark.
2000   *The Bible, Theology, and Faith: A Study of Abraham and
          Jesus*. Cambridge Studies in Christian Doctrine. Cambridge:
          Cambridge University Press.
2001   "Whose Justice? Which Righteousness? The Interpretation of
          Isaiah V 16." *Vetus Testamentum* 51.1:55–68.
2003   "'Holy, Holy, Holy': Isaiah's Vision of God." Pages 122–40
          in *Holiness Past and Present*. Edited by Stephen C. Barton.
          London: T&T Clark.
2006   *Prophecy and Discernment*. Cambridge Studies in Christian
          Doctrine. Cambridge: Cambridge University Press.

Morgan, Donn F.
2002   *The Making of Sages: Biblical Wisdom and Contemporary
          Culture*. Harrisburg, PA: Trinity.

Moyise, Steve, and Maarten J. J. Menken, eds.
2005   *Isaiah in the New Testament*. London: T&T Clark.

Mulder, Martin J.
1998   *1 Kings 1–11*. Vol. 1 of *1 Kings*. Historical Commentary on the Old Testament. Leuven: Peeters.

Müller, H.-P.
1999   "Chemosh." Pages 186–89 in *Dictionary of Deities and Demons in the Bible*. Edited by Karel van der Toorn, Bob Becking, and Pieter W. van der Horst. 2nd ed. Grand Rapids: Eerdmans.

Murphy, Nancey, Brad J. Kallenberg, and Mark Thiessen Nation, eds.
1997   *Virtues and Practices in the Christian Tradition: Christian Ethics after MacIntyre*. Harrisburg, PA: Trinity.

Musgrave, P. W.
1985   *From Brown to Bunter*. London: Routledge & Kegan Paul.

Na'aman, Nadav
1997   "Sources and Composition in the History of Solomon." Pages 57–80 in *The Age of Solomon: Scholarship at the Turn of the Millennium*. Edited by Lowell K. Handy. Studies in the History and Culture of the Ancient Near East 11. Leiden: Brill.

Nelson, Richard D.
1987   *First and Second Kings*. Interpretation. Atlanta: John Knox.

Netland, John
2007   "'Who Is My Neighbor?' Reading World Literature through the Hermeneutics of Love." Pages 67–82 in *Teaching Spiritually Engaged Reading*. Edited by David I. Smith, John Shortt, and John Sullivan. A special issue of the *Journal of Education and Christian Belief* 11.2.

Newbigin, Lesslie
1989   *The Gospel in a Pluralist Society*. London: SPCK.

Newsom, Carol A.
1996   "Bakhtin, the Bible, and Dialogic Truth." *Journal of Religion* 76.2:290–306.

Nietzsche, Friedrich
1968   "Twilight of the Idols." Pages 463–563 in *The Portable Nietzsche*. Translated and edited by Walter Kaufmann. New York: Viking.
1974   *The Gay Science*. New York: Vintage Books, Random House. Originally published in 1887.

Noth, Martin
1968   *Numbers*. Old Testament Library. London: SCM Press. German original published in 1966.

Nussbaum, Martha C.
   1986   *The Fragility of Goodness: Luck and Ethics in Greek Tragedy
           and Philosophy*. Cambridge: Cambridge University Press.
   1990   *Love's Knowledge: Essays on Philosophy and Literature*.
           Oxford: Oxford University Press.

Nygren, Anders
   1953   *Agape and Eros*. Translated by Philip S. Watson. Philadelphia:
           Westminster. Originally published in 1930.

O'Donovan, Oliver
   1980   *The Problem of Self-Love in St. Augustine*. New Haven: Yale
           University Press.
   1996   *The Desire of the Nations: Rediscovering the Roots of
           Political Theology*. Cambridge: Cambridge University Press.

Olegovich, Giorgy, ed.
   1999   *Ten Year Commemoration to the Life of Hans Frei (1922–
           1988)*. New York: Semenenko Foundation.

Olson, Dennis T.
   1996   *Numbers*. Interpretation. Louisville: John Knox.
   2007   "Between Humility and Authority: The Interplay of the
           Judge-Prophet Laws (Deuteronomy 16:18–17:13) and
           the Judge-Prophet Narratives of Moses." Pages 51–61 in
           *Character Ethics and the Old Testament: Moral Dimensions
           of Scripture*. Edited by M. Daniel Carroll R. and Jacqueline
           E. Lapsley. Louisville: Westminster John Knox.

Osiek, Carolyn
   1994   "Philippians." Pages 237–49 in vol. 2 of *Searching the
           Scriptures: A Feminist Commentary*. Edited by Elisabeth
           Schüssler Fiorenza. London: SCM Press.
   2000   *Philippians, Philemon*. Abingdon New Testament
           Commentaries. Nashville: Abingdon.

Parry, Robin
   2004   *Old Testament Story and Christian Ethics: The Rape of
           Dinah as a Case Study*. Paternoster Biblical Monographs.
           Milton Keynes, UK: Paternoster.

Pattison, Stephen, Margaret Cooling, and Trevor Cooling
   2007   *Using the Bible in Christian Ministry: A Workbook*. Using the
           Bible in Pastoral Practice Series. London: Darton, Longman
           & Todd.

Perdue, Leo G.
   1995   *The Collapse of History: Reconstructing Old Testament
           Theology*. Overtures to Biblical Theology. Minneapolis: Fortress.

2005   *Reconstructing Old Testament Theology: After the Collapse of History*. Overtures to Biblical Theology. Minneapolis: Fortress.

Peterson, Eugene H.
2006   *Eat This Book: A Conversation in the Art of Spiritual Reading*. Grand Rapids: Eerdmans.

Peursen, Wido T. van
2007   "Who Was Standing on the Mountain? The Portrait of Moses in 4Q377." Pages 99–113 in *Moses in Biblical and Extra-Biblical Traditions*. Edited by Axel Graupner and Michael Wolter. Beihefte zur Zeitschrift für die alttestamentliche Wissenschaft 372. Berlin: de Gruyter.

Pimpinella, Denise
2006   "Miriam in Numbers 12." *Concept: An Interdisciplinary Journal of Graduate Studies*. Online: http://www.publications.villanova.edu/Concept/2006/pimpinella.pdf.

Polaski, Sandra Hack
1999   *Paul and the Discourse of Power*. Gender, Culture, Theory 8. Biblical Seminar 62. Sheffield: Sheffield Academic Press.

Porter, Jean
1990   *The Recovery of Virtue: The Relevance of Aquinas for Christian Ethics*. Louisville: Westminster John Knox.
1995   *Moral Action and Christian Ethics*. New Studies in Christian Ethics. Cambridge: Cambridge University Press.
2001   "Virtue Ethics." Pages 96–111 in *The Cambridge Companion to Christian Ethics*. Edited by Robin Gill. Cambridge: Cambridge University Press.

Powell, Mark Allan
2001   *Chasing the Eastern Star: Adventures in Biblical Reader-Response Criticism*. Louisville: Westminster John Knox.
2007   *What Do They Hear? Bridging the Gap between Pulpit and Pew*. Nashville: Abingdon.

Provan, Iain W.
1995   *1 and 2 Kings*. New International Biblical Commentary on the Old Testament 7. Peabody, MA: Hendrickson; Carlisle, UK: Paternoster.
1997   *1 and 2 Kings*. Old Testament Guides. Sheffield: Sheffield Academic Press.
1999   "On 'Seeing' the Trees While Missing the Forest: The Wisdom of Characters and Readers in 2 Samuel and 1 Kings." Pages 153–73 in *In Search of True Wisdom: Essays in Old Testament Interpretation in Honour of Ronald E.*

Clements. Edited by Edward Ball. Journal for the Study
of the Old Testament: Supplement Series 300. Sheffield:
Sheffield Academic Press.

2002   "In the Stable with the Dwarves: Testimony, Interpretation,
         Faith, and the History of Israel." Pages 161–97 in *Windows
         into Old Testament History: Evidence, Argument, and the
         Crisis of "Biblical Israel."* Edited by V. Philips Long, David W.
         Baker, and Gordon J. Wenham. Grand Rapids: Eerdmans.

Pyper, Hugh S.

1993   "Judging the Wisdom of Solomon: The Two-Way Effect of
         Intertextuality." *Journal for the Study of the Old Testament*
         59:25–36.

Rad, Gerhard von

1962   *Old Testament Theology*. Vol. 1. London: SCM Press.
         Originally published in 1957.

1965   *Old Testament Theology*. Vol. 2. London: SCM Press.
         Originally published in 1960.

1980   *God at Work in Israel*. Translated by John H. Marks.
         Nashville: Abingdon. Originally published in 1974.

2005   "The Form-Critical Problem of the Hexateuch." Pages 1–58 in
         *From Genesis to Chronicles: Explorations in Old Testament
         Theology*. Fortress Classic in Biblical Studies. Minneapolis:
         Fortress. Originally published in 1938.

Rae, Murray A.

2005   *History and Hermeneutics*. London: T&T Clark.

Rawlinson, Henry C.

1852   "Outlines of Assyrian History, Collected from the Cuneiform
         Inscriptions." Pages xv–xlvi in *The XXIVth Annual Report of
         the Royal Asiatic Society*.

Rendsburg, Gary A.

1998   "The Guilty Party in 1 Kings iii 16–28." *Vetus Testamentum*
         48.4:534–41.

Rendtorff, Rolf

1993   "Isaiah 6 in the Framework of the Composition of the Book."
         Pages 170–80 in *Canon and Theology: Overtures to an Old
         Testament Theology*. By Rolf Rendtorff. Overtures to Biblical
         Theology. Minneapolis: Fortress.

Rey, Joshua

1999   *Persuading People to Be Good: Alasdair MacIntyre's "Three
         Rival Versions of Moral Enquiry" and Why We Should Read
         It*. Grove Ethical Series 112. Cambridge: Grove Books.

Rhoads, David, Joanna Dewey, and Donald Michie

    1999   *Mark as Story: An Introduction to the Narrative of a Gospel.*
            2nd ed. Minneapolis: Fortress.

Ricoeur, Paul

    1967   *The Symbolism of Evil.* Boston: Beacon.

    1970   *Freud and Philosophy: An Essay on Interpretation.* New
            Haven: Yale University Press.

    1974   *The Conflict of Interpretations: Essays in Hermeneutics.*
            Northwestern Studies in Phenomenology and Existential
            Philosophy. Evanston, IL: Northwestern University Press.

    1991   *From Text to Action: Essays in Hermeneutics 2.* Translated
            by Kathleen Blamey and John B. Thompson. Evanston, IL:
            Northwestern University Press.

    1992   *Oneself as Another.* Translated by Kathleen Blamey. Chicago:
            University of Chicago Press.

    1995   "The Summoned Subject in the School of the Narratives of
            the Prophetic Vocation." Pages 262–75 in *Figuring the Sacred:*
            Religion, Narrative, and Imagination. By Paul Ricoeur. Edited
            by Mark I. Wallace. Minneapolis: Fortress.

    1997   "The Self in the Mirror of the Scriptures." Pages 201–20 in
            The Whole and Divided Self. Edited by David E. Aune and
            John McCarthy. New York: Crossroad.

Rine, C. Rebecca

    2007   "Learning to Read with Augustine of Hippo." Pages 39–52
            in *Teaching Spiritually Engaged Reading.* Edited by David I.
            Smith, John Shortt, and John Sullivan. A special issue of the
            Journal of Education and Christian Belief 11.2.

Roberts, Robert C.

    2007   *Spiritual Emotions: A Psychology of Christian Virtues.* Grand
            Rapids: Eerdmans.

Roberts, Robert C., and W. Jay Wood

    2007   *Intellectual Virtues: An Essay in Regulative Epistemology.*
            Oxford: Oxford University Press.

Robinson, Geoffrey D.

    1998   "The Motif of Deafness and Blindness in Isaiah 6:9–10: A
            Contextual, Literary, and Theological Analysis." *Bulletin for*
            Biblical Research 8:167–86.

Rodd, Cyril S.

    2001   *Glimpses of a Strange Land: Studies in Old Testament Ethics.*
            Old Testament Studies. Edinburgh: T&T Clark.

Rogers, Cleon
1986   "Moses: Meek or Miserable?" *Journal of the Evangelical Theological Society* 29.3:257–63.

Rogers, Eugene F., Jr.
1996   "How the Virtues of an Interpreter Presuppose and Perfect Hermeneutics: The Case of Thomas Aquinas." *Journal of Religion* 76.1:64–81.

Römer, Thomas
1997   "Nombres 11–12 et la question d'une rédaction deutéronomique dans la Pentateuque." Pages 481–98 in *Deuteronomy and Deuteronomic Literature: Festschrift C. H. W. Brekelmans*. Edited by M. Vervenne and J. Lust. Leuven: Peeters.

Rost, Leonhard
1982   *The Succession to the Throne of David*. Translated by Michael D. Rutter and David M. Gunn. Sheffield: Almond. Originally published in 1926.

Routledge, Robin
1995   "*Ḥesed* as Obligation: A Re-examination." *Tyndale Bulletin* 46.1:179–96.

Rudman, Dominic
2000   "Is the Rabshakeh Also among the Prophets? A Rhetorical Study of 2 Kings XVIII 17–35." *Vetus Testamentum* 50.1:100–110.

Sakenfeld, Katharine Doob
1978   *The Meaning of Ḥesed in the Hebrew Bible*. Harvard Semitic Monographs 17. Missoula, MT: Scholars Press.
1985   *Faithfulness in Action: Loyalty in Biblical Perspective*. Overtures to Biblical Theology. Philadelphia: Fortress.
1999   *Ruth*. Interpretation. Louisville: John Knox.

Sanders, James A.
1972   *Torah and Canon*. Philadelphia: Fortress.
1984   *Canon and Community: A Guide to Canonical Criticism*. Guides to Biblical Scholarship. Philadelphia: Fortress.

Sasson, Gilad
2004   ["'Woe to You, O Land, When Your King Is a Child': The Criticism of the Sages regarding Solomon's Trial."] *Beit Mikra* 49:191–200 [in Hebrew].

Savran, George
2003   "Theophany as Type Scene." *Prooftexts* 23:119–49.

Sayre, Patricia A.
1993   "The Dialectics of Trust and Suspicion." *Faith and
        Philosophy* 10.4:567–84.

Schlabach, Gerald W.
1994   "Augustine's Hermeneutic of Humility: An Alternative
        to Moral Imperialism and Moral Relativism." *Journal of
        Religious Ethics* 22.2:299–330.

Schneiders, Sandra M.
1991   *The Revelatory Text: Interpreting the New Testament as
        Sacred Scripture.* San Francisco: HarperSanFrancisco.
1999   *The Revelatory Text: Interpreting the New Testament as
        Sacred Scripture.* 2nd ed. Collegeville, MN: Liturgical Press.

Schwartz, Regina M.
1997   *The Curse of Cain: The Violent Legacy of Monotheism.*
        Chicago: University of Chicago Press.

Scott, R. B. Y.
1955   "Solomon and the Beginnings of Wisdom in Israel." Pages
        262–79 in *Wisdom in Israel and in the Ancient Near East.*
        Edited by M. Noth and D. Winton Thomas. Supplements to
        Vetus Testamentum 3. Leiden: Brill.

Seibert, Eric A.
2006   *Subversive Scribes and the Solomonic Narrative: A Rereading
        of 1 Kings 1–11.* Library of Hebrew Bible. Old Testament
        Studies 436. New York: T&T Clark.

Seitz, Christopher R.
1991   *Zion's Final Destiny: The Development of the Book of Isaiah:
        A Reassessment of Isaiah 36–39.* Minneapolis: Fortress.
1993   *Isaiah 1–39.* Interpretation. Louisville: John Knox.
1998   *Word without End: The Old Testament as Abiding
        Theological Witness.* Grand Rapids: Eerdmans.
2001   *Figured Out: Typology and Providence in Christian Scripture.*
        Louisville: Westminster John Knox.
2007   *Prophecy and Hermeneutics: Toward a New Introduction to
        the Prophets.* Studies in Theological Interpretation. Grand
        Rapids: Baker Academic.

Seow, Choon-Leong
1984   "The Syro-Palestinian Context of Solomon's Dream."
        Harvard Theological Review 77.2:141–52.
1999   "The First and Second Books of Kings." Pages 1–295 in vol. 3
        of *The New Interpreter's Bible.* Edited by L. E. Keck. 12 vols.
        Nashville: Abingdon.

Sheppard, Gerald T.
1996   "The 'Scope' of Isaiah as a Book of Jewish and Christian
        Scriptures." Pages 257–81 in *New Visions of Isaiah*. Edited
        by Roy F. Melugin and Marvin A. Sweeney. Journal for the
        Study of the Old Testament: Supplement Series 214. Sheffield:
        Sheffield Academic Press.

Sherwin, Michael S., OP
2005   *By Knowledge and by Love: Charity and Knowledge in the
        Moral Theology of St. Thomas Aquinas*. Washington, DC:
        Catholic University of America Press.

Shults, F. LeRon
1999   *The Postfoundationalist Task of Theology: Wolfhart
        Pannenberg and the New Theological Rationality*. Grand
        Rapids: Eerdmans.

Silberman, Lou
1983   "Wellhausen and Judaism." *Semeia* 25:75–82.

Smith, David I., John Shortt, and John Sullivan, eds.
2007   *Teaching Spiritually Engaged Reading*. A special issue of the
        Journal of Education and Christian Belief 11.2.

Smith, R. Scott
2003   *Virtue Ethics and Moral Knowledge: Philosophy of Language
        after MacIntyre and Hauerwas*. Ashgate New Critical
        Thinking in Philosophy. Aldershot: Ashgate.

Spinks, D. Christopher
2007   *The Bible and the Crisis of Meaning: Debates on the
        Theological Interpretation of Scripture*. London: T&T Clark.

ST
        Summa theologiae. By Thomas Aquinas. 59 vols. London:
        Blackfriars, 1964–76.

Stade, Bernhard
1886   "Anmerkungen zu 2 Kö. 15–21." *Zeitschrift für die
        alttestamentliche Wissenschaft* 6:156–89.

Stavrakopoulou, Francesca
2004   *King Manasseh and Child Sacrifice: Biblical Distortions
        of Historical Realities*. Beihefte zur Zeitschrift für die
        alttestamentliche Wissenschaft 338. Berlin: de Gruyter.

Steiner, George
1988   Review of Robert Alter and Frank Kermode, eds., *The
        Literary Guide to the Bible*. *New Yorker*, January 11, 94–98.
1989   *Real Presences: Is There Anything in What We Say?* London:
        Faber & Faber.

1996 "A Preface to the Hebrew Bible." Pages 40–87 in *No Passion Spent: Essays 1978–1996*. By George Steiner. London: Faber & Faber.

Steinmetz, David C.
1987 "John Calvin in Isaiah 6: A Problem in the History of Exegesis." Pages 86–99 in *Interpreting the Prophets*. Edited by J. L. Mays and P. J. Achtemeier. Philadelphia: Fortress.

Steinweis, Alan E.
2006 *Studying the Jew: Scholarly Antisemitism in Nazi Germany*. Cambridge, MA: Harvard University Press.

Stern, Philip D.
1991 *The Biblical Ḥerem: A Window on Israel's Religious Experience*. Brown Judaic Studies 211. Atlanta: Scholars Press.

Sternberg, Meir
1985 *The Poetics of Biblical Narrative: Ideological Literature and the Drama of Reading*. Bloomington: Indiana University Press.

Stout, Jeffrey
1981 *The Flight from Authority: Religion, Morality, and the Quest for Autonomy*. Notre Dame, IN: University of Notre Dame Press.
1988 *Ethics after Babel: The Languages of Morals and Their Discontents*. Cambridge: James Clarke.
1999 "Hans Frei and Anselmian Theology." Pages 24–40 in *Ten Year Commemoration to the Life of Hans Frei (1922–1988)*. Edited by Giorgy Olegovich. New York: Semenenko Foundation.

Stuhlmacher, Peter
1977 *Historical Criticism and Theological Interpretation of Scripture: Toward a Hermeneutics of Consent*. Philadelphia: Fortress.

Swartley, Willard M.
2007 "Peacemaking Pillars of Character Formation in the New Testament." Pages 225–43 in *Character Ethics and the New Testament: Moral Dimensions of Scripture*. Edited by Robert L. Brawley. Louisville: Westminster John Knox.

Sweeney, Marvin A.
2005 *The Prophetic Literature*. Interpreting Biblical Texts. Nashville: Abingdon.

Tate, Marvin E.
1996 "The Book of Isaiah in Recent Study." Pages 22–56 in *Forming Prophetic Literature: Essays on Isaiah and the*

Twelve in Honor of John D. W. Watts. Edited by James
W. Watts and Paul R. House. Journal for the Study of the
Old Testament: Supplement Series 235. Sheffield: Sheffield
Academic Press.

Thiselton, Anthony C.
1992   *New Horizons in Hermeneutics: The Theory and Practice of
        Transforming Biblical Reading.* London: HarperCollins.
2000   *The First Epistle to the Corinthians.* New International Greek
        Testament Commentary. Grand Rapids: Eerdmans; Carlisle,
        UK: Paternoster.

Thomas Aquinas. *See DQVirtGen and ST*

Thomasset, Alain
2005   "Personnages bibliques et 'formation' éthique des lecteurs."
        Pages 73–94 in *Analyse narrative et Bible.* Edited by C. Focant
        and A. Wénin. Bibliotheca ephemeridum theologicarum
        lovaniensum 191. Leuven: Peeters.

Topping, Richard R.
2007   *Revelation, Scripture and Church: Theological Hermeneutic
        Thought of James Barr, Paul Ricoeur and Hans Frei.*
        Aldershot: Ashgate.

Torijano, Pablo A.
2002   *Solomon, the Esoteric King: From King to Magus, A
        Development of Tradition.* Journal for the Study of Judaism:
        Supplement Series 73. Leiden: Brill.

Treier, Daniel J.
2006   *Virtue and the Voice of God: Toward Theology as Wisdom.*
        Grand Rapids: Eerdmans.
2008   *Introducing Theological Interpretation of Scripture:
        Recovering a Christian Practice.* Grand Rapids: Baker
        Academic.

Trible, Phyllis
1994   "Bringing Miriam out of the Shadows." Pages 166–86 in *A
        Feminist Companion to Exodus to Deuteronomy.* Edited
        by Athalya Brenner. Feminist Companion to the Bible 6.
        Sheffield: Sheffield Academic Press. Originally published in
        Bible Review 5.1 (1989): 170–90.

Tull, Patricia K.
2006   "One Book, Many Voices: Conceiving of Isaiah's Polyphonic
        Message." Pages 279–314 in *"As Those Who Are Taught": The
        Interpretation of Isaiah from the LXX to the SBL.* Edited by
        Claire Mathews McGinnis and Patricia K. Tull. Society of

Biblical Literature Symposium Series 27. Atlanta: Society of
Biblical Literature.

Twain, Mark (Samuel Clemens)
1958   *The Adventures of Huckleberry Finn*. 1884. Repr. New York:
        Harper & Row.

Van Hooft. *See* Hooft

Vanhoozer, Kevin J.
1998   *Is There a Meaning in This Text? The Bible, the Reader, and the
        Morality of Literary Knowledge*. Grand Rapids: Eerdmans.
2002   *First Theology: God, Scripture and Hermeneutics*. Leicester,
        UK: Apollos.
2005a   *The Drama of Doctrine: A Canonical Linguistic Approach to
        Christian Theology*. Louisville: Westminster John Knox.
2005b   "Discourse on Matter: Hermeneutics and the 'Miracle'
        of Understanding." *International Journal of Systematic
        Theology* 7.1:5–37.
2006   "Imprisoned or Free? Text, Status, and Theological
        Interpretation in the Master/Slave Discourse of Philemon."
        Pages 51–93 in *Reading Scripture with the Church: Toward
        a Hermeneutic for Theological Interpretation*. By A. K. M.
        Adam et al. Grand Rapids: Baker Academic.

Vanhoozer, Kevin J., et al., eds.
2005   *Dictionary for Theological Interpretation of the Bible*. Grand
        Rapids: Baker Academic; London: SPCK.

Van Keulen. *See* Keulen

Van Peursen. *See* Peursen

Van Seters, John
1987   "Love and Death in the Court History of David." Pages
        121–24 in *Love and Death in the Ancient Near East: Essays
        in Honor of Marvin H. Pope*. Edited by John H. Marks and
        Robert M. Good. Guildford, CT: Four Quartets.

Van Wieringen. *See* Wieringen

Van Wolde. *See* Wolde

Vaughan, Andrew G.
1999   *Theology, History, and Archaeology in the Chronicler's
        Account of Hezekiah*. Archaeology and Biblical Studies 4.
        Atlanta: Scholars Press.

Venema, G. J.
2004   *Reading Scripture in the Old Testament: Deuteronomy
        9–10; 31; 2 Kings 22–23; Jeremiah 36; Nehemiah 8*.
        Oudtestamentische Studiën 47. Leiden: Brill.

Village, Andrew
    2007   *The Bible and Lay People: An Empirical Approach to
            Ordinary Hermeneutics*. Aldershot: Ashgate.

Volf, Miroslav
    1996   *Exclusion and Embrace: A Theological Exploration of
            Identity, Otherness, and Reconciliation*. Nashville: Abingdon.

von Rad. *See* Rad

Watson, Francis
    1994   *Text, Church and World: Biblical Interpretation in
            Theological Perspective*. Edinburgh: T&T Clark.
    1997   *Text and Truth: Redefining Biblical Theology*. Edinburgh:
            T&T Clark.

Wawrykow, Joseph
    2005   "Aquinas on Isaiah." Pages 43–71 in *Aquinas on Scripture:
            An Introduction to His Biblical Commentaries*. Edited by
            Thomas G. Weinandy, Daniel A. Keating, and John P. Yocum.
            London: T&T Clark.

Webster, John
    2001   *Word and Church: Essays in Christian Dogmatics*. Edinburgh:
            T&T Clark.
    2003   *Holy Scripture: A Dogmatic Sketch*. Current Issues in
            Theology. Cambridge: Cambridge University Press.
    2007   "Resurrection and Scripture." Pages 138–55 in *Christology
            and Scripture: Interdisciplinary Perspectives*. Edited by
            Andrew T. Lincoln and Angus Paddison. Library of New
            Testament Studies 348. London: T&T Clark.

Weems, Renita
    1988   *Just a Sister Away: A Womanist Vision of Women's
            Relationships in the Bible*. San Diego: LuraMedia.

Wells, Jo Bailey
    2000   *God's Holy People: A Theme in Biblical Theology*. Journal
            for the Study of the Old Testament: Supplement Series 305.
            Sheffield: Sheffield Academic Press.

Wengst, Klaus
    1988   *Humility: Solidarity of the Humiliated*. London: SCM Press.

Wenham, Gordon J.
    1980   "The Religion of the Patriarchs." Pages 157–88 in *Essays on
            the Patriarchal Narratives*. Edited by A. R. Millard and D. J.
            Wiseman. Leicester, UK: Inter-Varsity.
    2000   *Story as Torah: Reading Old Testament Narrative Ethically*.
            Old Testament Studies. Edinburgh: T&T Clark.

Westphal, Merold
1998   *Suspicion and Faith: The Religious Uses of Modern Atheism.*
        New York: Fordham University Press.

Whitelam, Keith W.
1979   *The Just King: Monarchical Judicial Authority in Ancient
        Israel.* Journal for the Study of the Old Testament:
        Supplement Series 12. Sheffield: JSOT Press.

Whybray, R. Norman
1968   *The Succession Narrative: A Study of II Sam. 9–20 and
        I Kings 1 and 2.* Studies in Biblical Theology 2/9. London:
        SCM Press.
2002   *The Good Life in the Old Testament.* Edinburgh: T&T
        Clark.

Widmer, Michael
2004   *Moses, God, and the Dynamics of Intercessory Prayer.*
        Forschungen zum Alten Testament 2.8. Tübingen: Mohr
        Siebeck.

Wieringen, Archibald L. H. M. van
1998   *The Implied Reader in Isaiah 6–12.* Biblical Interpretation
        Series 34. Leiden: Brill.

Wildberger, Hans
1991   *Isaiah 1–12.* A Continental Commentary. Minneapolis:
        Fortress. German original 1980.

Williams, Catrin H.
2006   "The Testimony of Isaiah and Johannine Christology." Pages
        107–24 in *"As Those Who Are Taught": The Interpretation of
        Isaiah from the LXX to the SBL.* Edited by Claire Mathews
        McGinnis and Patricia K. Tull. Society of Biblical Literature
        Symposium Series 27. Atlanta: Society of Biblical Literature.

Williams, Rowan
1988   "The Suspicion of Suspicion: Wittgenstein and Bonhoeffer."
        Pages 36–53 in *The Grammar of the Heart: New Essays in
        Moral Philosophy and Theology.* Edited by Richard H. Bell.
        San Francisco: Harper & Row.

Williamson, H. G. M.
1994   *The Book Called Isaiah: Deutero-Isaiah's Role in
        Composition and Redaction.* Oxford: Clarendon.
1997   "Isaiah 6.13 and 1.29–31." Pages 119–28 in *Studies in the
        Book of Isaiah: Festschrift Willem A. M. Beuken.* Edited by
        J. van Ruiten and M. Vervenne. Bibliotheca ephemeridum

theologicarum lovaniensum 132. Leuven: Leuven University Press.

1999   "'From One Degree of Glory to Another': Themes and Theology in Isaiah." Pages 174–95 in *In Search of True Wisdom: Essays in Old Testament Interpretation in Honour of Ronald E. Clements.* Edited by Edward Ball. Journal for the Study of the Old Testament: Supplement Series 300. Sheffield: Sheffield Academic Press.

2005   "Temple and Worship in Isaiah 6." Pages 123–44 in *Temple and Worship in Biblical Israel.* Edited by John Day. Library of Hebrew Bible. Old Testament Studies 422. London: T&T Clark.

2006   *Isaiah 1–5.* International Critical Commentary. London: T&T Clark.

Wilson, Jonathan R.

1997   *Living Faithfully in a Fragmented World: Lessons for the Church from MacIntyre's "After Virtue."* Christian Mission and Modern Culture. Harrisburg, PA: Trinity.

Wilson, Robert R.

1980   *Prophecy and Society in Ancient Israel.* Philadelphia: Fortress.

Wittgenstein, Ludwig

1953   *Philosophical Investigations.* Oxford: Blackwell.

1958   *Philosophical Investigations.* 2nd ed. Oxford: Blackwell.

Wolde, Ellen van

1995   "Who Guides Whom? Embeddedness and Perspective in Biblical Hebrew and in 1 Kings 3:16–28." *Journal of Biblical Literature* 114.4:623–42.

1996   *Stories of the Beginning: Genesis 1–11 and Other Creation Stories.* London: SCM Press.

1997   *Ruth and Naomi.* London: SCM Press.

Wolters, Al

2004   "Zechariah 14 and Biblical Theology: Patristic and Contemporary Case Studies." Pages 261–85 in *Out of Egypt: Biblical Theology and Biblical Interpretation.* Edited by Craig G. Bartholomew et al. Scripture and Hermeneutics Series 5. Grand Rapids: Zondervan; Milton Keynes, UK: Paternoster.

Wolterstorff, Nicholas

1996   *John Locke and the Ethics of Belief.* Cambridge Studies in Religion and Critical Thought. Cambridge: Cambridge University Press.

Wong, G. C. I.
1996   "A Cuckoo in the Textual Nest at Isaiah 7:9b." *Journal of Theological Studies* 47.1:123–24.

Wood, W. Jay
1998   *Epistemology: Becoming Intellectually Virtuous.* Contours of Christian Philosophy. Downers Grove, IL: InterVarsity.

Woods, Susanne, ed.
1993   *The Poems of Aemilia Lanyer: Salve Deus Rex Judaeorum.* Women Writers in English 1350–1850. Oxford: Oxford University Press.

Work, Telford
2002   *Living and Active: Scripture in the Economy of Salvation.* Sacra Doctrina. Grand Rapids: Eerdmans.

Wright, Christopher J. H.
2006   *The Mission of God: Unlocking the Bible's Grand Narrative.* Nottingham, UK: Inter-Varsity.

Wright, N. T.
1992   *The New Testament and the People of God.* London: SPCK.
2005   *Scripture and the Authority of God.* London: SPCK.

Wright, Stephen I.
2000   "An Experiment in Biblical Criticism: Aesthetic Encounter in Reading and Preaching Scripture." Pages 240–67 in *Renewing Biblical Interpretation.* Edited by Craig G. Bartholomew et al. Scripture and Hermeneutics Series 1. Grand Rapids: Zondervan; Carlisle, UK: Paternoster.

Wright, Terry R.
2007   *The Genesis of Fiction: Modern Novelists as Biblical Interpreters.* Aldershot: Ashgate.

Zagzebski, Linda Trinkhaus
1996   *Virtues of the Mind: An Inquiry into the Nature of Virtue and the Ethical Foundations of Knowledge.* Cambridge: Cambridge University Press.
1997   "The Place of *Phronēsis* in the Methodology of Theology." Pages 204–23 in *Philosophy and Theological Discourse.* Edited by Stephen T. Davis. Claremont Studies in the Philosophy of Religion. Basingstoke, UK: Macmillan; New York: St. Martin's Press.

Zimmermann, Jens
2004   *Recovering Theological Hermeneutics: An Incarnational-Trinitarian Theory of Interpretation.* Grand Rapids: Baker Academic.

Zlotowitz, Meir, ed.
1976   *The Book of Ruth = Megillas Ruth: A New Translation with
         a Commentary Anthologized from Talmudic, Midrashic
         and Rabbinic Sources.* ArtScroll Tanach series. New York:
         ArtScroll Studios; Brooklyn, NY: Mesorah.

SUBJECT INDEX

AUTHOR INDEX

261

Scripture Index